Final Cut Express 4
Editing Workshop

Final Cut Express 4
Editing Workshop

Tom Wolsky

AMSTERDAM • BOSTON • HEIDELBERG • LONDON • NEW YORK • OXFORD
PARIS • SAN DIEGO • SAN FRANCISCO • SINGAPORE • SYDNEY • TOKYO

Focal Press is an imprint of Elsevier

ELSEVIER

Focal
Press

Senior Acquisitions Editor: Paul Temme
Associate Acquisitions Editor: Dennis McGonagle
Publishing Services Manager: George Morrison
Project Manager: Mónica González de Mendoza
Assistant Editor: Chris Simpson
Marketing Manager: Amanda Guest
Cover Design: Alisa Andreola
Cover Image: iStock

Focal Press is an imprint of Elsevier
30 Corporate Drive, Suite 400, Burlington, MA 01803, USA
Linacre House, Jordan Hill, Oxford OX2 8DP, UK

 Recognizing the importance of preserving what has been written, Elsevier prints
its books on acid-free paper whenever possible.

Library of Congress Cataloging-in-Publication Data
Wolsky, Tom.
Final Cut Express 4 editing workshop / Tom Wolsky.
  p. cm.
Includes index.
ISBN 978-0-240-81077-5 (pbk. : alk. paper) 1. Digital video—Editing—
Data processing. 2. Motion pictures—Editing—Data Processing.
3. Final cut (Electronic resource) I. Title.
TR899.W659673 2008
006.6'96—dc22

                                             2008007677

British Library Cataloguing-in-Publication Data
A catalogue record for this book is available from the British Library.

ISBN: 978-0-240-81077-5

For information on all Focal Press publications
visit our website at www.books.elsevier.com

10 11 12 6 5

Typeset by Charon Tec Ltd (A Macmillan Company), Chennai, India
www.charontec.com

Printed in the United States

To all my friends on the Apple Final Cut Express forum: Ian B, Martin R, Alchroma, VJK, Piero F, Michel B, and many more

Contents

vii

CONTENTS

ix

CONTENTS

What's on the DVD?

The companion DVD for *Final Cut Express 4 Editing Workshop* includes unedited, raw footage and tutorial projects with sequences that guide you through the material. You will find the following on the disk:

- Almost 16 minutes of audio and video media files
- 27 graphics files
- 15 FCE4 tutorial project files
- Folder of AVCHD media
- XML files of the project
- QuickTime preview movies of all FCE transitions
- Extras folder with:
    - Demo filters from CGM
    - Timecode Calculator
    - Two custom button bars
    - Lens flare effect in DV and HD, both 1080i and 720p

Introduction

WHAT IS EDITING?

The first movies were single, static shots of everyday events. The Lumière brothers' screening in Paris of a train pulling into the La Ciotat train station caused a sensation. Shot in black and white, and silent, it nevertheless conveyed a gripping reality for the audience. People leaped from their seats to avoid the approaching steam locomotive. The brothers followed this with a staged comic scene. Georges Méliès expanded on this by staging complex tableaux that told a story. It wasn't until Edwin H. Porter and D. W. Griffith in the United States discovered the process of editing one shot next to another that movies were really born. Porter also invented the close-up, which was used to emphasize climactic moments. Wide shots were used to establish location and context. Griffith introduced such innovations as the flashback, the first real use of film to manipulate time. Parallel action was introduced, and other story devices were born, but the real discovery was that the shot was the fundamental building block of film and that the film is built one shot at a time, one after the other. It soon became apparent that the impact of storytelling lies in the order of the shots.

Films and videos are made in the moments when one shot changes into another, when one image is replaced by the next, when one point of view becomes someone else's point of view. Without the image changing, all you have are moving pictures. The idea of changing from one angle to another or from one scene to another quickly leads to the concept of juxtaposing one idea against another. The story is not in each shot but in the consecutive relationship of the shots. The story isn't told in the frames themselves so much as in the moment of the edit, the moment when one shot, one image, one idea, is replaced with another. The edit happens not on a frame but between the frames, in the interstices between the frames of the shots that are assembled.

INTRODUCTION

Editing is a poor word for the film or video production process that takes place after the images are recorded or created. It is not only the art and process of selecting and trimming the material and arranging it in a specific order but is very much an extension of script writing, whether the script was written before the project was recorded or constructed after the material was gathered and screened. The arrangement and timing of the scenes, and then the selection, timing and arrangement of the picture elements within each scene, are most analogous to what a writer does. The only difference is that the writer crafts his script from a known language and his raw imagination, whereas the editor crafts her film from the images, the catalogue of words, as it were—the dictionary of a new language—that have been assembled during the production. The editor's assembly creates a text that, although a new, never before seen or heard language, is based on a grammatical traditional—one that goes back to Porter and Griffith—that audiences have come to accept as a means for conveying information or telling a story.

Unlike the written language, a novel, or an essay that can be started and stopped at the reader's whim, video or film production is based on the concept of *time*, usually linear time of a fixed length. Nowadays, of course, many forms of video delivery—the Web, computer or portable player, or DVD player—can be stopped and started according to the viewer's desires. Nonetheless, most productions are designed to be viewed in a single sitting for a specified duration.

Film and video are designed to accommodate the temporal rigidity of the theater but with the spatial fluidity and freedom of a novel. Whether it is 10 minutes, 30 minutes, one hour, two hours, or more, the film is seen as a single, continuous event of fixed duration. On the other hand, time within the film is infinitely malleable. Events can happen quickly: We fly from one side of the world to another, from one era to a different century, in the blink of an eye. Or every detail and every angle can be slowed down to add up to a far greater amount than the true expanse of time or seen again and again.

Because film and video production are based on the notion of time, the process of editing—controlling time and space within the story—is of paramount importance. This process of editing, of manipulating time, does not begin after the film is shot but as soon as the idea is conceived. From the time you are thinking of your production as a series of shots or scenes and as soon as the writer puts down words on paper or the computer, the movie is being edited, and the material is being ordered and arranged, juxtaposing one element against another, one idea with another.

This process of writing with pictures that we call editing has three components:

1. *Selection*, choosing the words, deciding which shot to use
2. *Arrangement*, the grammar of our writing, determining where that shot should be placed in relation to other shots, the order in which the shots will appear
3. *Timing*, the rhythm and pace of our assembled material, deciding how long each shot should be on the screen

Timing is dictated by rhythm—sometimes by an internal rhythm the visuals present, sometimes by a musical track, and often by the rhythm of spoken language. All language, whether dialog or narration, has a rhythm, a cadence or pattern, that is dictated by the words and based on grammar. Grammar marks language with punctuation: Commas indicate short pauses, semicolons are slightly longer pauses, and periods mark the end of a statement. The new sentence begins a new idea, a new thought, and it is natural that as the new thought begins, a new image is introduced to illustrate that idea. The shot comes not at the end of the sentence, not in the pause, but at the beginning of the new thought. This is the natural place to cut, and this rhythm of language often drives the rhythm of film and video. Editing creates the visual and aural juxtaposition between shots. That's what this book is about: how to put together those pieces of picture and sound.

WHY DO I GET TO WRITE THIS BOOK?

I have been working in film and video production for longer than I like to admit (okay, about 40 years). I worked at ABC News for many years as an operations manager and producer, first in London and then in New York. I went on to teach video production at a small high school in rural northern California. I also have written curriculum for Apple's Video Journalism program and taught training sessions for them, and during the summer, I have had the pleasure of teaching Final Cut at the Digital Media Academy on the beautiful Stanford University campus.

The structure of this book follows that of my *Final Cut Pro Editing Workshop* books. It is organized as a series of tutorials and lessons that I hope have been written logically to guide the reader from one topic to a more advanced topic. The nature of your work with Final Cut Express, however, may require the information in Lesson 10, for example, right away. You can read that lesson by itself. There may, however, be elements in Lesson 10 that presuppose that you know something about using the Viewer in conjunction with the Canvas.

WHO SHOULD READ THIS BOOK?

This editing workshop is intended for all FCE users. So the broader question should really be "Whom is FCE intended for?" It appeals, I think, to serious hobbyists, the so-called prosumer market, event producers, and even small companies with video production requirements. I also think it's a great video application for education—fully featured, able to go beyond the limitations that frustrate many students who use iMovie, but without the professional features of its older sibling, Final Cut Pro. Institutional education pricing makes it affordable for schools even in these penny-pinching times. Final Cut Express is not a simple application to use; it's not plug-and-play. It requires learning your way around the interface, its tools, and its enormous capabilities.

WHAT'S ON THE DVD?

The DVD included with this book contains some of the lessons, projects, and clips used in the book. Not all of the lessons require materials from the DVD. For some, such as Lessons 1, 3, 4, and 19, you don't need any clips at all. For others, you may want to substitute your own material—clips you want to work with or are more familiar with. I hope you find this book useful, informative, and fun. I think it's a good way to learn this kind of application.

Acknowledgments

First, as always, my gratitude to all of the people at Focal Press who make this bookwriting process relatively painless, particularly Paul Temme, Acquisitions Editor, for his thoughtful advice and guidance, and for bringing this project to life. My thanks also to Mónica González de Mendoza, Project Manager, and Chris Simpson, Assistant Editor, for their help and ready answers to my questions and for shepherding the project through the production process. Many thanks are due to Deborah Prato for her stylish copyediting and to Macmillian Publishing Solutions for their work on the layout. My thanks to Alisa Andreola for her wonderful work on the covers, Janet Cocker for proofreading, and Keith Shostak for carefully indexing the book. Any errors in text or substance remain mine alone.

So many people helped make this book possible and deserve thanks: Sidney Kramer for his expert advice; Dion Scoppettuolo, FCE product manager, for his assistance; Rich Corwin and Anita Lupattelli Corwin for their gracious cooperation; and Toby Malina for her kind help. Thanks also to Klaus Eiperle for letting me put demo versions of his wonderful CGM effects on the DVD.

A great many thanks are due to my partner, B. T. Corwin, for her insights, her endless encouragement, her engineering technical support, and her patience with me. Without her, none of this would have been possible. Finally, again my thanks to the wonderful people of Damine, Japan, who welcomed us into their homes and whose lives provided the source material for many of these lessons.

LESSON 1

Installing Final Cut Express

1

Welcome to Final Cut Express, version 4—the newest version of Apple's video editing software for DV and HDV users, and now the newest high-definition, consumer format for AVCHD users. This version is based on its older cousin, Final Cut Pro 6. It is a universal binary application, which means it will run on either older PowerPC Macs or Apple's Intel-based computers. If you are working with AVCHD material, you will need to have one of Apple's Intel computers, a MacPro, iMac, MacBook, MacBook Pro, or MacBook Air.

Final Cut Express (FCE) has a unique niche in video editing applications; nothing else of its caliber is available in its price range. FCE occupies the space between Apple's free iMovie editing application and its high-end, resolution-independent suite of applications called Final Cut Studio. With the introduction of the latest version of iMovie 08, many of its users have been frustrated with what appears to be a dumbing down of the application. It is now very significantly an amateur consumer product and not enough for the serious hobbyist or even the small business professional. Though iMovie 06 is still available, it's clearly been dead-ended by Apple. For the serious hobbyist or professional who is working in DV, HDV, or AVCHD, Final Cut Express is a good choice for those who don't want or need to pay the price of Final Cut Studio. iMovie and FCE are similar in some ways, but they differ not only on the surface but in the applications' underlying architecture. We will examine these differences in workflow as they come up in the book.

NOTE
New Operating System:
If you have to
upgrade your operating system to run your new software, or if you
want to upgrade to Leopard, the new Mac OS 10.5, most professionals
recommend that you do a clean erase and install of the new operating
system, rather than simply archiving and installing it. Professional applications,
especially video applications, call on many system functions to operate, and
making a minor change or failing to correctly place or update a minor Library file
will make the application function incorrectly. If you must upgrade, the best way is to
make a clone of your existing system, using Carbon Copy Cloner or Super-Duper!
Erase your main drive, which you can do from the system installation discs, and then
install a clean, new operating system. Install your software, and then from the
cloned drive, transfer your users and other files you want to keep. If you're
really careful, you can even move over and install many simple
applications this way, but you cannot do that with video
or other professional applications.

2

I'm sure you want to dive right into it, but FCE 4 first must be installed correctly on a properly functioning system. Video editing software is not simple
shareware but a complex, system-integrated piece of software that requires
your system to be running in optimal condition. This means all of the correct
system software must be installed on hardware, computer, and hard drives that
can support digital video. Your hard drives must be fast, clean, and running
properly, ready for moving large amounts of data at high speed.

WHAT YOU REALLY NEED

Final Cut Express 4 works only with Apple's OS X 10.4.10 or higher. It runs
well on Leopard, OS 10.5 and on a G4 or G5 Mac that is 1.25 GHz or higher.
This also applies to dual processor machines. Each processor has to be
1.25 GHz or faster. FCE will, of course, run best on the Intel dual-core (Core
Duo) computer. The computer must have an AGP or PCI Express graphics card
or the Intel GMA integrated processor in the MacBook. All of these machines
should come with the necessary graphics card as standard. Though the application will run with the MacBook integrated graphics process, it will not run
some of new the FxPlug filters that come with FCE 4. I would no longer recommend used a MacBook with this application, and though it will also run
on a Mac mini, it is not approved as a system by Apple, and I would not advise

it. The application will run on a G4 PowerBook, MacBook Pro, or iMac, and, of course, it will run beautifully on a top-of-the-line 8-core MacPro tower. As just noted, if you're working in the AVCHD format, you must have an Intel-based computer, not a G4 or G5.

Memory: How Much and What Kind?

Applications have to deal with two distinct types of memory: RAM and storage. They perform quite distinct functions. RAM (random access memory) is the chips that hold the system and applications while they are running. FCE is stored in RAM while it's open, as is the operating system. To do this, you will need at least 1 G of RAM, but I recommend that you have at least 2 G of RAM and even more if you can. You'll also need 500 MB of storage space available for installation applications, Final Cut Express, and LiveType, together with their ancillary application support media.

NOTE
Do Not Upgrade LiveType: If you are upgrading from an older version of FCE, do not upgrade LiveType. There is nothing new in it, and the new version that comes with the latest version of FCE has had a significant amount of the LiveType content removed. Keep your old LiveType, and for safety, rename it so the FCE installation doesn't accidentally erase it. Also, if you have Soundtrack from an older version of FCE, this application will still work with the new Final Cut Express, though it has been removed from the FCE package. It is unclear how much longer Soundtrack will work with FCE and the current versions of the operating system, but if you have it, you can use it. If you want a purely music creation tool, you're probably better off working with Garage Band than with the old Soundtrack.

3

Your finances almost invariably dictate which computer you purchase for editing video. It's a good idea to get the biggest, fastest, and most powerful computer you can afford. If you have budget constraints, start with an iMac. If you need to be on the road a lot, get a MacBook Pro. If you have a larger budget, go for it: an 8-core Mac Pro loaded with lots of RAM.

Multiple Drives

Storage is an essential part of any video system. DV consumes about 3.6 MB per second of storage space. That translates to 216 MB per minute, approximately

1 GB for five minutes, and almost 13 GB for an hour. Fortunately, cheap hard drives are available in ever-increasing sizes, with platter speeds, seek times, and caches ample for working with DV-quality material. HDV material has the same amount of storage space as DV when recorded, but it gets converted to a high-resolution format when ingested into FCE. AVCHD uses even less storage space when recorded, and an hour or more can be fitted onto a single 4 G memory card. However, when this material, HDV and AVCHD, is ingested, it is transcoded into the Apple Intermediate Codec, which is approximately 12 MB per second, about 40 G per hour of footage, ten times larger than AVCHD natively.

Because a digital video editing system needs to move large amounts of data at high speeds, you should use separate drives purely for storing video data. You should have one internal hard drive dedicated to your operating system and applications, such as Final Cut Express, LiveType, Photoshop or Photoshop Elements, iTunes, your iLife applications, iDVD, iWeb, Garage Band, and so on, and everything else from Internet-access software to word processing and spreadsheets. All of these should be on one drive—your system drive—and all the applications should be in the system's *Applications* folder.

You should also have at least one other hard drive that's both large and fast. This drive should carry only your media. A separate drive is much more efficient at moving large amounts of data at high speed. The media drive needs to get that data off the drive very quickly and play it back. In addition, it needs to play back multiple tracks of audio from various places on the drive simultaneously. That's quite enough work for any one drive to be doing at any one time! Expecting it to access both the application and the operating system can be the straw that breaks the camel's back. You are much less likely to have video playback or capture failure through dropped frames and other issues if you have the media on a separate, dedicated hard drive. This drive should run at 7,200 rpm and have at least an 8 MB cache. For MacBook, MacBook Pro, or iMac users, external FireWire drives are a good solution, such as are those from Seagate, WiebeTech, or boxes from Granite Digital in which you can put a number of different fast, bare drives. With a G5 or a MacPro, the best solution is to put a second, large drive inside your computer.

Optimizing Your Computer for FCE

In addition to the hardware, you can optimize your computer for video editing with Final Cut Express, using a few simple procedures. In **System Preferences**, you can switch off a few items that might interfere with the application's

NOTE
Reformatting a New Drive:
Most hard drives come formatted for Windows.
Before you use them, you should reformat them to
Mac OS Extended (Journaled). You do this with Disk Utility.

1. Open Disk Utility, which should be in the Utilities folder of your Applications folder.

2. Select the drive you want to format, and click on the Erase tab (see Figure 1.1).

3. Set the Volume Format pop-up to Mac OS Extended (Journaled).

4. Name the drive.

5. Click on Security, and check Zero Out Data, as in Figure 1.2. You only have to zero out on a new drive that has not been properly formatted. If you need to reformat it or erase the drive later, you can do a simple erase that deletes the directory file without having to zero out.

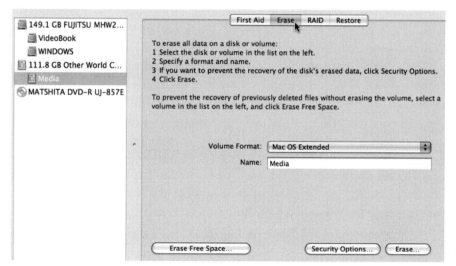

FIGURE 1.1
Disk Utility Erase panel.

operations while it's running. You should set **Software Update** to *not* check for updates automatically. That way, it won't take off and try to run while you're working in FCE.

For the **Desktop**, most professionals recommend switching off screen savers and working in a neutral, usually medium-gray desktop, because it is more

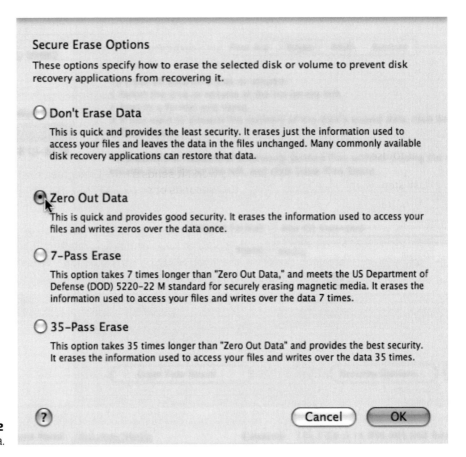

FIGURE 1.2
Zero Out Data.

restful for the eyes and does not affect the color rendition of your eyes. (You'll see this tonal display in the application—mostly gray shades.)

The **Displays** should be set so that your computer monitor is running in **Millions of Colors** and at the resolution settings the system recommends for your display, which should be a minimum of 1,024 × 768. The application will not run properly at lower resolutions.

The **Energy Saver** should be set so that the system never goes to sleep. It's less critical, however, that the monitor doesn't go to sleep. I usually set it around ten minutes, but the system and the hard drive should *never* shut down, which would wreak havoc with slow renders.

I also recommend that you switch off **AppleTalk** and networking. This is done easily by going to **Network Preferences** and creating a new location called **None**. Set up your **None** location without any active connections—no internal modem, no Airport, no Ethernet—everything unavailable and shut off. To reconnect to the network, simply change back to a location from the **Apple** menu that allows access to whatever connection you want to use.

NOTE
No Spin: The Energy Saver controls do not affect secondary and external drives like FireWire drives, but this can be a problem for FireWire drives. If you find your secondary or media drive spinning down or going to sleep (for example, if you take a break), get a simple shareware utility like No Spin (http://software.electriceelprod.com) to keep the drive awake while you work. It sends a polling ping to the drive every 60 seconds or so to keep it from dosing off and going to sleep.

One last step is in what's now called Leopard's System Preferences **Exposé and Spaces**. This feature also allows you to call up your Dashboard widgets, separate your windows to see them all, and create separate rooms or spaces for doing different types of work. For example, I have one space for e-mail, another for Internet browsing, a third for writing tasks, and a fourth for video and media work. Exposé and Spaces is, unfortunately, a little problematical for FCE users. The default shortcuts for Exposé's functions are **F9**, **F10**, and **F11**, which are critical to working efficiently in FCE. I recommend that you change the default Exposé keyboard shortcuts to **Option-F9**, **Option-F10**, and **Option-F11**. You can do this in your System Preferences in the Exposé and Spaces panel, as shown in Figure 1.3. Hold down the **Option** key before selecting the item in the pop-up. You should change the default Dashboard shortcut as well. I like to use **F1**, because it doesn't do anything in FCE.

Monitors

In addition to your computer display, you should also have a video monitor. These monitors, like television sets, reproduce images very differently from computer monitors, which have much greater color depth, resolution, and contrast range. In addition, video monitors have an interlaced scan line display, which computer monitors do not. These attributes are all critical to how your video will finally look. One reason this is so important is because your material is being made into a video format. Whether you shot it with a DV, HDV, or AVCHD camera, because FCE is resolution specific, it always generates video in one of these formats, which are usually interlaced video formats designed for display on a television. If you work in DV and your project is intended to be seen on a television set, you must edit with a video monitor that shows true color and

7

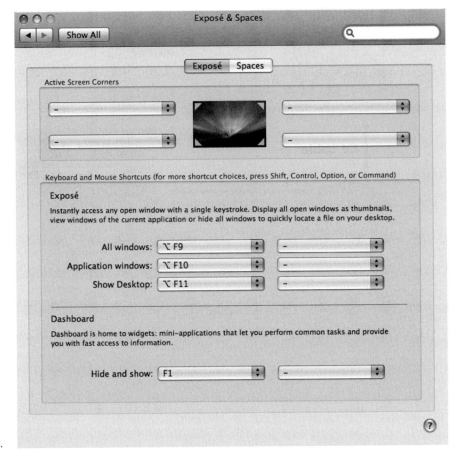

FIGURE 1.3
Exposé and Spaces
system preferences.

interlacing output. The high-definition format that FCE uses cannot be displayed directly on a video monitor while you work.

Even if you intend the final product to be seen only on the Internet, the application still makes it into one of these video formats, so you should monitor on an interlaced display to properly assess your material's output. Another way to monitor your material more closely is to view it in FCE at full 100 percent resolution. (We'll see how to do that later.)

You may also want a second computer display for the large number of windows that video editing applications need. This is helpful for long-form video production, but it is by no means as essential as a video monitor or, at the very least, a television display.

TIP
Monitoring HD: You can best monitor HD by using the Digital Cinema Desktop display function while you work. This lets you view the video full screen on your computer monitor, and it's easy to toggle in and out of it with a keyboard shortcut. We'll see how to set this up in a later lesson.

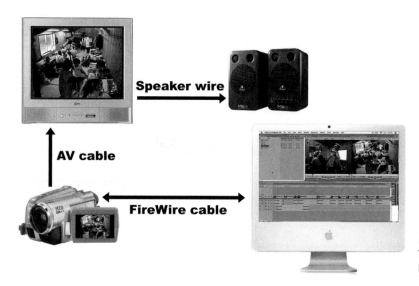

FIGURE 1.4
Typical DV connection layout.

9

To get the video out of your computer and onto the video monitor or TV, you need to use some kind of digital-to-analog conversion device. The simplest one for most people is a camcorder. The video and audio come out of the computer's FireWire port, which gets connected to the camcorder, DV deck, or DV converter box, such as the DataVideo DAC-100. The output of the camcorder in turn is connected to the video monitor. That's the best place to watch your movie while you work. The audio from the camera or the video monitor is fed into speakers. Figure 1.4 shows a typical DV connection layout. The camera is the hub that passes the digital signal to and from the computer and sends the analog signal to the video monitor and speakers.

If you are using an external FireWire hard drive, in most cases the system works best by daisy-chaining the FireWire connection. A six-pin to six-pin FireWire cable connects the computer to the hard drive, and a six-pin to four-pin cable connects the hard drive to the camcorder, a six-pin to six-pin cable connects to a converter box, and standard video cables connect the camcorder or converter to your TV or video monitor. Avoid using USB drives for video work. Although they are fast, they transfer data in bursts, which doesn't work well for video and is not supported by Apple for use with video applications.

Speakers

Good-quality speakers are very important. They should be connected to the same source as the video you're monitoring. The rule of thumb here is that audio

NOTE

Canon Cameras: Generally, Canon cameras do not support daisy-chaining and require a separate FireWire bus to work correctly with an external FireWire drive. Unfortunately, all Apple computers, although they may have multiple FireWire ports, have only one FireWire bus controlling them. For tower computers and laptops with PCMCIA cardbus or Express Card slots, third-party hardware can be added that will add a second bus and allow you to use external drives with these cameras. This is a real problem for iMac users, who don't have these options. Generally, with these setups, it's best to capture your material in the internal drive and then move it to the external drive for editing.

follows video, so if you are looking at your video on a television monitor, you should listen to your audio from the same source. If you have a deck or a DV camera that is feeding the signal from your computer to your TV monitor, that device should also be feeding your audio speakers. Switchable speakers would be ideal, with two inputs to monitor either the video source or the computer output.

NOTE

Updates: After installing the software, it's probably a good idea to check the Apple Final Cut Express web page (http://www.apple.com/finalcutexpress) to see if there have been any updates to the application. Applications are constantly being refined and updated to fix problems or to accommodate developments in hardware or the operating system. You can also do this by choosing **Software Update** in the **System Preferences** or directly from under the Apple menu. Also, don't forget to register your new software.

FIRING UP THE APPLICATION

FIGURE 1.5
Final Cut Express icon.

Now it's time to launch that program. Double-click on the icon in the *Applications* folder or, better yet, make an alias in the Dock and click on that (see Figure 1.5). After you start up the application, the first window asks you to register your application. Once you've done this, the screen will not appear again.

After a new installation, or after you have trashed your Final Cut Preferences file (see page 58), you will next see the new setup preferences screen. The default setting is **DV-NTSC** with audio at 48 kHz, as shown in Figure 1.6. There are two new pop-ups that let you limit your selection choices to make it easier to choose the correct setting. The Format pop-up (see Figure 1.7) lets you pick the format you want to work with—HD, NTSC, or PAL—or the codec you want to work in—Apple Intermediate Codec or DV/Panasonic DVCPRO. If you're using HD, select that and the Use pop-up will be limited to the three available HDV Apple Intermediate Codec presets, as shown in Figure 1.8. The Rate pop-up lets you select the frame rate you're working in. If you change it to 25 fps, as in Figure 1.9, the default setup will immediately change to DV PAL, as 25 fps is the basic PAL frame rate.

NOTE
Registering: If you don't register your software, every fifth time you launch the application the registration screen will appear. There is no way to switch this off, short of hacking the application.

If you are working in DV with audio recorded using 12-bit audio, also called 32 kHz audio, more choices will appear, such as in Figure 1.10. For now, choose **DV-NTSC**. That's the format in which we'll be working.

The pop-up at the bottom makes you choose your primary scratch disk. The pop-up defaults to your system partition, setting the scratch disk inside the user's *Documents* folder. It also offers you the choice of any hard drives attached to your system. You should set this to your dedicated media drive whenever possible, as shown in Figure 1.11.

11

If you do not have a camcorder or DV deck connected to your computer, you will get the warning dialog shown in Figure 1.12. If you will be working consistently without a deck or camera

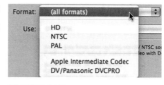

FIGURE 1.7
Format pop-up.

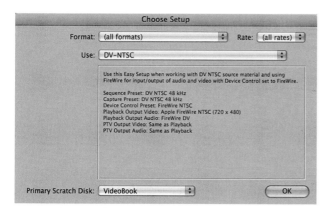

FIGURE 1.6
Choose Setup Dialog box.

FIGURE 1.8
HD options.

FIGURE 1.9
Choose Frame Rate Dialog box.

FIGURE 1.10
DV options.

FIGURE 1.11
Setting the scratch disk.

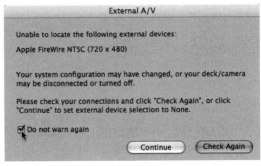

FIGURE 1.12
External A/V warning.

NOTE

Codec: Codec stands for "compression-decompression." FCE works using QuickTime, which is a multimedia architecture that handles video, audio, still images, and other data. Any video that's brought into Final Cut Express should be in QuickTime and compressed into one of the three codecs that FCE uses: DV/Panasonic DVCPRO in either NTSC (the North American and Japanese standard) or PAL (the standard used by the rest of the world). The third codec is the Apple Intermediate Codec, which is a high-resolution codec used for HD material, either HDV or the new AVCHD format. FCE does not work with other formats or codecs like MPEG-2 or MPEG-4. That material must be converted to QuickTime using one of the three FCE compatible codecs.

NOTE

Sample Rates: Audio is recorded digitally by cutting up the sound into samples. The more samples per second into which the audio is divided, the more accurately it will represent the original sound. DV has two sample rate options: 32 kHz (kiloHertz) and 48 kHz, which means sampling the audio either 32,000 times per second, or 48,000 times per second. The camera manufacturers designate these sample rates as 12-bit for 32 kHz and 16-bit for 48 kHz. You should always set your camera to record at 16-bit or 48 kHz. If you haven't and you recorded at 32 kHz, then you should use one of the 32 kHz presets.

connected, notice the little check box in the lower left that allows you to switch off this warning. You can turn it back on in **User Preferences** under the **Final Cut Express** menu.

UNDERSTANDING THE INTERFACE

Launching a new application for the first time is always an adventure, especially when it's as complex as Final Cut Express. Some software can be intimidating, and some can be downright confusing. When FCE launches, it fills your screen with lots of windows, buttons, and tools to explore. Figure 1.13 shows you the default arrangement called **Standard**.

The Primary Windows

The screen is divided into four primary windows, with two large, empty screens as your principal monitors:

1. The **Browser** is the first window at the top left of the screen, which is empty except for one sequence. The Browser is the equivalent of the Clips pane in iMovie HD or the Event pane in iMovie 08.
2. The **Viewer**, the empty black window in the middle of the screen, allows you to look at individual video clips. You can open clips either from the Browser or from the Timeline window.
3. The **Canvas**, the empty monitor on the right, displays the output of your material as you edit it. The Canvas is linked directly to the Timeline.

13

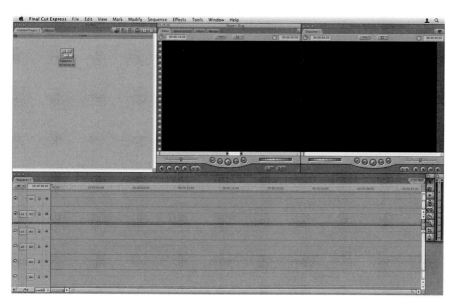

FIGURE 1.13
The Final Cut Express interface.

FIGURE 1.14
Tools palette.

4. The **Timeline** for your video is the window with the horizontal sections in the bottom half of the screen. This is where you lay out your video and audio material in the order you want them. The Timeline that's open in the interface is the item called *Sequence 1* in the Browser.

The materials that you're working with in the project, such as video clips, audio files, and imported graphics, are all listed in the Browser. Think of the Browser as a giant folder. You can nest folders within folders, just as you can on the Desktop. You can make folders in FCE and keep them in your Browser to organize your material. The Browser is not where your clips are stored; it is only a list. Your clips are physically stored on your media hard drives.

You'll also notice small vertical bars to the right of the Timeline that contain the **Tools** and **Audio Meters**. Some of the tools are hidden, nested inside the Tools palette. Figure 1.14 shows all the tools displayed. There is a Selection tool, which is the arrow at the top. There are Edit and Range Selection tools; Track Selection tools; editing tools such as Roll, Ripple, Slip, and Slide; Blade tools; Zoom and Hand tools; Crop and Distort tools; and various Pen tools for creating and editing keyframes.

Window Arrangements

Many people like to work with multiple monitors or large Cinema displays or to attach a second monitor when working on a PowerBook. With multiple monitors you can move the Browser onto a separate screen and leave just the Viewer, Canvas, Timeline, and Tools on the main monitor. In FCE, you can create new window arrangements by moving the screens into new positions, such as in Figure 1.15, with a long, tall Browser on the left. You can save this, or any other window arrangement, by holding down the **Option** key and selecting from the **Window** menu, **Arrange**>**Set Custom Layout** (see Figure 1.16). In this menu some other presets are available to you.

Once the arrangement has been set, it can be called up at any time from the **Window**>**Arrange** menu or by using the listed keyboard shortcut. You can always return to the Standard window arrangement from the **Window** menu or use the keyboard shortcut, **Control-U**.

In FCE, you can resize windows dynamically by grabbing the edges where the cursor changes to a Resizing tool (see Figure 1.17). When you pull with the

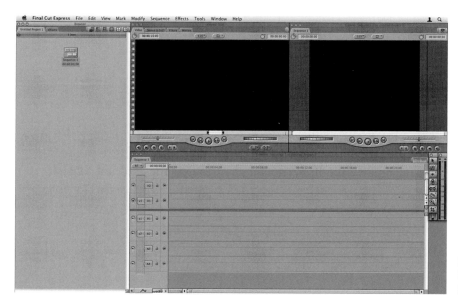

FIGURE 1.15
Long Browser
arrangement.

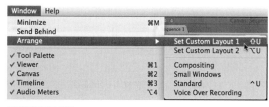

FIGURE 1.16
Window>Arrange>Set Custom arrangement.

FIGURE 1.17
Resizing tool for window
arrangements.

15

Resizing tool, the windows will move proportionately, expanding and contracting as needed to fill the available space.

Tabbed Palettes

You have probably also noticed that most of these windows have tabs with other windows behind them. Let's take a quick look at what's back there. Tabbed in the Browser is the **Effects** window. Video and audio effects, transitions, and generators are stored here, including any favorites you want to access frequently.

> **TIP**
>
> **Open Sequence:** Should your project ever open and you don't see a Canvas or Timeline, it means that no sequence is open. There needs to be at least one sequence in a project. Double-click the sequence icon in the Browser, and it will open the Timeline with its Canvas.

The **Viewer** has tabs behind it as well:

- **Stereo (ala2)** or **Mono (al)** and **Mono (a2)**, which hold the two channels of audio associated with a video clip. This is where you can see a video clip's audio waveform and manipulate the sound by raising and lowering the levels or panning the tracks from left to right.
- **Filters** is where you control the effects that are applied to clips.
- **Motion** lets you view and change settings for properties such as Scale, Rotation, Center, Crop, and others.

Most of the Motion properties can be animated. You can also change the image's opacity, making it more transparent. At zero opacity it will be invisible. You can add a Drop Shadow that will appear on any underlying layers, and you can add Motion Blur, which simulates the amount of smearing, created by a fast movement across the screen. We will look at these Motion tools in more detail in Lessons 13 and 14. The Canvas and the Timeline window can also have tabs. If you have more than one sequence open at a time, they will appear as tabs in the Timeline window and in the Canvas.

SUMMARY

So ends Lesson 1. This lesson helped you to get started correctly, making sure your system is set up to edit digital video with a professional application. We looked briefly at the application and its interface. In the next lesson, we'll look at the interface in greater detail with an existing project.

LESSON 2

The Final Cut Express Interface

Now that you've set up your system, let's look more closely at each of the components of Final Cut Express's interface and each of its windows. To do so, we must open a project that has something in it, and to do that, we need to load the material from the DVD that accompanies this book onto your computer.

LOADING THE LESSON

Let's begin by loading the book's DVD into your DVD drive. To simplify the process for you, the materials you need for the projects are combined into a single folder on the disc. On the DVD you will see a folder called *FCE_Media&Projects*. Drag the entire folder onto your computer. Though the media for the projects is included in this folder, most computers' internal drives should be fast enough to play these short DV clips, unless the drive is overly full.

Ideally you would place the project files in the *Projects* folder on your system drive and the clips inside the *Media* folder on your dedicated media drive. The sound and video clips included in the *Media* folder will play much more easily from your computer's high-speed media drive than your internal drive. If you want to do this, use the following steps:

1. From the *FCE_Media&Projects* folder, drag the folder called *Media* onto your media drive.
2. Next, drag the *Projects* folder onto your internal system drive. It's not very large, so probably the best place to put it is inside your home *Documents* folder.

3. Before you do anything else, eject the DVD.

4. Open the *Projects* folder on your hard drive, and double-click the project file *Lesson 2* to open the project. There is no project for Lesson 1, so for convenience there's no project named *Lesson 1*.

NOTE

Right-Clicking: If you do not have a three-button mouse, either an Apple Mighty Mouse or a third-party mouse, you really should get one. Any inexpensive USB three-button mouse with a scroll wheel will do. The application uses right-clicking to bring up shortcut menus, and the scroll wheel will move sliders as well as window displays. Until you get the three-button mouse, whenever I say "right-click," you should hold down the Control key while clicking to bring up the shortcut menu.

RECONNECTING THE MEDIA

Before the project finishes loading, you may see the dialog box in Figure 2.1. This will happen if the projects and the media are in separate locations. Because the media is in a new location from where it was previously, you will have to reconnect the files:

1. Click on the **Reconnect** button in the Offline Files dialog box. Do not click **Continue**.

2. In the next window that comes up, check the **Search Single Location** box, and specify the drive where your media is located (see Figure 2.2).

3. Click the **Search** button.

4. FCE will find one of the items. If it's the correct item, make sure it's selected and click the **Open** button in the dialog box (see Figure 2.3). If it doesn't find it, use the **Locate** button in Figure 2.2 to find it manually. It should find the rest of the files as well.

5. All of the files should then have moved to the bottom of the Reconnect Files dialog box. Click the **Connect** button to reconnect the files (see Figure 2.4).

You must do this for each of the projects from this book that you open.

FIGURE 2.1
Offline Files
dialog box.

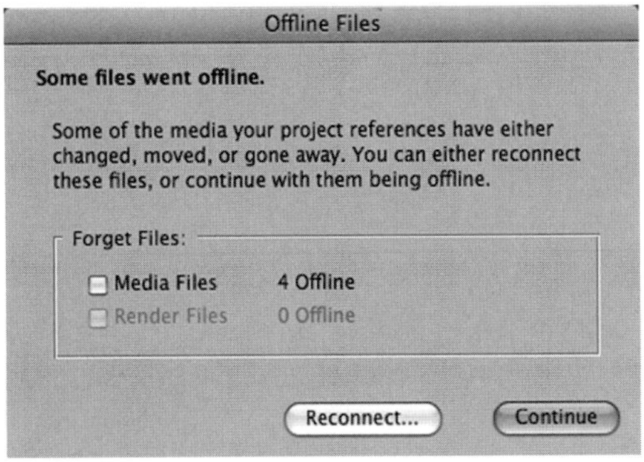

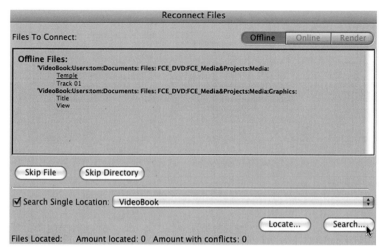

FIGURE 2.2
Reconnect Files dialog
box.

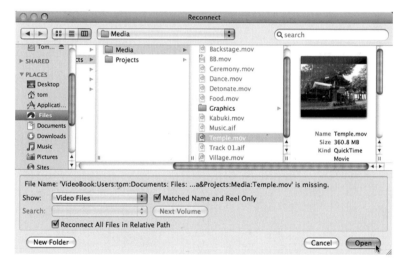

FIGURE 2.3
Reconnect dialog box.

19

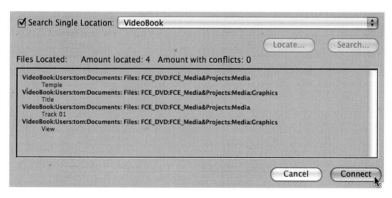

FIGURE 2.4
Items ready to be
reconnected.

NOTE

XML Files: In some instances, the project files will not open, especially when they are opened by secondary users on a system. It's possible you will get an error message like the one in Figure 2.5. This appears to be a bug in the application that has not been corrected as of this writing. This is why the projects have also been provided as XML files on the DVD disc.

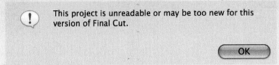

> ⚠ This project is unreadable or may be too new for this version of Final Cut.
>
> [OK]

FIGURE 2.5
Project fails to open.

1. If this does happen, begin by copying the XML folder from the disc onto your system drive.
2. Then simply open FCE, and from the **File** menu, select **Import > FCP XML from iMovie**.
3. Navigate to the *XMLs* folder and select *Lesson 2*.
4. When you get a noncritical error message, click **No** and ignore it.

   Your project file will open, and you just have to go through the Reconnect process listed previously.

5. Start by selecting everything in the Browser and going to **File . Reconnect Media**.
6. When the reconnect process is complete, save the project as *Lesson 2*.

THE BROWSER

When the project called *Lesson 2* has finished loading, the Browser should look like Figure 2.6. This default view for the Browser in Final Cut Express is called a Medium Icon view. You will see icons for video clips; notice the small speaker to indicate that the clip has audio. You will also see an audio track with its speaker icon, and you will see a couple of folders. Although it uses a folder icon, in FCE-speak this folder is called a *bin*, an old film term. Think of long bits of processed film hanging from pins into a large, cloth-lined bin, but whatever you call it, it behaves like a folder.

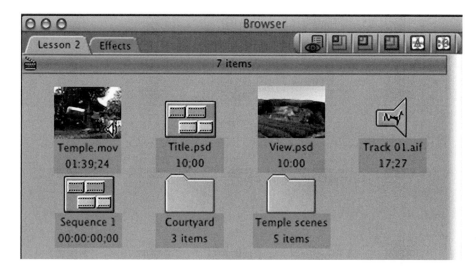

FIGURE 2.6
Lesson 2 Browser window in Medium Icon view.

Renaming Items

You can rename items in the Browser, clips, or sequences, just as you would any file in the Finder. Click twice on the name to highlight it. (Don't quickly double-click, as this will open the item.) With the name selected, type in a new name. You can also select the item and press the **Enter** key on the keyboard to select the name for editing. (See the note on **Clip Name Changes**.)

You can have as many sequences as you want in a project, and you can place sequences within sequences, which is called nesting sequences. We'll look at nesting in Lesson 12. FCE allows you to have more than one project open at a time, which is very useful because it allows you to easily move elements from one project to another. However, you may get confused about which window belongs to which project, so try not to have more than one project open at a time unless it's really necessary.

To close the open projects, click the little round button in the upper left corner of the Browser. This is the **Close** button that is red in the Mac operating system's windows. This closes the Browser, and all the projects close with it. You can also close the project by right-clicking on the tab and selecting **Close**, or by simply pressing **Control-W** when the Browser is the active window. You can identify the active window by the window title bar at the top, which is highlighted and brighter than the other window title bars in the application.

NOTE
Clip Name Changes: Selecting a clip and pressing the Enter key is the only instance in the application in which the Enter key and the Return key have different functions. Although the Enter key will let you rename an item, the Return key will open the item, a clip into the Viewer, and a sequence into the Timeline window.

Browser Views and Buttons

You can change the Browser view by clicking one of the tiny buttons in the upper right corner of the window (see Figure 2.7). These buttons let you choose List view or three different icon views—Small, Medium, and Large—as well as buttons for arranging by Name or by Duration. Small icon view is pretty useless, and the large icons take up a lot of screen space.

FIGURE 2.7
Browser buttons.

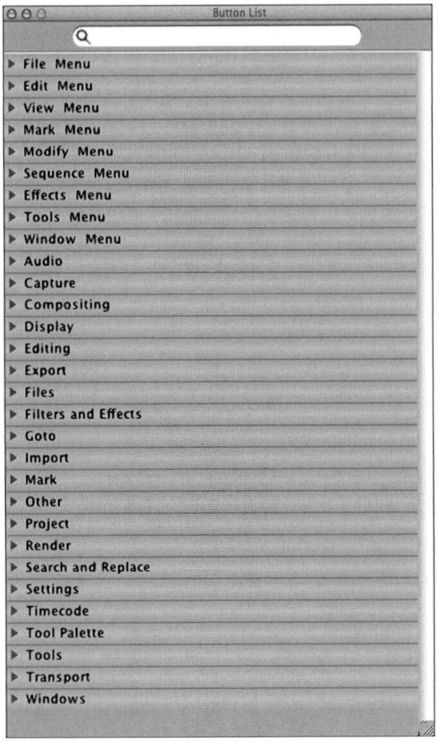

You can also change views by selecting **View>Browser Items**. Finally, as in much else in FCE, you can use a keyboard shortcut. **Shift-H** will cycle through the four Browser view options.

FIGURE 2.8
Button list.

FCE has the ability to create buttons that you can place in the various windows of the interface. To create a new button, open the **Button List** from the **Tools** menu (or use the keyboard shortcut **Option-J**). This calls up the Button List shown in Figure 2.8. To find the function for which you want to create a button, start typing in the search field at the top of the list, and all the functions that have that word will appear in the list.

To make a button for Export to QuickTime Movie, for instance, type *export*, and three items will appear. Drag the item you want to any one of the little coffee-bean-like holders in the upper right corner of any of FCE's windows. The buttons can be further customized by adding colors to the buttons and spacers to group them into sections. You can even color the spacers by using the shortcut menu, with which you can also save your

22

Button List

- ▶ File Menu
- ▶ Edit Menu
- ▶ View Menu
- ▶ Mark Menu
- ▶ Modify Menu
- ▶ Sequence Menu
- ▶ Effects Menu
- ▶ Tools Menu
- ▶ Window Menu
- ▶ Audio
- ▶ Capture
- ▶ Compositing
- ▶ Display
- ▶ Editing
- ▶ Export
- ▶ Files
- ▶ Filters and Effects
- ▶ Goto
- ▶ Import
- ▶ Mark
- ▶ Other
- ▶ Project
- ▶ Render
- ▶ Search and Replace
- ▶ Settings
- ▶ Timecode
- ▶ Tool Palette
- ▶ Tools
- ▶ Transport
- ▶ Windows

button configurations for all of your windows (see Figure 2.9). To remove a button, drag it out of the bean. It will disappear, like an item from the Dock, in a puff of smoke.

FIGURE 2.9
Button holder
shortcut menu.

In the *Extras* folder on the DVD that came with this book is a Button List called *Editing Workshop Button Bars*. By right-clicking in the button folder and using the **Load All Button Bars** function and navigating to that file on the DVD, you can load a group of very useful buttons. There aren't many of them because I'm not a great advocate of mousing around the desktop and clicking buttons, but you can add your own favorites to any of the button holders.

23

NOTE

The *Modify Clip Name to Match File* and *Modify File Name to Match Clip* which were available as buttons in FCE4 have been removed in 4.0.1. The toolbars in the DVD's *Extras* folder includes these buttons, but they may not work in 4.0.1.

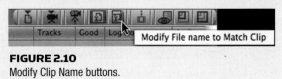

FIGURE 2.10
Modify Clip Name buttons.

Let's change the Browser to List view. Right-click in the empty Browser space, and select **View as List**. To see the contents of the bins, (1) click the twirly disclosure triangle to expand the folder view, *or* (2) double-click on the folder icon.

If you double-click the icon, the bin will open in a new window. To close the window, click on the little button in the upper left corner of the window, or use the keyboard shortcut, **Command-W**.

TIP

Default Buttons: Final Cut does not provide an easy way to get back to the default button bar set. The only way to easily revert to the default set is to actually save the button bar set when it is in its default state. To do that, right-click on each button bar to restore the default, and then right-click on one, and from the shortcut menu select **Save All Buttons Bars**. Now if you've added or deleted any buttons and you want to go back to the default state, simply select in the same shortcut menu **Load All Button Bars** and navigate to your saved buttons, which is normally in your *Final Cut Express User Data* folder in your *Preferences* folder. A *Default Button Bars* is already saved for you in the *Extras* folder of the DVD, along with the *Editing Workshop Button Bars*.

TIP

Tabbed Bins: You can open a bin tabbed into the project window by holding down the Option key as you double-click to open it. To close a tab, right-click on the tab, and select Close Tab, or use the keyboard shortcut, Control-W.

The Browser contains two sequences: *Sequence 1* and *Title.psd*. When opened, a sequence appears in the Timeline window. Here you lay out your video, audio, and graphics clips. A sequence can have multiple tracks of video and audio. You can also place sequences within sequences, as we shall see later. Whenever you create a new project, FCE always creates a default empty sequence called *Sequence 1*. The *Title.psd* also has a sequence icon because FCE imports Photoshop files as layered sequences, with each of the layers in the PSD file appearing as a separate video layer in the Final Cut sequence, one stacked on top of the other. The other Photoshop file, *View.psd*, is a single-layer file and imports as a single-layer graphic and has a different icon. We'll look at working with graphics in Lesson 12.

Browser Details

With the Browser in List view and the window arrangements set to Standard, stretch out the Browser window to the right (or use the maximize button, the one on the right of three in the upper left corner), and you will see just some of the many things the Browser displays in List view (see Figure 2.11).

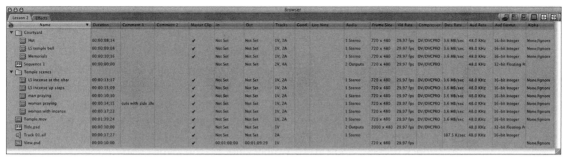

FIGURE 2.11
Browser List view.

NOTE

Sequence Settings: The *Sequence 1* that appears in the Browser is in the format and specification you selected when you launched the application. In this case, the sequence is in DV NTSC format. If you change the easy setup, as we'll see in the next chapter, this does not affect the sequence that has already been created. Only any new sequences you create will be in that format.

The Browser shows the duration of clips and the In and Out points, which are probably marked Not Set at this stage. You also see track types (whether video and/or audio) and how many audio tracks are present. Note that the Photoshop sequences tell you how many layers are in the sequence. Also notice that *Sequence 1* by default has two video tracks and four audio tracks.

FIGURE 2.12
Subclips in the Browser.

The Master Clip column has some items that are checked. We'll look at this more closely on page 78. In Figure 2.12, the clips in the bin called *Courtyard* have torn edges on the left and right. These are subclips, which we will discuss in more detail in Lesson 5.

The Browser also shows the type of audio, frame size, and frame rate (in the case of these clips, 29.97 frames per second, the standard frame rate for all NTSC and HD video in North America and Japan); the type of video compression used; the data rate; the audio sampling rate; and much, much more information than you will probably ever need!

> **TIP**
>
> **Ordering:** You can arrange the order in which clips are shown in List view by selecting the column header. By clicking the little triangle that appears in the header, you can change the order from descending to ascending. Also, if you Shift-click on the header of other columns, another triangle will appear and will be added as secondary ordering lists. Secondary sorting allows you to organize and arrange your material to suit your workflow. To clear secondary sort orders, choose a new primary sort, and click on an unsorted column header without the Shift key.
> You can move any of the columns by grabbing the header at the top of the column and pulling it to wherever you want the column to appear. Only the Name column cannot be moved. It stays displayed on the left side of the window.

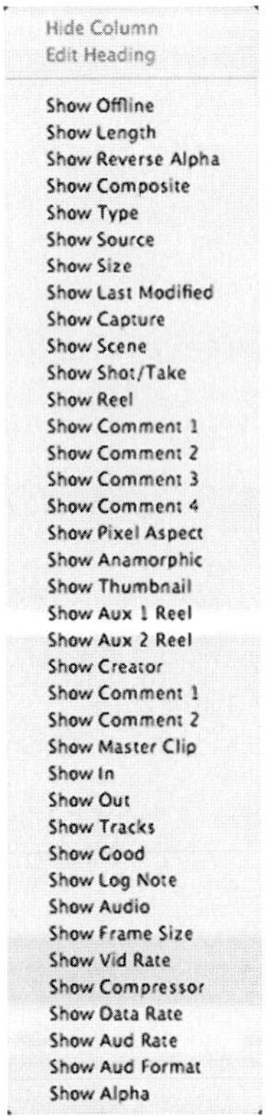

FIGURE 2.13
List of available Browser items.

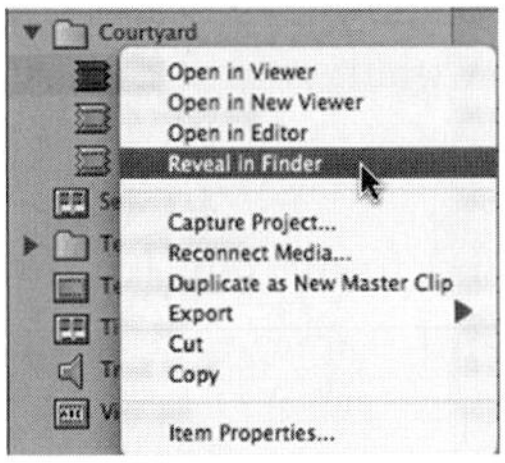

FIGURE 2.14
Clip Shortcut menu.

If your cursor is over the column headers in the Browser and you right-click your mouse, you get a shortcut menu. Figure 2.13 shows the list of the available categories, except for Name and Duration, that are active columns in the Browser.

One of the important items you can call up here is Source, which tells you the file path to a clip's location on your hard drive. Another way to locate a file on your hard drive and what it's called is to right-click on the clip and select **Reveal in Finder** (see Figure 2.14). If you right-click on the clip *Hut* and go to the media in the Finder, you will see the media file is called *Temple.mov*. Renaming a clip in the Browser does not rename the media file on the hard drive and vice versa (see "The Browser Façade").

Another item that is hidden in the Browser columns is **Show Thumbnail**. This cool feature brings up a thumbnail that shows the first frame of the video. Grab the thumbnail and drag the mouse. This is called *scrubbing*, and you're dragging through the video clip itself so you can see what's in it. Viewing media in the Browser can save time. You can quickly scan through a shot to see if it's the one you're looking for. You can also change the Poster frame—the frame that appears in the thumbnail. The default is the first frame of the video (or the In point), but if you scrub through the video and find a new frame you would like to set as the thumbnail, press the **Control** key and release the mouse. A new Poster frame has

THE BROWSER FACADE

The FCE Browser is a facade. In other words, whatever you're bringing into the FCE project—the media you are importing into your Browser—is equivalent to the aliases of your media (see Figure 2.15). While you are working with these aliases, you are using them to pass instructions to the computer about which pieces of video and audio to play when and what to do with them. The conveniences created for you in the application are an elaborate way of telling the computer what to do with the media on your hard drives and how to play it back. All of the clips in the project, whether in the Browser, the Viewer, or the Timeline, are simply pointers to the media on the hard drive. This is a nondestructive, completely nonlinear, random-access artifice. This means that your media is not modified by anything you do in the application but that you can arrange the clips and work on any portion of your project at any time. It also means you can access any piece of media from anywhere on your hard drive at any time. The clips are not brought into the Browser or placed in the Timeline. They never leave their place on the hard drives. They are never in the project at all except as a list. You can change the names in the list to anything more convenient, and it has no effect at all on the data stored on your hard drive. All you are doing is changing how you give instructions to the data, not the data itself. On the other hand, if you change the names of the clips on your hard drive, that *will* confuse FCE, and you will have to reconnect each clip to establish the links between the two.

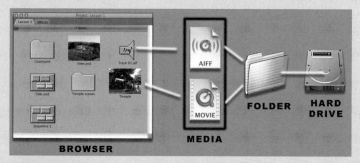

FIGURE 2.15
Media and FCE workflow.

27

been set. If you change the Poster frame for a clip here or in any other Browser window, the poster will change for each instance of that clip anywhere in the Browser and will also display as the poster when the Browser is set to Icon view.

When the Browser is in Icon view, the clips are shown with their Poster frame. Like the thumbnails we saw earlier in List view, these icons have the same scrubbable property. To do this, you must select the **Scrub** tool from the **Tools**

FIGURE 2.16
Scrub tool.

FIGURE 2.17
Browser shortcut menu.

FIGURE 2.18
Item Properties format
panel.

palette (see Figure 2.16). Or, if you hold down **Control-Shift**, the cursor will change to the **Scrub** tool, which is the **Hand** tool with forward and reverse arrows that will let you scrub the icons.

As everywhere in the application, right-clicking in the Browser will call up several useful items (see Figure 2.17), allowing you to make new bins and sequences, as well as importing and arranging material. The clips themselves hold a shortcut menu that can do a variety of useful things, as we've already seen.

Another very useful option in the clip's shortcut menu is Item Properties. Item Properties, which can also be called up by using the keyboard shortcut **Command-9**, calls up an information window that tells you everything about a clip (see Figure 2.18). You can rename a clip here, as well as see technical information about the clip and its specifications.

One of the most important functions of the Browser is that it allows you to organize and catalog material. This is especially important for long projects or projects with a great deal of media. The Browser allows you to add descriptions

Format				
	Subclip	V1	A1	A2
Name	Hut	Hut	Hut	Hut
Type	Subclip			
Creator	QuickTime Player	QuickTime Player	QuickTime Player	QuickTime Player
Source	Media:Media:Temple.mov	Media:Media:Temple.mo	Media:Media:Temple.mo	Media:Media:Temple.mo
Offline				
Size	360.8 MB	360.8 MB	360.8 MB	360.8 MB
Last Modified	Tue, Aug 12, 2003, 11:46 PM	Tue, Aug 12, 2003, 11:4	Tue, Aug 12, 2003, 11:4	Tue, Aug 12, 2003, 11:4
Tracks	1V, 2A			
Vid Rate	29.97 fps	29.97 fps		
Frame Size	720 x 480	720 x 480		
Compressor	DV/DVCPRO – NTSC	DV/DVCPRO – NTSC		
Data Rate	3.6 MB/sec	3.6 MB/sec	3.6 MB/sec	3.6 MB/sec
Pixel Aspect	NTSC – CCIR 601	NTSC – CCIR 601		
Anamorphic				
Field Dominance	Lower (Even)	Lower (Even)		
Alpha	None/Ignore	None/Ignore		
Reverse Alpha				
Composite	Normal	Normal		
Audio	1 Stereo		Left	Right
Aud Rate	48.0 KHz		48.0 KHz	48.0 KHz
Aud Format	16–bit Integer		16–bit Integer	16–bit Integer

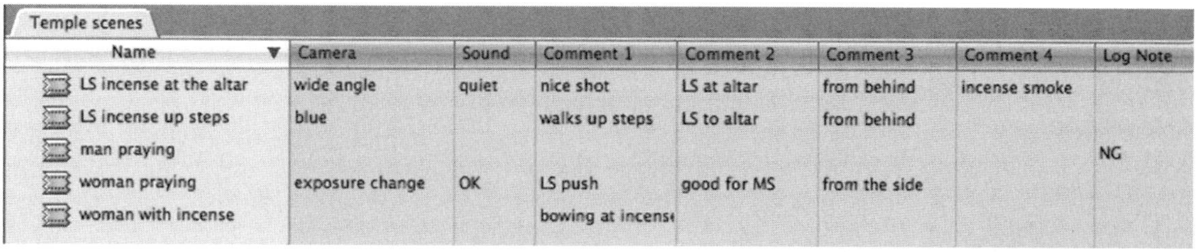

Temple scenes							
Name ▼	Camera	Sound	Comment 1	Comment 2	Comment 3	Comment 4	Log Note
🎞 LS incense at the altar	wide angle	quiet	nice shot	LS at altar	from behind	incense smoke	
🎞 LS incense up steps	blue		walks up steps	LS to altar	from behind		
🎞 man praying							NG
🎞 woman praying	exposure change	OK	LS push	good for MS	from the side		
🎞 woman with incense			bowing at incens(				

FIGURE 2.19
Browser comments.

and other information about your clip. The descriptive information and comments can be entered in the Browser columns (see Figure 2.19). To get from one comment field to the next, press the **Tab** key, and the cursor will move to the next editable window.

FIGURE 2.20
Editing a column heading.

Notice that two of the column headers have been renamed Camera and Sound to add information about the technical quality of the material. You can change the names of any of the comments columns by right-clicking in the column header and choosing **Edit Heading** from the shortcut menu (see Figure 2.20). There are Comments A and B as well as Master Comments 1 to 4.

THE VIEWER

29

Much of the editing in Final Cut Express takes place in the Viewer. This is where you manipulate individual clips, mark where you want them to start and

TIP

Shortcut Menus: Using shortcut menus in List view lets you change items for multiple clips with a few clicks of the mouse. For instance, to add a comment to the Log Note, I select a number of clips and then use the shortcut menu in the Log Note column. This will bring up a list with all of my recent notes in that column. I select the one I want, and all of the selected clips will have their log notes changed (see Figure 2.21).

FIGURE 2.21
Log Note shortcut menu.

FIGURE 2.22
The Viewer.

end, and prepare them for your timeline. To load a clip into the Viewer, double-click on it, or select it and press the **Return** key. You can also drag it into the Viewer, or right-click on it and select **Open in Viewer**. Start by double-clicking on the clip *Temple* to open it into the Viewer (see Figure 2.22).

Viewer Buttons

Figure 2.23 shows the buttons clustered around the bottom of the Viewer. The **Shuttle** tab lets you shuttle the clip forward and backward. Grab it with the mouse and move right and left. The farther from the default center position you go, the faster the video will play. The **Jog** wheel lets you roll back and forth through the frames slowly. The central button in the middle is the **Play** button. Starting from the left in the group around the Play button, the first button is **Go to Previous Edit** (**Up** arrow). The next button is quite useful; it lets you play from your In point to your Out point. The keyboard shortcut is **Shift**-\. The next button to the right of the central Play button is **Play Around Current Point** (\). The default is for playback to start five seconds before where the playhead is and play for two seconds past where the

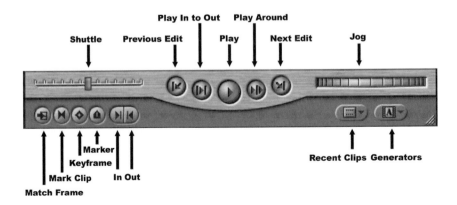

FIGURE 2.23
Viewer buttons.

playhead is. We'll look at how to use these functions in later lessons. The play-head shows you where you are in the clip and is designated by a little yellow triangle with a line hanging off it. There are many playheads in the application; the three we see in the Viewer, the Canvas, and the Timeline just happen to be visible. The last button is **Go to Next Edit** (**Down** arrow).

Another cluster of smaller buttons sits at the bottom left of the Viewer. From the left, the first button is **Match Frame (F)**, which although very useful, will not work for you yet. If you open a clip that's in a timeline, it allows you to match back to the same frame in the Canvas. The next button is **Mark Clip (X)**, which selects the In and Out points the entire length of the clip. The diamond-shaped button adds a keyframe, which you need when creating animation, although the Viewer is not the best place to do this. The next button adds a marker to the clip (**M**). Markers are very useful; they let you set visible marks on clips that appear in the Timeline window. You can mark the beat of a piece of music, where a phrase appears in dialog, or where a pan or zoom starts or ends. Practically anything you can imagine noting about a clip can be made to appear on the screen. Think of them as onscreen Post-it® notes for a video editor.

Next to the **Marker** button is a group of two buttons: **Mark In (I)** and **Mark Out (O)**. These allow you to designate where you want a clip to start and end before you place it in the Timeline. Two more buttons appear at the bottom right of the Viewer. The one with the **Clip** icon lets you load recently opened clips. The

31

NOTE

Match Frame Variations: A match frame button, which is also activated by the F key, appears on the Canvas. When the Canvas or the Timeline is the active window, Match Frame has a different function from match frame in the Viewer. Here, the button or shortcut will match frame back to the same clip and frame of video in the Browser from which the Timeline clip was taken. Another useful Match Frame tool to remember is Command-Option-F, which is a variation of Match Frame that takes you back to the same frame from a new clip of the original piece of media called up directly from your hard drive. Another useful shortcut is Shift-F, which doesn't open the clip into the Viewer but finds it and selects it in the Browser. This can be very handy if you have lots of bins or even bins within bins. It lets you locate a clip in the Browser.

button with the large **A** opens a menu that accesses the **Generators**, such as Bars and Tone, Render Gradients, Color Mattes, Slug, Text, Title 3D, and the Title Crawl tool. We'll delve into this button in later lessons.

Put your cursor in the white bar directly below the video image. As you mouse down, the playhead will jump to where you are. This is the scrubber bar. If you drag the playhead left or right it lets you scrub through the video that's loaded in the Viewer.

Top of the Viewer

Let's look at the top portion of the Viewer for a moment (see Figure 2.24). In the center are two buttons, actually pop-up menus. The one on the left, the **Zoom** pop-up menu (see Figure 2.25), adjusts the size of the image displayed in the Viewer. You can set it to **Fit to Window (Shift-Z)**, or to a percentage from very small to so large that you can see all of the pixels at their blocky best.

FIGURE 2.24
Top of the Viewer.

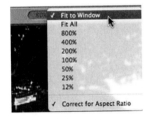

FIGURE 2.25
Zoom pop-up menu.

The other button, the **View** pop-up menu, changes the view from **Image** mode to **Image + Wireframe** (see Figure 2.26). You need this mode especially for compositing in the Canvas when you're combining and animating multiple layers of video. The pop-up also lets you turn on overlays, including the **Title Safe** overlay.

Viewer Time Displays

At the top of the Viewer are two sets of numbers. The time display on the left is the duration of the clip from its marked In point to its marked Out point. If the In and Out are not set, it will show the duration of the media from start to finish. This clip is 1 minute, 39 seconds, and 24 frames long. See "What Is Timecode?" for an explanation of video frame counting.

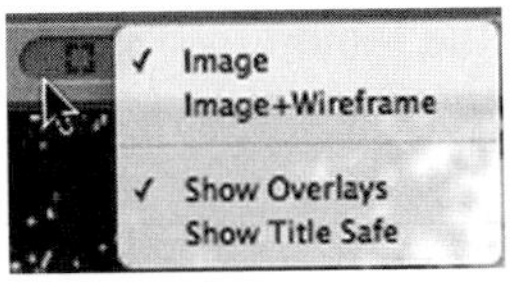

FIGURE 2.26
View pop-up menu.

The time display on the right shows the current time for the frame where its playhead is sitting. This is not the timecode for the clip, which FCE does not display, but timecode is crucial to accurate editing, and FCE does keep track of the timecode internally for DV material, although it is not viewable. Like all time displays in FCE, it's addressable. Click in it to type a new number or to add and subtract a value. When you change the time in the current time display, the playhead immediately jumps to that time.

PLAYING CLIPS

You can play a clip to look at your video in several different ways. The most apparent is the big Play button in the middle of the Viewer controls. If you like working with the mouse, this is just for you, but it is not the most efficient way to work by any means. There are also the Jog and Shuttle controls on the Viewer to view your video at other than real speed. The keyboard is your friend. Learn how to use it because it makes it much easier to control your editing than using the mouse.

Spacebar

Press the **Spacebar** to play the clip. To pause, press the spacebar again—**Spacebar** to start, **Spacebar** to stop. To play the clip backward, press **Shift-Spacebar**. This method is much quicker, and it keeps your hands on the keyboard and off the mouse. You can play and manipulate clips in the Viewer with great efficiency using only the keyboard.

WHAT IS TIMECODE?

Timecode is a frame-counting system that is almost universal to video cameras. A number is assigned to every frame of video and is physically recorded on your tape or disk. The numbers represent time, and on most consumer cameras, they begin at 00:00:00:00, zero hours, zero minutes, zero seconds, and zero frames. On professional and some prosumer cameras, the start number can be set to anything you like. A timecode number is assigned to every frame of video—25 frames per second in the European PAL system and 30 frames per second in the North American and Japanese NTSC system.

This can be a problem for NTSC because the true frame rate of all NSTC video isn't 30 fps but 29.97 fps. Because of this, NTSC has created two ways of counting timecode called Drop Frame and Non-Drop Frame.

Non-Drop Frame (NDF) displays the numbers based on a simple 30 fps frame rate. The problem with this is that when your timecode gets to the one-hour mark, one hour of real-world time has already come and gone. The one hour of clock time finished almost four seconds earlier, so your program is running too long.

Drop Frame (DF) uses a complex method of counting that compensates for the difference between 29.97 fps and 30 fps. No actual frames of video are dropped. DF drops two frames per minute in its count, except every tenth minute. This means that at the one-minute mark, your DF video will go from 59;29 to 1:00;02. There is no 1:00;00 or 1:00;01. Notice the semicolons. The convention is to write DF timecode with semicolons, or at least one semicolon, but NDF is written only with colons. The DV standard uses Drop Frame timecode as its counting method, although some prosumer and all professional cameras can be switched between the two.

Some consumer cameras, particularly inexpensive Canon cameras, must have their date/time clock set so they can generate timecode. It is crucial that the clock on your camera be set to some date or time; otherwise, every time you press Record, the camera may restart the timecode at 0:00:00;00, which will create a break in what should be continuous timecode.

If you are working in HD, either HDV or AVCHD, you should also be aware that in FCE the timecode in those formats are, unfortunately, lost during capture.

Keyboard Shortcuts

Another common way to play the clip is with the **L** key: **L** is play forward, **K** is pause, and **J** is play backward. On your keyboard, the keys are clustered together, but you're probably thinking, "Why not comma, period, and slash?" There is a method to the madness. **J**, **K**, and **L** were chosen because they're directly below **I** and **O**, which are used to mark the In and Out points on clips and in sequences. They are also probably the most frequently used keys on the editing keyboard. Hence, **J**, **K**, and **L** are positioned conveniently for the finger of your right hand with the **I** and **O** keys directly above them.

You can view your video at other speeds. You can fast forward by repeatedly pressing the **L** key. The more times you press **L**, the faster the clip will play. Similarly, hitting the **J** key a few times will make the clip play backward at high speed. These are your VCR controls.

To play a clip one frame at a time, press the **Right** arrow key. To play it slowly, hold down the key. To play slowly backward, hold down the **Left** arrow key. To jump forward or backward one second, use **Shift** with the **Left** or **Right** arrow keys. Pressing **K** and **L** together will also give you slow forward, and **K** and **J** together give you slow backward. To go back to the previous edit—the cut prior to the point where you are currently—use the **Up** arrow key. To go to the next edit event, use the **Down** arrow key. To go to the beginning of the clip, press the **Home** key, and to go to the end, press the **End** key. A list of important keyboard shortcuts can be found in Table 2.1.

Table 2.1	Some Principal Keyboard Shortcuts
Play	L
Pause	K
Play backward	J
Fast forward	Repeat L
Slow forward	L + K or hold Right arrow
Fast backward	Repeat J
Slow backward	J + K or hold Left arrow
Forward one frame	Right arrow
Backward one frame	Left arrow
Forward one second	Shift-Right arrow
Back one second	Shift-Left arrow
Go to previous edit	Up arrow
Go to next edit	Down arrow
Go to beginning	Home
Go to end	End
Mark the In point	I
Mark the Out point	O
Go to In point	Shift-I
Go to Out point	Shift-O
Play Around Current Point	\
Play from In point to Out point	Shift-\
Match Frame	F
Mark Clip	X
Add Marker	M

This is just the surface of the Viewer. We'll be visiting it repeatedly in the lessons to come, especially the tabbed windows behind the video window.

EXPLORING THE CANVAS AND TIMELINE

You'll probably first notice that the Canvas window (see Figure 2.27) is similar to the Viewer. Most controls are duplicated. Some have been placed in mirrored

TIP

Keyboard Shortcuts: When working in
complex applications like a video editing application,
it is far more efficient to use the keyboard shortcuts than menus,
buttons, or even shortcut menus. The keyboard is more efficient than
the mouse and less likely to produce health issues like carpal tunnel
syndrome. The FCE keyboard is pretty comprehensively mapped, and
it would be very beneficial to learn the most important shortcuts. A complete
list of shortcuts can be found at http://manuals.info.apple.com/en/FinalCutExpress
HD_QuickRef.pdf. If trying to remember all of the keyboard shortcuts is shorting out
your brain, you can get color-coded special keyboards with keys that display the
shortcuts. A great tool is Loren Miller's KeyGuide, a laminated color-coded
keyboard display of all FCE's shortcuts. No FCE editor should be without
one. Miller makes them for a number of applications, including Final
Cut Express. You can find out more about them and order
them from http://www.neotrondesign.com.

positions, such as the cluster in the lower right corner, which mirrors the cluster in the lower left of the Viewer. Note that the Match Frame button here has a different function than the Match Frame button in the Viewer. (See the Note about Match Frame on page 31.) The Shuttle and the Jog are also in mirrored positions in Canvas, but they have the same function. The time displays at the top function the same as in the Viewer. The two pop-up menus in the top center are also the same. The Canvas is missing the Recent and Generators pop-ups, which are available only in the Viewer window.

FIGURE 2.27
The Canvas window.

The Timeline Window

Let's take a look at the Timeline window (Figure 2.28) that, because it's empty at this stage, isn't all that much to look at. The Timeline window is made up of tracks. Above the horizontal central double bar are the video tracks. FCE defaults to the two video tracks visible, marked V1 and V2. Below the horizontal bar are four visible audio tracks. A1 and A2 are set as destination tracks, awaiting a stereo pair of audio clips, and A3 and A4 are ready for additional sound tracks. You can change the number of tracks with which a sequence opens in Preferences, which we'll look at in the next lesson. An FCE sequence can have up to 99 tracks of video and 99 tracks of audio.

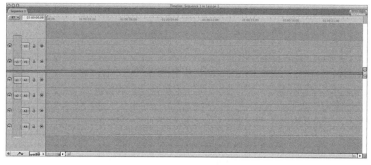

FIGURE 2.28
The Timeline window.

At the top of the window is the like a ruler and displays the current time position for an item in the Timeline window. Just to the left of the ruler is the current time display, where the playhead is at the moment. In an empty sequence that has just been opened, the playhead will be at the beginning at 0:00:00;00.

The Patch Panel

One of the video tracks, V1, has a small v1 button attached to it. This is the source button, and it indicates what selected destination track the source video will be sent to. This area, which sets the source video and audio to the destination video and audio tracks, is called the **patch panel**. You can separate the source button from the destination track by clicking the small source button, which separates it from the track icon, as shown in Figure 2.29. You can reset the destination track by clicking the link together. You can also reassign source buttons to destination tracks by pulling the patch to the desired track. We'll talk about the patch panel more in later lessons.

There are simple keyboard shortcuts to select each of FCE's windows. The principal window shortcuts are shown in Table 2.2.

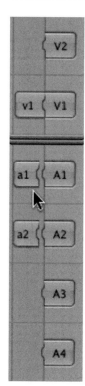

FIGURE 2.29
Setting destination tracks in the patch panel.

37

Table 2.2	Principal FCE Windows Shortcuts
Window	**Shortcut**
Viewer	Command-1
Canvas	Command-2
Timeline	Command-3
Browser	Command-4
Effects	Command-5
Toggle Between Viewer and Canvas	Q

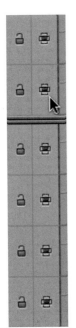

FIGURE 2.30
Track locks and Auto Select features.

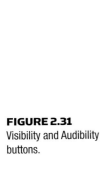

FIGURE 2.31
Visibility and Audibility buttons.

More Timeline Functions

To the right of the patch panel are track locks, which let you lock and unlock specific tracks as necessary (see Figure 2.30). Just to the right of that, next to the tracks themselves, is FCE's Auto Select feature. **Auto Select** is used to perform copy, lift, add edit, and some paste functions to specific tracks. It also controls FCE's match frame function.

To the left of the patch panel are the green **Visibility** and **Audibility** buttons (Figure 2.31), which can be toggled on and off as needed. We'll look at those more in later lessons. More controls for the Timeline windows appear along the bottom and the left edge of the window (see Figure 2.32). The slider on the far right lets you change the horizontal scale at which your clips are displayed in the Timeline window. Drag the clip *Temple* from the Browser into the Timeline. You don't have to be very precise—just drop it anywhere! It's a pretty long clip, so use the slider to adjust the scale of the Timeline to see how it functions.

The triangle to the left of the slider is a pop-up menu that lets you set different displays in the Timeline window (see Figure 2.33), audio waveforms, or filmstrip display.

The buttons to the left of that set the track height. Four settings of track height can be toggled with the keyboard shortcut **Shift-T**. Choose whichever height is comfortable for you and your monitor's resolution. You can also set individual track heights by putting the cursor between the tracks and dragging up or down to resize the track height (see Figure 2.34).

The second button from the left displays **Clip Overlays**, which allow you to adjust the clip's audio levels and video opacity. On the far left edge of the Timeline window is a little button that opens up the **Mute/Solo** buttons on the left edge of the window (see Figure 2.35). These buttons allow you to selectively mute tracks or solo a track so you hear only the selected tracks. The difference between muting and switching off audibility is that a muted track will still export or record to tape, whereas a track with audibility switched off will not export or be heard during recording to tape.

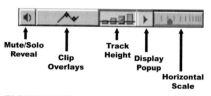

FIGURE 2.32
Timeline buttons.

FIGURE 2.33
Timeline pop-up menu.

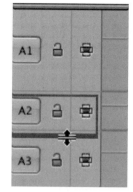

FIGURE 2.34
Resizing individual track heights.

FIGURE 2.35
Mute/Solo buttons.

39

FIGURE 2.36
Track Mover and Static Display Line closed.

FIGURE 2.37
Track Mover and Static Display Line split.

FIGURE 2.38
Snapping and Linked Selection on.

The **Track Mover** tool lets you change the proportions of the video and audio panels in the Timeline window by moving the **Static Display Line** (see Figure 2.36). This can also be split to show different sections of the video and audio panels simultaneously, which can be very useful when you're working with multiple tracks of video or audio. By pulling the tabs on the right edge, you can pull apart the Static Display Line (see Figure 2.37). Much like word processing software, this function lets you keep several tracks displayed while scrolling through the rest of the tracks independently.

In the upper right corner of the Timeline window are two tiny icons that tell you if **Snapping** and **Linked Selection** are turned on (see Figure 2.38). The buttons are green when they are turned on and blacked when they are turned off.

If Snapping is on, the playhead, clips, and anything you move in the Timeline will automatically want to butt up against one another as if they are magnetized.

FIGURE 2.39
RT pop-up.

Turn on **Linked Selection** if you want the sound and the picture together when you grab a sync clip. With **Linked Selection** on, they'll move in unison. With it off, the two elements can be moved separately. I recommend leaving **Linked Selection** on at all times, bypassing it only when necessary with a simple keyboard modifier instead of using the button.

The last button in the Timeline window is the **RT** pop-up in the upper left corner, which lets you set your real-time playback capability (Figure 2.39). The default is **Safe RT**, whereas **Unlimited RT** allows more real-time playback on fast computers but at the expense of dropped frames during playback. You should leave it on Safe RT for now.

SUMMARY

You should now be familiar with the interface and the terminology used in Final Cut Express. I'm sure at this point that you have many questions, and I hope to answer as many of them as possible over the course of these lessons so you can work smoothly and efficiently with the application. Spend some time clicking around in the Final Cut Express windows. You can't hurt anything. And remember to try right-clicking to bring up shortcut menus. In the next lesson, you'll learn how to edit your material into a sequence and start to build up your movie.

TIP

Help: If you have problems with your computer, or with Final Cut Express in particular, help is available in two places: the Apple Final Cut Express discussion forum, which you can link to from http://discussions.info.apple.com, or my website at http://www.fcpbook.com.

LESSON 3
Setting Up Your Application Preferences

Digital video editing is divided into three phases:

1. Getting your material into the computer
2. Editing it (which is the fun part!)
3. Getting it back out of your computer

This lesson is about setting up your computer so it's ready for number 1. Before you capture your material, you must set up your application correctly. In Final Cut Express 4, as in most video editing programs, that means setting up your preferences and selecting the correct choices for your material.

After setting your preferences, we'll proceed to capturing your media. These fundamentals are absolutely necessary for FCE to function properly. Set it up right, get your material into your project properly, and you're halfway home. You cannot overestimate how important this is.

SETTING UP A NEW PROJECT

There is no Lesson project on the accompanying DVD, so let's begin by creating a new project. Start by double-clicking the Final Cut Express icon in the *Applications* folder. Or better yet, if you've created a Dock alias for FCE, click on the icon in the Dock. FCE will launch the last project that was open. If a previous project opens, close the Browser, which will close the project.

1. Go up to **File>New Project (Command-Shift-N)**.
   You will get a new project called *Untitled Project*, with the empty sequence in the Browser called *Sequence 1*. Because FCE uses your project name to

41

create folders that organize your material inside designated folders, such as the *Capture Scratch* and *Render* folders, it's a good idea to give your project a name right away. At this stage you can't save the project because there's nothing to save. However, you can use **Save Project As** to save it with a name. FCE will use that name to create files in designated places on your hard drive.

2. Give the project a name, and save it inside your *Documents* folder.

TIP
Opening a New Project: If you ever want FCE to open a new, blank project rather than the existing project, you can simply hold down the Shift key when you double-click on the icon or on the Dock alias. This will open a blank project and is a new feature in version 4. You must hold down the Shift key through the whole launch process.

USER PREFERENCES

Final Cut Express has three separate preferences settings:

- **User Preferences**, which sets up how you want to work with the application
- **System Settings**, which sets preferences that control your computer
- **Easy Setup**, which is for audio/video preferences and deals with how you get your material in and out of your computer

To access **User Preferences**, go up to the **Final Cut Express** menu and select **User Preferences (Option-Q)**. As soon as you open **User Preferences**, you will see the pane in Figure 3.1, which is the General Preferences panel.

GENERAL PREFERENCES

The User Preferences may seem daunting because it's made up of four tabbed windows. We'll work through it, however, starting with **General Preferences**, the first window. Fortunately, most of the items here can be left at their default setting.

The first item you should change is the **Levels of Undo**, which defaults to ten actions. This is the same default used when Final Cut was first introduced in 1999, when we could run the application on a PowerMac 300 MHz G3 using

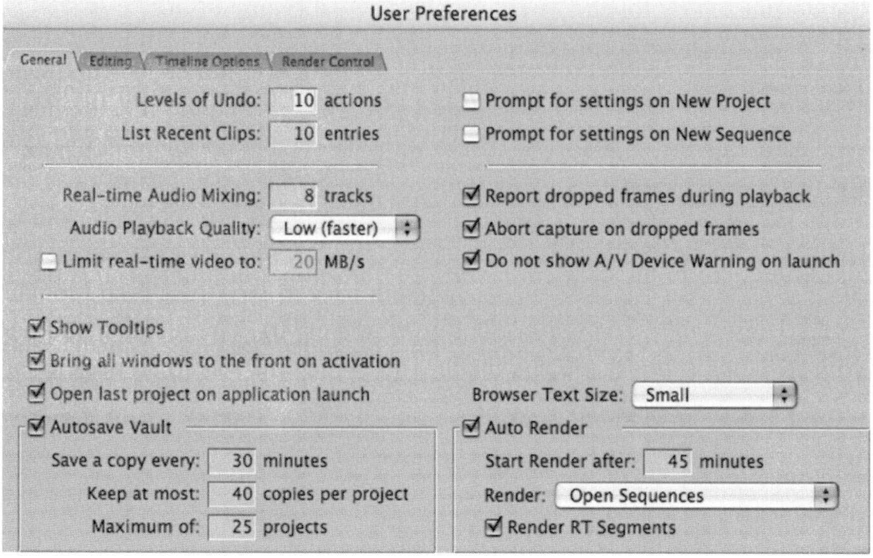

User Preferences

General \ Editing \ Timeline Options \ Render Control \

Levels of Undo: 10 actions   ☐ Prompt for settings on New Project
List Recent Clips: 10 entries   ☐ Prompt for settings on New Sequence

Real-time Audio Mixing: 8 tracks   ☑ Report dropped frames during playback
Audio Playback Quality: Low (faster) ⇕   ☑ Abort capture on dropped frames
☐ Limit real-time video to: 20 MB/s   ☑ Do not show A/V Device Warning on launch

☑ Show Tooltips
☑ Bring all windows to the front on activation
☑ Open last project on application launch   Browser Text Size: Small ⇕
☑ Autosave Vault   ☑ Auto Render
Save a copy every: 30 minutes   Start Render after: 45 minutes
Keep at most: 40 copies per project   Render: Open Sequences ⇕
Maximum of: 25 projects   ☑ Render RT Segments

FIGURE 3.1
User Preferences
General tab.

OS 8.5 with 128 MB of RAM. You should increase the number to 32, which is as high as it will go.

For **List of Recent Clips**, 10 seems like a good number. This is the number of clips retained for the pop-up at the bottom of the Viewer (see Figure 3.2). The limit is 20.

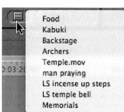

Food
Kabuki
Backstage
Archers
Temple.mov
man praying
LS incense up steps
LS temple bell
Memorials

Real-time Audio Mixing determines how many tracks the application will try to play back in real time before it requires rendering. This is no guarantee that it will be able to do it, but it will try. The default is fine, although if you're mixing a lot of tracks, most computers and hard drives can support more tracks, so you should raise the number to something like 24.

FIGURE 3.2
Recent clips in the
pop-up menu.

NOTE
More Audio Less Video: The more you increase the number
of real-time audio tracks, the more the application will prioritize in favor of
real-time audio playback rather than real-time video playback. If you're doing a
lot of video compositing and image manipulation, keep the real-time audio mixing
preference low. When you're ready to mix and build your audio tracks,
render all your video and then increase your real-time
audio preference.

The default setting for the **Audio Playback Quality** pop-up menu is Low. It's fine to work in Low; it will allow a greater number of real-time tracks for playback. When you're outputting to tape, exporting, or doing an audio mixdown, these are automatically done at High quality. You don't need to reset this. Changing this item will also reduce the number of audio tracks that you can preview without rendering.

The **Limit real-time video** option is of little value in FCE. It is a holdover from Final Cut Pro, where you can work with a very high data rate video. It's best to simply leave it unchecked. Neither DV nor HDV, the two formats FCE works with, exceeds 20 MB/per second of data.

The next two items, **Show Tooltips** and **Bring All Windows to the Front on Activation** should probably be left checked. The third item, **Open Last Project on Application Launch**, I usually leave checked as well. Most single users will probably find it easiest for the application to work this way. In schools, however, or other multiuser environments, I would strongly suggest that this item be unchecked so you either manually open the project you're working on or open a blank project when you launch the application. It helps prevent people from capturing material into the wrong project folders.

In the lower left of this panel are the **Autosave Vault** preferences. Autosaving saves your project incrementally with a date and time stamp. Here you can assign how often you want the project saved, how many copies to keep, and how many projects you want to be held. Saving a project to disk can take a moment or two. The larger the project gets, the greater the number of clips and sequences, and the longer the save will take. So interrupting your workflow by setting the **Save a Copy** box too small might be an annoyance. I have found that 30 minutes is a good number. You probably won't lose too much if the application does crash, plus you'll save a couple of days' worth of work in the vault. If you make the save time too quick—say, 10 minutes or less—you may want to increase the copies per project that are saved. The saved files can be called up from the *Autosave Vault* folder from the **File** menu by selecting **Restore Project**. You'll be given a dialog that offers you a list of time-stamped copies of that project (see Figure 3.3).

You can save up to 100 copies of each project, with a maximum of 100 projects. It works on a first-in/first-out basis. The oldest project saved is dumped into the Trash as new autosaves are added. Because it's not deleted from your hard drive, you can still retrieve an autosaved project from the Trash if you haven't emptied it.

On the right side of the General Preferences panel is a list of check boxes. The default settings for the first five are probably best left the way they are. It's probably wise to leave **Report Dropped Frames During Playback** checked on, as well as **Abort Capture on Dropped Frames**. You may find that FCE is giving dropped frame warnings immediately when a capture begins. If this is happening, you might try switching this feature off and seeing if you can capture your material cleanly. Also, if it aborts 55 minutes into a one-hour capture, you've lost everything and must start all over again. The most common cause of dropped frames can be traced to two things: (1) your media drive is not fast enough for digital video, and (2) your computer is trying to do too many things at the same time.

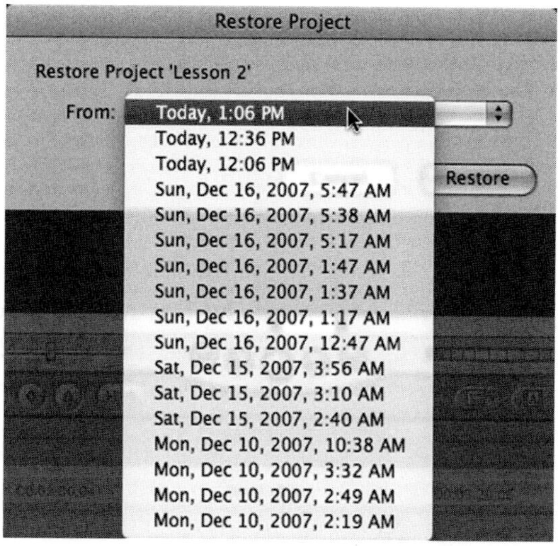

FIGURE 3.3
Restore Project dialog box.

You can set the Browser Text pop-up to Small, Medium, or Large. If your eyes are good, I suggest Small. The Medium and Large settings use too much Browser space and also increase the size of the text in the Timeline clips, which makes it difficult to see clip names of short shots.

The **Auto Render** settings allow you to set a time for which the application will start rendering material based on your settings when your computer is idle. It's great to find all of your rendering done when you come back from lunch or after you leave your computer on overnight.

That's it for the first window of Preferences!

TIP
Restoring Project: When you restore a project, the application gives you a warning first. The project then opens with the project name, and when you save it, it saves in the location of the original project. You can also use Revert Project, which, as in other applications, will take you back to the last saved state. Note that neither Restore nor Revert will bring back arrangements. These are in your preferences and will not be restored.

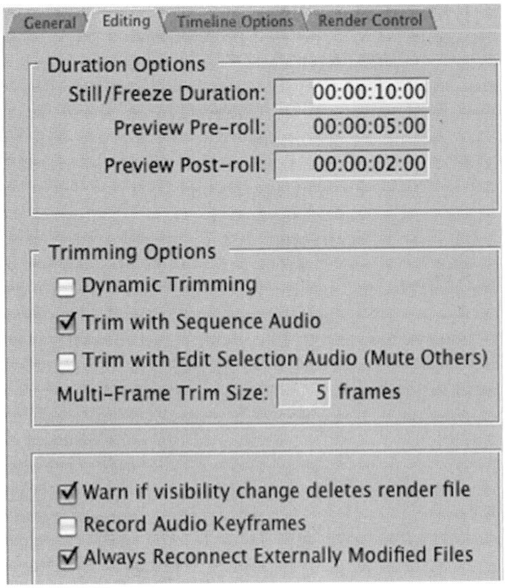

FIGURE 3.4
Left side of Editing
Preferences panel.

Editing Preferences

Open the next tab, Editing Preferences, which gives you control over your editing functions and a couple of functions new to this version of FCE. The left side of the panel looks like Figure 3.4.

Still Image Duration sets the length of imported single-frame graphics and freeze frames made in FCE. You can change them after you've made them in FCE, but they'll appear at this length in the Browser. The default setting of 10 seconds seems long to me, so I usually set it to 5 seconds, a reasonable length for most stills or graphics from applications such as Photoshop. If you're doing training or other videos that require many full screen graphics, leaving it at 10 seconds might be better for you. Although stills and freeze frames have a default duration of 10 seconds, they're actually two minutes and 10 seconds long when they're imported. The duration can be changed to any length you want. You have to set the maximum duration for the still inside the Browser before it is placed inside a sequence. After that, the still cannot be extended beyond its designated duration unless you use the Fit to Fill edit function, which we look at in Lesson 6. It can be made shorter but not longer. There is also a sequence time limit of 12 hours that you cannot exceed. Previous versions were limited to four hours.

In the last lesson, we talked about playing around the current time. If you hit the **Play Around** button or use the keyboard shortcut \, playback will begin a defined amount of time before the playhead and play for a defined amount of time past it. You define those times here. The default Preview preroll is five seconds, a traditional preroll time for VTR machines. The default Preview postroll is two seconds. Five seconds for a preroll always feels long to me, so I set it to three seconds. I leave the postroll at two seconds. When we get to use this feature, you can play with it and see what feels right for you.

In the Trimming Option section, I would leave this at the default. It can be changed at a later time when you're using the Trim Edit window.

Multi-Frame Trim Size sets the number of frames that can be trimmed in the Trim Edit window or the Timeline. Five is the default, which seems fine to me, but after you've worked with the tools, you might prefer to pick a different value that suits you better. We'll look at items such as multiframe trimming in closer detail in later lessons.

The next two items I would leave as they are. The visibility warning is useful, and it can also be turned off when it comes up. The **Record Audio Keyframes** check box lets you adjust and record audio levels in real time while you control the levels of a clip in the Viewer. It's a feature that we'll look at in Lesson 10, although it has limited use in FCE because you can't really mix tracks with it in the application. The last of these three items, **Always Reconnect Externally Modified Files**, now defaults to being checked on. It's a useful function if you edit images like still files in an application such as Photoshop or Photoshop Elements.

The right side of the Editing Preferences panel (see Figure 3.5) is new to FCE4. The **Auto Conform Sequence** defaults to **Ask**, which is probably the best setting. How this works is, when you first put a clip into a sequence, if the sequence properties don't match the media, it allows you to auto-matically conform the sequence to match the media. This is a great new fea-ture that will probably save a lot of people from a lot of trouble and a lot of headaches. You should be aware, however, that the sequence will only conform to one of the formats FCE uses. If you try to put in an MPEG-4 file that's in the H.264 codec, it will not create a sequence setting for that and will instead conform the media to that sequence. It will simply drop the media into the Timeline without warning.

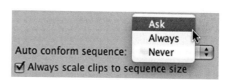

FIGURE 3.5
Right side of Editing Preferences panel.

47

The second line in this section sets the application to automatically scale material to fit the sequence. Small clips, big clips, HD into DV, or vice versa, will all be scaled up or down as needed to fit the Canvas. This is another really useful feature and works for all media, video and graphics files. If you don't like this behavior, simply switch it off here.

Timeline Options

The next tab, **Timeline Options** (see Figure 3.6), is where you define your personal preferences for your sequence timeline layout. You can set the track

FIGURE 3.6
Timeline Options tab.

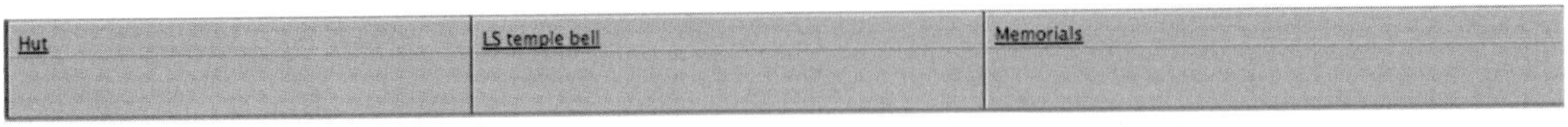

FIGURE 3.7
Name.

FIGURE 3.8
Name Plus Thumbnail
style.

FIGURE 3.9
Filmstrip style.

> **TIP**
> *Filmstrip:* Although Filmstrip style may look like the best way to edit, it is very taxing on any computer. Using Filmstrip style on anything but the fastest computer can make the application work very slowly.

size, the default number of tracks with which a new Timeline opens, and a thumbnail display style. The style the tracks are displayed in **Name, Name Plus Thumbnail,** or **Filmstrip** (see Figures 3.7 to 3.9).

I leave the two check boxes, **Show Keyframe Overlays** and **Show Audio Waveforms**, turned off. It's easier to just toggle them on and off in the Timeline as needed.

As the warning at the bottom indicates, all of these settings in Timeline Options affect only *new* sequences. Existing sequences will not be affected. To change the Timeline Options of an existing sequence, you'll have to open the sequence and use **Sequence>Settings (Command-zero)** and change them there, or use the triangle pop-up in the lower left of the Timeline window that we saw in the last lesson in Figure 2.33.

Render Control

The **Render Control** panel (see Figure 3.10) allows you to change the render quality of your material from the default high-resolution to quite low-resolution rendering at low frame rates. The advantage of this is that low-resolution material will render out much more quickly than full DV or HD resolution settings. Here you can also set to render Filters or just motion, as well as adding in **Motion Blur** and **Frame Blending**. These last two, which produce better results, will slow down rendering considerably. Render Control for individual sequences, which is where you're more likely to need it, can also be accessed from **Sequence>Settings**. Be careful with changing these settings. See the lesson on outputting for the issues this potentially creates.

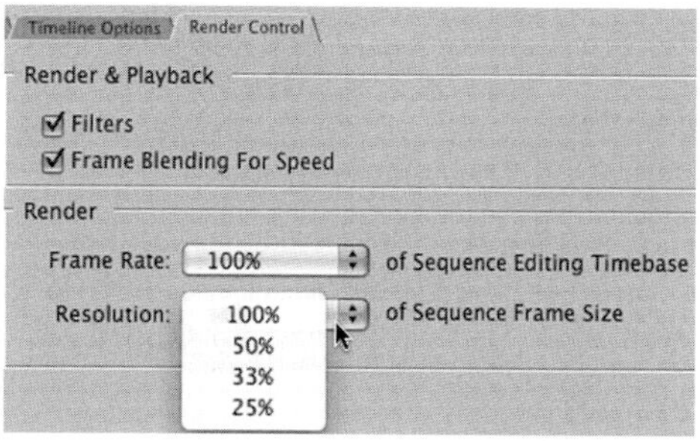

SYSTEM SETTINGS

Systems Settings (Shift-Q) has several important function controls, especially in the first panel.

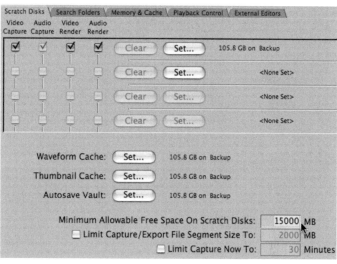

FIGURE 3.10
Render Control.

Scratch Disks

The first panel in the tabbed window is **Scratch Disks** (see Figure 3.11). This is perhaps the most important of all the preference panels. Let's look at the bottom portion of the panel first. The locations of **Waveform Cache, Thumbnail Cache,** and **Autosave Vault** all default to the drive that you set when you first launched the application, which should be your media drive and is probably where you should leave them.

Minimum Allowable Free Space on Scratch Disks defaults to a low number, much lower than it should be. Most people feel that at this setting, the hard drive will fragment heavily and slow down. Some go so far as to say that

FIGURE 3.11
Scratch Disks panel.

TIP
Scratch Disk Preferences: FCE's preferences are system based, a separate set of preferences for each user. They are not project based. Unfortunately, there is no way to have the Scratch Disks change with whatever the open project is. However, inside the Capture Scratch folder, the capture material is segregated into separate folders based on the project name. So when you open a project and go to capture, whatever you capture goes into a folder that keeps its material separate from that of other projects.

you should leave 25 percent of your drive free. For large drives, this seems a bit excessive. Experienced users recommend 10 percent or at least 10 GB. If you have a single partition larger than 100 GB, I would suggest setting this number to at least 10 GB to 15 GB, or 10,000 MB to 15,000 MB, as in Figure 3.11.

Unless you have a particular reason, you should leave **Limit Capture/Export Segment Size To** and **Limit Capture Now To** unchecked. These features limits the size of segments FCE can capture or export. There isn't any particular reason to limit it.

Let's get back to the main body of the **Scratch Disks** panel. Here you assign scratch disks for your ingested material and for your render files. This is the location of where these files will go when they are copied off your tape or your camera disk. Normally, you set a project's video, audio, and render files in the same location. By default, FCE assigns separate render folders for audio and video. When you click the **Set** button, a navigation window allows you to select the location for these files. Usually I go to the media drive I want to use for a project and select the drive itself.

Selecting the drive will create folders with names like *Capture Scratch, Render Files,* and *Audio Render Files.* As you ingest your video material, it is stored in *Capture Scratch.*

If you have more than one hard drive or partition, you can set multiple locations in the Scratch Disks panel. In FCE you can set up to 12 drives or partitions. The application automatically switches from one partition to another as they fill.

TIP
Choose the Top Level: If you've selected the top level of the drive as your scratch and render location, the next time you need to set a scratch disk, be careful not to select the *Capture Scratch* folder; select the drive or partition. Selecting the folder rather than the drive will make another *Capture Scratch* folder inside the current one.

50

NOTE

Scratch Disk Warning: If the assigned scratch disk is not available when you launch the application, a warning appears asking you to reassign the scratch disk. In the warning dialog box that appears (see Figure 3.12), you are given a choice to either Quit, mount drive and Check Again, or Reset Scratch Disks to choose an available partition or disk. If the scratch disk with your media is missing, both the items in your Browser and your render files will go offline. So it may be worth reconnecting that missing drive rather than reassigning the scratch disk to another location.

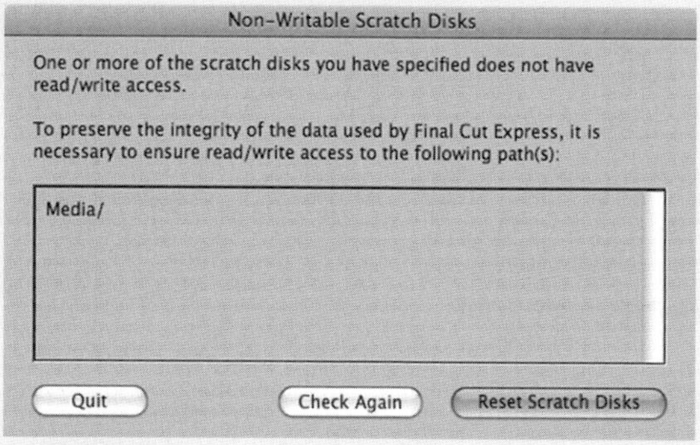
Non-Writable Scratch Disks
One or more of the scratch disks you have specified does not have read/write access.
To preserve the integrity of the data used by Final Cut Express, it is necessary to ensure read/write access to the following path(s):
Media/
Quit
Check Again
Reset Scratch Disks

FIGURE 3.12
Missing disks warning.

Search Folders

The second panel, **Search Folders** (see Figure 3.13), lets you set what drives or folders you want FCE to search when looking to reconnect material. If you have large drives or a lot of them, you can set the search locations here. It will let the application reconnect automatically and also improve search and reconnect speed.

Scratch Disks
Search Folders
Clear
Set...
Media

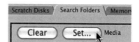

FIGURE 3.13
Search Folder panel.

Memory & Cache

The next panel, **Memory & Cache** (see Figure 3.14), allows you to control the amount of memory used by the application. Normally, the default values are fine. If you want to work in other applications (e.g., if you have an application such as Adobe After Effects that you would like to render in the background

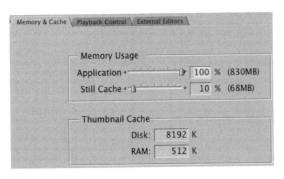

FIGURE 3.14
Memory & Cache panel.

while you work in FCE), then you can lower the application RAM to allow other applications to have RAM to work with.

Also, if you're working with a lot of large images in a sequence, you might want to raise the **Still Cache** memory allocation. If you're working with a lot of intense applications or large stills, adding more physical RAM to your computer might also be a good idea.

Thumbnail Cache (Disk) and (RAM) values are relatively small. It's probably best to keep them at the default values unless you like to work in the Browser with lots of bins in Icon view or like to keep thumbnails open in List view. If you do, you may want to raise these values from the default. Make sure you have extra RAM available. Some people make these numbers quite high, 30 MB or more. I don't use icons much, so I leave it low.

Playback Control

Playback Control (see Figure 3.15) is best left at its default settings. As with **Timeline Options**, these settings are best changed for individual sequences and can easily be done with the handy **RT** pop-up in the upper left corner of the Timeline window that we saw in Lesson 2.

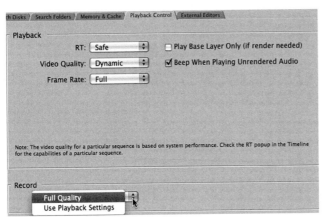

> **TIP**
> **Remember:** Using Filmstrip in your sequences will require considerably more system overhead and a larger Thumbnail Cache size.

FIGURE 3.15
Playback Control panel.

Video Quality can be set to **High, Medium**, or **Low**. The lower the settings, the poorer the image quality, but the greater the real-time playback capabilities.

These settings affect only playback quality and do not change your render quality at all.

This panel also has a check box for **Beep When Playing Unrendered Audio** and the Record quality pop-up at the bottom. The first lets you switch off the beeping sound you get with unrendered material—like material captured in iMovie or MP3 audio files. Switching it off lets you ignore the warning, which you obviously can't otherwise.

The **Record** quality pop-up, which, unlike the video quality and frame rate controls does not appear in the Timeline RT pop-up, lets you record to tape at reduced level for a quick preview copy without having to render out your material. It may be a useful feature for you.

External Editors

The last panel is the **External Editors** tab. Here you can define which applications are used to work on different types of files outside of FCE (see Figure 3.16). This allows you to launch an application to alter a clip in either the Browser or the Timeline. Select a clip and right-click for the shortcut menu choice **Open in Editor** (see Figure 3.17). This will launch the application that you specify in this preferences panel. After you edit the clip—such as a still image in Photoshop—those changes will be reflected in FCE.

53

Scratch Disks	Search Folders	Memory & Cache	Playback Control	External Editors

Still Image Files	Clear	Set...	VideoBook:Applications:Adobe P...toshop CS3:Adobe Photoshop CS3.app
Video Files	Clear	Set...	VideoBook:Applications:QuickTime Player.app
Audio Files	Clear	Set...	VideoBook:Applications:Audacity:Audacity.app

FIGURE 3.16
External Editors panel.

You can set **External Editors** for stills, video, and audio. Be aware, though, that if you set the QuickTime Player as your editor for video files, when you select **Open in Editor** for the audio portion of a sync sound clip using an application like Soundtrack or Audacity, FCE will open the QuickTime Player, not the audio editor preference. FCE thinks of the audio track as part of a single video clip and so uses the QT Player. Single audio files, even if the creator type is QuickTime, will still open with the specified audio editor.

FIGURE 3.17
Open in Editor.

NOTE

Application Reduction: A number of functions have been removed from the Final Ct Express package. Those familiar with earlier versions of FCE will realize that Soundtrack is no longer available with the editing application and that the number of LiveFonts and other content available with LiveType have been removed. The options available in the shortcut menu for clips in the Timeline have also been substantially reduced. The options available in the previous version of FCE can be seen in Figure 3.18. These functions are all still available in the application, but they are no longer available in the shortcut menu.

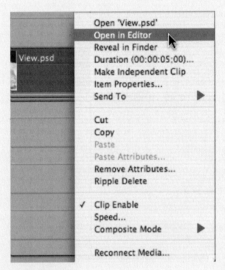

FIGURE 3.18
FCE3.5 Shortcut menu.

NOTE

Changes in Photoshop: Sometimes changes made to a file in Photoshop, particularly to the layer structure and opacity, will cause the file to appear to be offline. Select Reconnect and navigate to the Photoshop file on your hard drive. If the dialog does not come up and the file still appears to be offline, select the item in the Browser, and from the shortcut menu, choose Reconnect Media.

EASY SETUP

From the **Final Cut Express** menu, select **Easy Setup**, or use the keyboard shortcut **Control-Q**. When you open Easy Setup, it brings up the panel in Figure 3.19. The default setting is DV NTSC, based on standard DV with an audio sampling rate of 48 kHz. Like the opening screen that we saw in Lesson 1, Final Cut Express 4 gives you pop-ups that allow you to limit the number of formats you see in the windows to the ones most relevant to you.

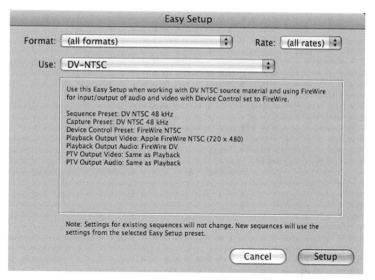

FIGURE 3.19
Easy Setup dialog box.

The trick to **Easy Setup** is to base it on the specifications used in your camera. If you're working with an audio sampling rate of 32 kHz, choose one of those presets. If you work in anamorphic—sometimes called widescreen or 16:9—choose one of those settings. If your camera or deck needs to use FireWire Basic instead of the standard FireWire, choose that. All Canon cameras and some Panasonic and JVC cameras need FireWire Basic, but all Sony devices work with standard FireWire, also called iLink and IEEE 1394. You should check your camcorder manual for its specifications.

There is a list of qualified devices, cameras or decks, for Final Cut Pro that Apple has tested. The list can be found here: http://www.apple.com/finalcutstudio/resources/devicelist.php. These will all work with FCE. Unfortunately this list does not include any AVCHD devices. A list of devices that work with iMovie '08 can be found at: http://docs.info.apple.com/article.html?artnum=306171. These include AVCHD cameras that will almost certainly also work in FCE.

NTSC, which some wags claim stands for Never Twice the Same Color, is actually the now-defunct National Television Standards Committee, which established the format used by television broadcasting in the United States. All of North America and Japan use this format as well. Europe and most of the rest of the world use PAL, which stands for Phase Alternating Lines, and refers to the way color is handled. PAL uses a frame rate of 25 fps and a DV frame size of 720 × 576 (720 pixels wide and 576 pixels tall). NTSC has a standard frame rate fixed at 29.97 fps, not, as many think, a more manageable 30 fps. The NTSC DV frame size is 720 × 480.

Notice that there is no difference in HD between European and North American frame sizes, just in their frame rates, 1080i50 (for 25 fps) and 1080i60 (for 30 fps, or 29.97). Unfortunately, FCE only supports 720p at the North American frame rate of 30 fps (really 29.97). The HD frame sizes are 1,920 × 1,080 (compressed to 1,440 × 1,080 in many HD formats), and 1,280 × 720.

If you are working with AVCHD, you should select one of the HDV settings, the correct one for your frame rate and frame size as FCE uses the same codec, the Apple Intermediate Codec, when ingesting AVCHD or capturing HDV from tape.

If you are using a DV converter box or using your camera in digital pass-through mode, to capture from analog material, choose one of the DV

NOTE
AVCHD 1920 × 1080: Some AVCHD cameras allow you to shoot in full frame 1920 × 1080. Unfortunately this format does not work with FCE. You need to shoot using the 1440 × 1080 setting. You can ingest material that's in 1920, but it will have to rendered when placed in an FCE 1080i sequence.

NOTE
Canon DV Cameras and FireWire Drives:
Because of the way FireWire Basic works, it does not play well with external FireWire drives. This has caused problems for many users, particularly those using Canon DV cameras as a capture device. One drive manufacturer, LaCie, has gone so far as to say that they do not support the use of their FireWire drives with these Canon cameras while they are on the same bus. All Macs only have one FireWire bus, so additional hardware is needed. In a desktop tower computer, an inexpensive card can be added to give an additional FireWire bus. The PowerBooks and MacBook Pros have a cardbus or Express Card slot that can be used for this as well. This is a real problem for iMac users, who don't have these options. Their usual recourse is to capture to the internal system drive and then move the media to the external drive. Or they can capture from a cheap Sony camera or other device that uses the full FireWire device control protocol. This works for material that's been shot at 29.97 fps or 25 fps.

Converter options. This is for use with a noncontrollable device, a device that will not provide the machine with any timecode, which is what the application is looking for when it captures DV material.

The settings you choose here are for both your ingest and for your sequences. The two need to match. Be careful that you don't use one setting to bring in your material and then later change the settings for other material. Any sequences you create after changing the settings will reflect the new settings and will not work properly with material captured using the original settings.

WHAT DOES ANAMORPHIC MEAN ANYWAY?

Anamorphic is a 16:9 widescreen video that is compressed and squeezed horizontally into the standard 4:3 frame. Though widescreen televisions are only slowly being introduced in the United States, and usually as HD televisions, they have been fairly common throughout Japan and Europe for some time. Consequently, Japanese manufacturers have included this capability in many DV camcorders for quite a few years. The camera squeezes the pixels anamorphically (so that everything looks squashed, as though it's tall and narrow) to fit into a 4:3 frame and then unsqueezes them for playback on a widescreen TV.

The problem with this is that many people want to do 16:9 but don't have the equipment to do it properly. To monitor it, you need a widescreen monitor or one that can switch between 4:3 and 16:9. FCE will output the correct 16:9 display if the presets are correct, but you won't see it correctly without the right monitor. You will not see a letterboxed version. Some fairly expensive decks will take a 16:9 image and output it as letterboxed 4:3. You can also place your 16:9 material in a 4:3 sequence and force it to render out the whole piece as letterboxed 4:3.

Most DV camcorders will flag 16:9 material as such and tell the software that the material is anamorphic. The camera and the application will, in most cases, read this regardless of whether you use the 16:9 setup. If it doesn't do this, you will have to set it manually in the clip's Item Properties panel by checking in the Anamorphic line item. If you are shooting true 16:9 (i.e., with an anamorphic lens or with 16:9 CCDs), the correct setup has to be used to force FCE to treat it as widescreen material, even though it doesn't get the 16:9 DV flag from the camera. Even true 16:9 CCDs will squeeze the image to conform to the 4:3 frame size specification of the DV format. If you import material into a project, as opposed to capturing or ingesting it, FCE will not know whether the material is anamorphic or not. You have to tell it. You can do this in the Browser by right-clicking in the Anamorphic column and selecting Yes. You can do it for multiple clips at once by selecting them all first.

Button Bars

Custom Settings

Final Cut Express 4.0 Prefs

Final Cut Express Obj Cache

Final Cut Express Prof Cache

Plugins

FIGURE 3.20
Final Cut Express User Data folder contents.

Preferences Folder

If you have problems with FCE, one of the first remedies anyone will suggest is to trash your *Preferences* file. If there is a problem with your system, it's often your FCE preferences that are corrupt. To delete them, go into your user home folder, **Command-Option-H** from the Finder. Go to your *Library*, choose *Preferences*, and find the file *com. apple.FinalCutExpress.plist*. This file should be deleted. In the same folder, find the *Final Cut User Data folder* (see Figure 3.20).

Inside you can find four or five items, including two or three folders (*Custom Settings, Button Bars,* and *Plugins*). The other items should be your *Final Cut Express 4.0 Prefs, Final Cut Express Obj Cache,* and *Final Cut Express Prof Cache.* If you need to trash your preferences, the only files you should remove from the folder are the three document files: the 4.0 Prefs and the two Cache files. You should do this with the application closed. Put them in the trash and empty the trash.

TIP
Mixing Settings: Do not try to mix settings. If you shot your video in 32 kHz, do not think that by capturing it in 48 kHz, your material will become 48 kHz. All that will happen is that your audio will drift out of sync.

SUMMARY

In this lesson you learned how to set up your system so you will be ready to ingest. Doing this right is critical to the next step: getting your media onto your hard drive and into your project.

LESSON 4
Getting Material into Final Cut Express

Now that we have set up our preferences and everything is ready, we can start bringing our own material into the application. The process is called *capturing* or *ingesting*. Capturing is bringing in material from tape, either DV or HDV, and ingesting is bringing in material from a camera card or DVD camera disc. Either method is essentially a file transfer of the digital data on your camera tape or media to put that binary information that makes up your video and audio and other data onto your computer hard drive. In the case of DV material, the material is converted from its native format to a QuickTime file with separate audio tracks. In the case of HD material, it is converted to a QuickTime file using the Apple Intermediate Codec.

CAPTURE

To capture from DV or HDV tape, go to **File> Capture (Command-8)**. In DV this brings up the **Capture** window (see Figure 4.1). The window is divided into two sections. On the left is a Viewer like the standard FCE Viewer, but this viewer is for your tape deck or camera. The control buttons—**J**, **K**, **L**, **I**, and **O** keys, and the spacebar—work the same as in the FCE Viewer, except they control your deck or camera through the FireWire cable.

> **TIP**
> **Name Your Project:** Always name your project *before* you open the Capture window. The application uses the project name to create a folder in the *Capture Scratch* folder in which your media will be placed. If you don't name the project, the media will go into a folder named *Untitled Project*.

In addition to your keyboard shortcuts for **Mark In** and **Mark Out**, you also have buttons and timecode displays at the bottom of the Viewer for these functions (see

FIGURE 4.1
Capture window.

FIGURE 4.2
Capture Viewer controls.

Go to In   Mark In   Mark Out   Go to Out

Figure 4.2). The two inner buttons mark the In and Out points: **In** on the left, **Out** on the right. The timecode on the left is the In point, and the timecode on the right is the Out point. The left button on the far outside takes the tape deck to the assigned In point, and the far right button takes it to the assigned Out point, or you can use the keyboard shortcuts **Shift-I** to go to the In point and **Shift-O** to go to the Out point.

TIP

Capture Window Size: The size of the Capture window is determined by the size of your Canvas. If you want a large display for the Capture window, set your window arrangement so that you have a large Canvas. If you want a smaller screen on your computer monitor, set the arrangement to the default Standard or even Small Windows before you launch the capture window.

> **NOTE**
> **HDV:** If you're working in HDV, the Capture window is very simple. You have no device control, no mark In and Out functions, and only the Now button to capture your material. You simply put your camcorder in play and press the Now button. HDV contains no device control; the camera must be controlled manually.

Total Free Space	105.4 GB	Total Free Time (AV) 472.3 min
00:00:11;12		00:01:12;27

FIGURE 4.3
Current time and Duration displays in the Capture window.

The timecode in the upper right of the Viewer portion of the Capture window is your current time-code on your tape, and the Duration on the upper left is the duration you set with your In and Out points as you mark the tape (see Figure 4.3). Notice the displays at the top of the window that tell you how much available drive space you have on the designated scratch disk and how many minutes of video you can store on it.

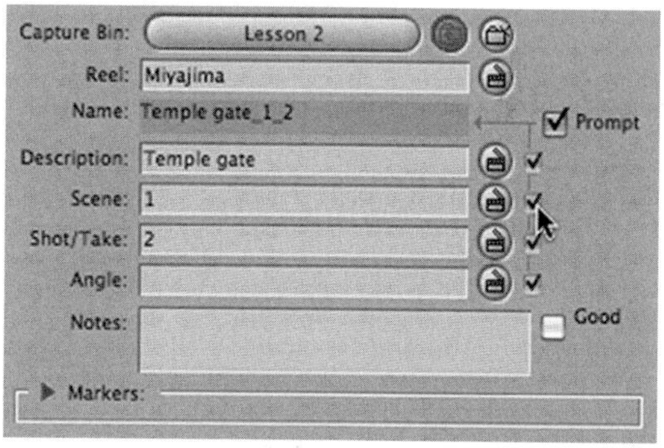

FIGURE 4.4
Capture panel.

On the right half of the Capture window is the panel where you add information that is used to organize your media (see Figure 4.4). At the top of this panel is a button that has the project name. The button to the far right of the name adds a bin to the Browser and designates it as the capture bin. Clicking the button again adds a new bin inside the previously designated bin. Using the button to the left, right next to the bin name, takes the capture bin up one level. If you click it enough times, it will go right up to the Browser level. There is, however, no button to take you back down through the hierarchy. The button with the project name takes you to the designated capture bin and opens it.

Creating a capture bin means that any material you capture is added directly to that designated bin. The bin appears in the Browser with a clapperboard icon on it when in Icon view or next to the bin's name when in List view.

FIGURE 4.5
Set Capture Bin.

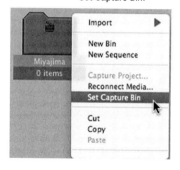

You can also select a capture bin directly in the Browser with a shortcut menu. Right-click on a bin, and from the shortcut menu, choose **Set Capture Bin** (see Figure 4.5). One critical piece of information in the Capture panel is the **Reel** name or number. This just means the videotapes you shot, but it uses the film term *reel*. It is extremely important that reel or tape numbers be assigned properly. Every reel should have a separate number or name. The number should be written on the tape and put in the Capture window. This number is actually attached to the QuickTime file when it's captured, and it enables FCE to recapture material if necessary. This is so important that when the application is in Capture mode, it will auto-detect when the reel in your camera or deck has been ejected and a new reel inserted and will post a warning message. The little clapperboard next to the reel name to the right can be clicked to increment it numerically.

In the Capture panel you can enter information about your clips before you capture them. You can't enter a name for the clip in the Name area of the Capture window, but you can give the clips names by combining Description, Scene, and Shot/Take number or other information. You probably want to keep these as short as possible. They can be combined through the check boxes, next to the tiny clapperboard icons, into the name for the clip. It's important that some information be added into the clip name, or the media file on your hard drive will be called *Untitled*, which is not very useful.

FIGURE 4.6
Markers window.

At the bottom of the Naming portion of the panel is an area where you can add notes about a clip or the section of material that you're capturing. This can be useful for organizing and searching through your material while you're editing. Below the Naming portion of the window is a box that you can twirl open with a disclosure triangle. This box allows you to add and name markers (see Figure 4.6). We'll look at markers more closely Lesson 5, but right now markers are a way of letting you add more information about a clip, keyed to a specific point somewhere inside the material. Once the clip has been captured, markers will appear attached to the clip, where they can be accessed from the Browser, as we'll see in the next lesson.

NOTE

Angle: The Angle function that you see in Figure 4.4 is a holdover from Final Cut Pro and serves no function in Final Cut Express. It is used to designate angles in multicamera editing, a feature that is only available in FCP.

STRATEGIES FOR CAPTURING

At the bottom of the **Capture** window (see Figure 4.7) are three buttons you can use to capture DV material three different ways: **Clip, Now** and **Project**.

Capture Now

Capture Now is the simplest method, but it gives you the least control. It also requires that your material be properly shot, preferably without timecode breaks. Breaks in the timecode can cause havoc with any capture, particularly if you use **Capture Now**. FCE captures around timecode breaks, but

FIGURE 4.7
Capture buttons.

it should be avoided if at all possible, because it will still lose audio/video synchronization if it comes across a section of unstable video or a section of tape with no video at all, even if timecode is present.

FCE handles the capture around timecode breaks automatically, albeit slowly. If the tape has a break on it, but the timecode continues to get higher, a new clip will start at the break, but the same reel number will be maintained. If the timecode resets to zero at the break, which is what usually happens on consumer cameras, the reel number will be changed and incremented, as well as make a new clip. This will treat each portion of the tape where the timecode resets to zero as a separate tape. Avoid having breaks in your timecode if you can. It will make your life a lot easier.

Capturing large chunks of video with the Now function is a common work strategy. To use Now, you should name the material you're about to capture, as described previously, and then put the deck in play and click the **Now** button. A capture screen comes up and begins recording as soon as it's checked your drives and found a video signal from your camera or deck.

If you are working with a noncontrollable device using the **DV Converter** preset, **Now** is the only capture choice available to you. It is a good idea, if possible, to dub your analog material to DV tape and then use the tape—properly reel-numbered—as your master. Dubbing allows you to easily access the material again if you ever need to recapture.

63

TIP
Monitoring: When capturing, audio should be monitored through external speakers connected to the camcorder or deck you're playing back from. You will not be able to hear the sound through the computer's speaker while the Capture window is open or during capturing itself. See the sections "Monitors" and "Speakers" in Lesson 1.

FCE records the clip on your designated scratch disk until one of the following three events occurs:

- It runs out of hard drive space.
- It hits your preference time limit.
- You hit the **Escape** key and stop the process.

If you press the **Escape** key or the capture stops because of the time limit, the deck also stops.

After your capture is complete, if you did not name the video before capturing, it appears as a clip called *Untitled* inside the Browser or designated capture bin. Whenever a clip is captured, it is saved inside the *Capture Scratch* folder on the drive you selected in your Preferences. Inside *Capture Scratch* is a folder with the project's name, one folder for each project.

Your captured material is stored inside that folder, and your clip is in that project's folder with the same name *Untitled* or the name you gave it. If you capture a clip using Now and you decide you don't want to use it, you'll have to go into your *Capture Scratch* folder, dig it out, and throw it into the Trash to get it off your hard drive and retrieve that drive space.

Using Capture Now, you can bring all of your video material into your computer for editing into smaller subclips rather than using your deck to select clips. FCE has a wonderful tool for those working with DV material called DV Start/Stop Detect that we'll look at in the next lesson. This gives the application the ability to automatically mark up shot changes and then break them up into separate clips. We will see this in Lesson 5.

TIMECODE BREAKS

Timecode breaks, or control track breaks, have been the bane of video editors since tape machines were invented. Many editors have mentally cursed the cameraperson who failed to keep good timecode on the tapes. These days, most consumer and prosumer cameras are designed to generate frame-accurate timecode, and that's the way tape should be delivered. FireWire uses the timecode recorded on tape when the video was shot to find your clips and control the deck during capture. This timecode information is passed to the application and remains with the clip throughout the editing process.

You can make sure there are no breaks in your DV timecode in many ways. The simplest way (which I recommend for beginners and students in particular) is to *prestripe* your tapes (i.e., record black and timecode on your tape before you shoot). You can do this in any camera or deck: (1) connect a video signal into the recording device; (2) put it in VCR mode if you're using a camera; and (3) press the Record button. With some cameras you may not be able to do this and will have to use it in camera mode; just put a lens cap on it or point it at a wall and put it into Record. If you can, stick a minijack plug into the mic input to kill the microphone. Now whenever you shoot, your tape will have the timecode written on it. The camera will then read the timecode and start writing from whatever it reads. **No breaks.**

If you don't want to prestripe the tape, then you just have to be careful when you shoot. After you shut off the camera to change batteries or play back your tape to review what you shot, for instance, don't simply stop it after a shot. It's a good idea to back up the tape just a second to get back into the area of timecoded material. This is why it's always a good idea when shooting to let the camera run for a few moments after the action you're shooting is complete, before you stop the recording. That way, you will have that moment or two of unnecessary material to back up into.

Any loss of video in the data stream is liable to cause a sudden loss of audio/video sync when you capture across it. So if you do have a tape with breaks in it, one of the simplest ways to get around the problem is to dub the tape. By dubbing it from one deck or one camera to another, the video and audio portions of the tape are actually cloned exactly as it was on the original, whereas the recording deck is creating new, unbroken timecode. Unfortunately, this often means that you lose the ability to work with DV Start/Stop Detect. Aside from shooting carefully, or prestriping the tape, another way around the problem is to use the Clip method to capture material between the timecode breaks.

Clip Capture

Another option in the Capture window is the **Clip** button. This requires that you enter In and Out points for where you want the capture to begin and where it should end. In the Clip method, you mark up the section of video you want to capture and then press the Clip button. This is a controlled form of Capture Now.

1. Mark an In point near the beginning of the reel and then an Out point near the end.
2. Click **Clip**.

FIGURE 4.8
Prompt check box.

If you have checked the Prompt box in Figure 4.8, you will get a dialog box asking to confirm the name (see Figure 4.9). If you didn't name the clip in the Capture panel, you must enter one. Notice the little clapperboard to the right of the name box. This lets you increment the name numerically.

FIGURE 4.9
Clip Name Window.

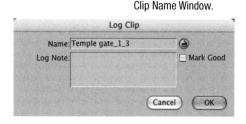

3. Click the **OK** button, and let the deck and the computer do their thing.

> **NOTE**
> **Preroll and Postroll:** Camcorders and
> decks cannot start and stop instantly. They require some time to
> get up to speed and to stop after they're playing, called preroll and postroll.
> This is a fixed preset in FCE of three seconds, so when you mark In and Out points
> to capture a clip, you need to make sure that your marked In point is no earlier than
> 03;00 from the beginning of the tape or from the last timecode break and that the Out
> point is no closer than three seconds to the end of the video material. In reality, most
> cameras need a bit more than three seconds of preroll, so you should
> set 04;00 as the minimum. Most cameras don't need as much as three
> seconds of postroll and usually stop within one second. Still it's better to
> be safe than to lose a long capture because the camera ran
> out of timecode during postroll.

FIGURE 4.10
Duplicate Item
Filename Dialog box.

If you enter a clip name that already exists in the project's scratch folder, you'll get the dialog box in Figure 4.10 asking you to rename the clip, skip capture, or abort it. If the clip is not active in your project, or if it mistakenly got captured into the scratch folder, you'll also get an option to Overwrite the existing clip.

During capture you will get a large black window and, at the bottom, information about what's happening (see Figure 4.11), which shows that the deck is *Cueing* source material, the clip that's being captured, the duration, and how much more to capture off that reel. When capture begins, you'll see the image in the Capture window, and the display in the bottom will change to the **Now Capturing** message in Figure 4.12.

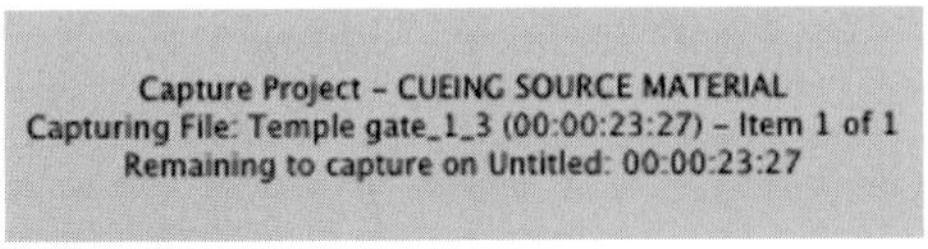

> **Capture Project – CUEING SOURCE MATERIAL**
> Capturing File: Temple gate_1_3 (00:00:23:27) – Item 1 of 1
> Remaining to capture on Untitled: 00:00:23:27

FIGURE 4.11
Cueing source material
message.

Do not be dismayed that the quality of the video in the Capture window seems poor and stuttering. The computer monitor cannot display a full-screen, interlaced image with full motion at full resolution during capture.

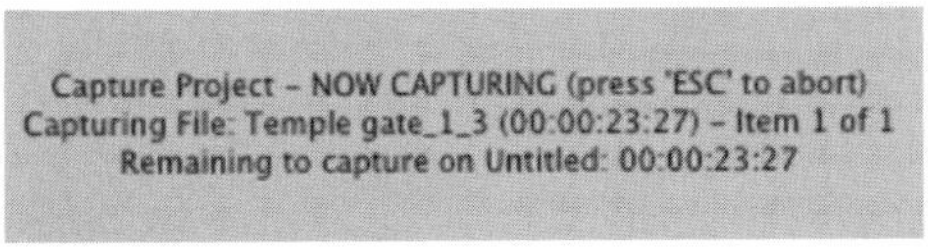

After you've captured your material, you are ready to edit. Close the Capture window before you start; don't try to play video while Capture is open. Once you've captured your material, it appears in the Browser. If you switch to List view, each clip will have a duration but with no In or Out points defined. Capturing only sets the media limit, and FCE assumes you want to edit the

> **Capture Project – NOW CAPTURING (press 'ESC' to abort)**
> Capturing File: Temple gate_1_3 (00:00:23:27) – Item 1 of 1
> Remaining to capture on Untitled: 00:00:23:27

FIGURE 4.12
Now Capturing message.

material further, so no In or Out points are designated. The clip has the de facto In and Out points marked by the limits of the media; they're not displayed in the Browser in the In and Out columns.

> **TIP**
>
> ***Renaming Clips:*** If you have to rename the clip because the name you've chosen is already used (as in Figure 4.10), the original incorrect name you assigned will appear in the Browser. This can mean that you have two clips in the Browser with the same name. The actual media file name will be correct, but the one in the Browser will not be. If you do rename a clip in the warning dialog box, it is a good idea to immediately rename the clip in the Browser to match the media file name you gave the clip before capture.

Project Capture

Project capture is designed to let you recapture material for old DV projects to reconstruct them. To do this, reopen the project. If the material is not available, you will get the Reconnect dialog box we've seen at the beginning of the earlier lessons. Click the **OK** button and let the project open.

All of the media will probably appear offline, with the Browser displaying clips with red slash marks through them (see Figure 4.13) and the words Media Offline across a red Canvas (see Figure 4.14). You could at this point evoke the Capture window and press the Project button. This will bring up the dialog box in Figure 4.15.

Normally the pop-up at the top would display only **All Items**, but if some of the clips are available to you while others are offline, then you'll get the choice of picking **All Items, Offline Items Only**, or **Selected Items**.

Notice the box that allows you to **Add Handles**. This will set the computer to capture a designated amount of material beyond the

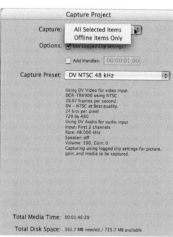

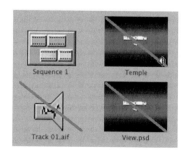

FIGURE 4.13
Browser with offline clips.

FIGURE 4.14
Browser with offline clips.

FIGURE 4.15
Capture Project dialog box.

67

In and Out points defined in your clips. You can select any of the available Capture Presets, and the window will display what your selected settings are. At the bottom you get an indication of the hard drive requirements for Total Media Time and Total Disk Space. Check that you have enough drive space for the capture. Also, look closely at the media time to make sure it looks about right—that you're capturing all the media you need but not too much.

When you click **OK**, you'll get a window telling you what tapes will be required for the project capture and how much will be captured off each tape. Load the first reel and click Continue. FCE will prompt you whenever a reel change is required.

If you capture with handles, the clips will come into the Browser with your designated In and Out points marked already, not the usual **Not Set** indication, and if you open the clip into the Viewer, you'll see the extra media beyond the marked In and Out points. It's important to understand the way project capture works. It works best if you've captured your material using the Clip method (i.e., selected the portions of the video you want to use and captured them as separate clips). But if you haven't, you can still use the **Project** button to trim down your material to just what you need, provided you've cut up your material into clips. If you have, this is how you do it:

1. Start by reopening your project file with the missing material that needs to be recaptured.
2. Delete everything except the sequence or clips you need to recapture. You may get a warning message that one or more clips are Master clips. Just click **OK** and push on.
3. Select the sequences in the Browser, and from the **Modify** menu, choose **Make Sequence Clips Independent**. This will separate the edited clips from the long masters you may have captured.
4. Start up the Capture window and click the Project button.

The application will now recapture only those clips that it needs to reconstitute your sequence. It will not capture any of the clips that you didn't use, that you deleted from your project, or the rest of the material that is not part of your sequence. If you captured whole reels of tape or large chunks, FCE would want to recapture all of the pieces that use even a very small portion of your clips. So if you originally captured a 60-minute reel and used only 10 seconds of it, the application would still want to capture the entire 60 minutes just to get those 10 seconds it needed to reconstitute your sequence.

Project capture does not work with HD material; it works only for the DV material. When your HDV or AVCHD material is ingested, it is converted to the

Apple Intermediate Codec during capture or transfer, and the timecode information is lost. This does not happen with DV material. The timecode information is retained for each media clip, even though it is not displayed within the application.

When a project is complete, you should separately back up imported audio and graphics files. You should also be aware that tracks recorded using the **Voice Over** tool are not able to be recaptured because they have no useful timecode. It's a good idea to build an *Import* bin that contains audio files, still images, graphics files, and your voiceover tracks. The **Source** column in the Browser or the clip's Item Properties will help you find the file path to where the media such as stills and voiceovers are stored. These should be backed up separately if you want to recreate the project at a later time. It may be simplest to burn this data material onto a CD or DVD for storage.

LOG AND TRANSFER

Log and Transfer is new to Final Cut Express 4 and is used for ingesting material that's been shot with AVCHD-based cameras. You can only transfer AVCHD material using an Intel-based Mac and not an older PowerPC, but if you do have an Intel computer and want to try the process, a folder on the book's DVD called *NO NAME* has a little AVCHD media for you to practice on.

69

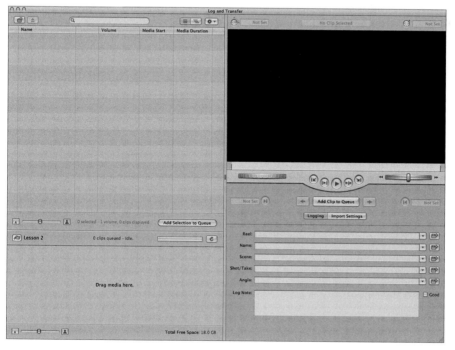

FIGURE 4.16
Log and Transfer window.

Name	Volume	Media Start	Media Duration
Clip #1	NO NAME	00:00:00;00	00:02:50;28
Clip #2	NO NAME	00:00:00;00	00:05:25;22
Clip #3	NO NAME	00:00:00;00	00:07:46;00
Clip #4	NO NAME	00:00:00;00	00:00:54;14
Clip #5	NO NAME	00:00:00;00	00:00:16;05
Clip #6	NO NAME	00:00:00;00	00:00:25;01
Clip #7	NO NAME	00:00:00;00	00:00:14;23
Clip #8	NO NAME	00:00:00;00	00:00:12;13
Clip #9	NO NAME	00:00:00;00	00:00:08;21
Clip #10	NO NAME	00:00:00;00	00:02:09;10
Clip #11	NO NAME	00:00:00;00	00:00:25;15

1 selected – 1 vol...21 clips displayed (Add Selection to Queue)

Miyajima   0 clips queued – Idle.

Drag media here.

FIGURE 4.17
Clips in the Transfer window.

70

FIGURE 4.18
Add Folder button.

NOTE
Frame Sizes: Some cameras can shoot AVCHD video in a variety of different sizes: 1920 × 1080 as well as 1440 × 1080. Be sure you update to version 4.0.1, which allows you to use any of the AVCHD formats. The first release was restricted to 1440 × 1080.

When working with AVCHD material, make sure you update to 4.0.1 and use one of the AVCHD Apple Intermediate Codecs as your preset. Use the one appropriate for your media: 1920 × 1080, 1440 × 1080, or 1280 × 720, at the correct frame rate. To access Log and Transfer use **File>Log and Transfer (Cmd-Shift-8)**, which brings up the window in Figure 4.16.

If you have your camera with the memory card connected via USB or have the card in a card reader, the application will sense the device and immediately populate the left side of the window with the clip on the card (see Figure 4.17). If the Transfer window doesn't recognize your card, or you've copied your material off the card (see the important note on *Copying the Memory Card*) use the little Add Folder button in the upper left corner of the Transfer window (see Figure 4.18) to navigate to and select the folder

NOTE
Copying the Memory Card: Many people copy the data off the memory card before they ingest their material, usually because they want to get the media off the card so they can reuse it. If you do this, make sure you do it right. Connect the camera or card reader to your computer. It should appear on your desktop as a drive. If not, use the Disk Utility to mount the card, which will appear as *NO NAME*. Make a folder on your computer and then open *NO NAME*. There will be a folder structure inside the card. Do not try to get the media out of the folders. Copy all the folders on the memory card into a folder you create on your computer. The folder structure is a wrapper for the data and critical to being read by the application. You can name the folder on your computer anything you want; a date or subject might be useful.

with your media. The little button on the opposite side with the gear icon (see Figure 4.19) lets you customize where the material goes and allows you to change the settings used for ingest. The settings here should be for the Apple Intermediate Codec.

FIGURE 4.19
Settings button.

Like the Capture window, the Transfer window sends your ingested material into a folder in the *Capture Scratch* with your project's name. The Transfer window allows you to prepare the video before ingesting it into your *Capture Scratch*. When you select a clip, it appears in the viewer on the right-hand side of the window (see Figure 4.20). Just as in the Capture window, you can play the clip here with the Play button or with the spacebar. You can also use **L** to play forward and the **K** key to pause. The **J** key for playing backward does not seem to work for some reason. It may work with some devices and not with others. You can also scrub through the video by dragging the playhead in the scrubber bar. If you don't want to ingest the entire clip of video, you can select portions by marking In and Out with the buttons below the viewer or by pressing the **I** or **O** keys, respectively. When you select a portion of the clip, the duration of the selection will appear in the upper left.

FIGURE 4.20
Right side of the Transfer window.

Below the viewer, just as in the Capture window, is the **Logging** panel (see Figure 4.21), where you can name the clip and give it a reel number. Reel number information is less critical here because the material cannot be recaptured. Resist using meaningless names like *Clip #1*. The name you use is the name that FCE will apply to the media when it's converted from the AVCHD format to the Apple Intermediate Codec. The little folder buttons next to each line item let you increment the name numerically with a click. If you switch to the **Import Settings** panel (see Figure 4.22), you can select to ingest either video or audio or both.

TIP
Removing In and Out Points: If you want to remove an In point that you've marked, press Opt-I. To remove a marked Out point, use Opt-O, and if you want to remove both the In and Out points, press Opt-X.

71

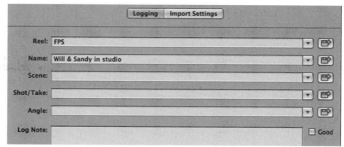

FIGURE 4.21
Logging panel.

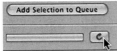

FIGURE 4.22
Import Settings panel.

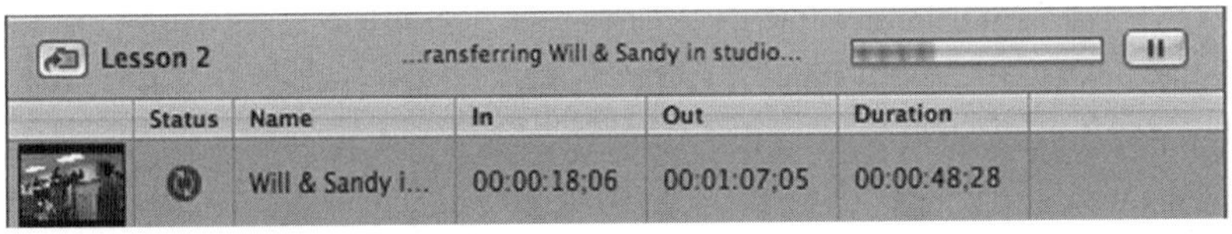

FIGURE 4.23
Clip ingesting.

FIGURE 4.24
Queue toggle.

To begin the ingest process, you either click the **Add Clip to Queue** or the **Add Selection to Queue** buttons, or you can simply drag the clip from the viewer or from the clip list into the lower left pane of the Transfer window. As long as the clip is being ingested, it will appear in that portion of the window, as in Figure 4.23. If you don't want the process to begin immediately, toggle the button just below **Add Selection to Queue** (see Figure 4.24). When the button has the curved arrow, icon clips can be added to the queue without being ingested. This lets you select multiple clips or multiple portions of a single clip before ingesting them. When you're ready to begin converting them and bringing them into FCE, simply click the button to toggle the queue and begin the process.

NOTE
File Sizes: You should be aware that although AVCHD can hold up to one and a half hours of material on a 4G card and up to three hours on an 8G card, and only take 4G and 8G, respectively, when it's copied from the card onto your computer, the material will take up significantly more space when it's converted to the Apple Intermediate Codec. One hour of material converted to AIC will take up approximately 49G at 1080i60 and 42G at 1080i50. This applies to HDV material as well. HDV natively is about 12G per hour, whereas AIC is about four times larger.

NOTE
Ingesting AVCHD Material: If you are having problems ingesting AVCHD material, check a few settings in the little gear popup near the center of the Log and Transfer window. You should use the Clear Logging Autofill Cache button. Also make sure AVCHD is set to Apple Intermediate Codec and that AC-3 Audio is set to Plain Stereo. FCE does not support 5.1 surround audio from AVCHD cameras.

TIP
Backing Up Media: Most AVCHD cameras use 4G or 8G cards, which is a very convenient size. 4G cards can easily and cheaply be burned as data onto a single-layer DVD, and 8G cards can be burned onto dual-layer DVDs, which are ideal ways to archive your AVCHD raw media for posterity or if you need to reuse the material.

Once the clips have been ingested, they will appear in the list with a blue button next to them, as in Figure 4.25. If only a portion of the clip has been ingested, the button will be half blue. When you close the Log and Transfer, your clips will be in the Browser with the names you gave them.

FIGURE 4.25
Clips after transfer.

IMPORTING FILES

In addition to capturing and ingesting material, you can also import material into FCE. QuickTime movies should be converted outside of FCE into the format you're working with in the application—either DV or HD. FCE does not directly accept MPEG-2, DV Stream, MPEG-4, or other types of QuickTime or AVI that are not in the correct formats the applications work with. FCE also allows you to import sound files, still images, and more. There are a couple of different ways to import material. You could use **Command-I** to import a single item or groups of items from one folder, or the **File** menu under **Import**>**Folder** to bring a folder full of clips or other material. Another way is to move the Canvas to the left, grabbing it with the bar at the top and sliding it out of the way to access your Desktop. You can drag and drop folders and files from anywhere on your drives directly into the Browser. This is the simplest, quickest way to bring lots of material into your project. You can also right-click in the Browser window and choose **Import**>**Files** or **Folder** from the shortcut menu.

Converting Files

Before you import media in other formats, it's best to convert it to a format FCE can work with natively in its Timeline. There are a number of tools you can use to do this. One is the QuickTime Pro player, which you can upgrade to at the Apple website, http://www.apple.com/quicktime. Another excellent conversion utility is the free tool MPEG Streamclip, which can be downloaded from http://www. squared5.com. MPEG Streamclip can also be used to convert unprotected DVD content into a format that can be edited in FCE. DVD conversion does require purchasing the MPEG-2 Playback Component from Apple. Another useful tool is ffmpegX, which can be found at http://ffmpegX.com/index.html.

To convert your material to DV in either tool, use export to QuickTime and set the codec to DV, either NTSC or PAL, and the frame rate to either 29.97 fps or 25 fps. The frame sizes should be 720 × 480 for NTSC and 720 × 576 for PAL. If you're converting your material to HD, use the Apple Intermediate Codec and select one of the standard frame sizes 1440 × 1080 or 1280 × 720, and again set the frame rates to either 29.97 for North America and Japan, or 25 fps for Europe and most of the rest of the world.

For its Everio HD cameras, using the 1440 format, JVC has provided a QuickTime component that allows it to work with Macs. You can find out details of how to work with this camera here: http://media2.jvc.com/camcorder/macHD.mov.

IMPORTING MUSIC

Importing music from either a CD or other formats (such as MP3) is slightly different from importing video. FCE can work with audio CD files, but they do raise some problems. Audio CDs use an audio sample rate of 44.1 kHz. This is not the sampling rate used by the DV format, which uses either 32 kHz or, most commonly, 48 kHz. MP3s should also be converted to the AIFF format while being resampled and having their compression removed. Although FCE can deal with resampling the audio while it plays it back, it doesn't do it very well, and it requires processor power, which may limit your ability to do real-time effects or to play back video or multiple tracks of audio without dropping frames (i.e., the audio or video stuttering). To avoid this, I highly recommend resampling the audio to the correct sampling rate you want to use before importing it into FCE. This can be done in many ways, but one of the best ways is to use the QuickTime Pro Player. The standard QT player will not be sufficient, but by upgrading to the pro version, you will get the ability to change files into several different formats. You can also do basic video and audio editing in the QT Pro Player. It's a great value and can easily be purchased from Apple at http://www.apple.com/quicktime.

FIGURE 4.26
QuickTime icon.

To resample the audio of a CD track or an MP3 file, drag the track(s) from the CD onto the QuickTime icon, which should probably be stored in your Dock (see Figure 4.26). This will launch the QT Pro Player and open the files into it.

1. Once the files are open, choose **File>Export (Command-E)**.
2. From the **Export** pop-up menu, select **Sound to AIFF** (see Figure 4.27).
3. Click on the **Options** button, and use the settings as in Figure 4.28. In this panel, choose the correct settings: Linear PCM for Format, Stereo LR for Channels, and either 48,000 Hz, which is most commonly used in DV, or 32,000 Hz, if that's the setting the rest of your material uses.
4. Give the new file a name, such as *SongName48k*, and save it onto your media drive.

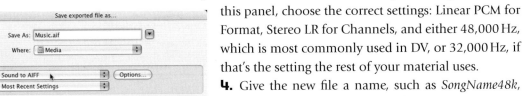
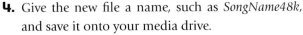

FIGURE 4.27
Export>Sound to AIFF.

The file will be copied from the audio CD onto your hard drive, converted, and resampled to the correct sampling rate. This is the file you should import into and work with in FCE.

Another way to do this if the QuickTime Pro Player is not available to you is with iTunes. To do this, you must have set up your iTunes preferences.

1. Under the **iTunes** menu, go to **Preferences**, select **Advanced**, and go to the **Importing** tab (see Figure 4.29).
2. From the **Import Using** pop-up menu, select **AIFF Encoder**.
3. From the second pop-up menu, select **Custom**.
4. Set the sampling rate to 48,000 Hz or whatever sampling rate you're working with.
5. Set the **Channels** to **Stereo** and the **Sample Size** to **16-bit**, as in Figure 4.30.

Now you're ready to import the music.

6. In the **iTunes** window, **Command**-click on one of the checked track boxes. This will deselect all of the tracks.
7. Check the tracks you want, and click the **Import** button in the lower right corner of the window (see Figure 4.31).

iTunes will copy the track from the CD to your iTunes library, which can be a labyrinthine place to find a track. You want to find the track because you want to move it from your iTunes library, which is on the internal system drive of your computer, onto your media drive. The simplest way to find the track is to right-click on the track in your iTunes library and from the contextual menu choose **Show Song File** (see Figure 4.32). This will open a Finder window for the folder that holds the file and select the file for you. Copy

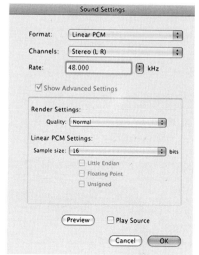

FIGURE 4.28
Sound settings dialog box.

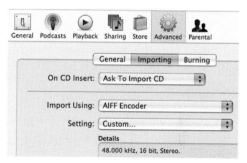

FIGURE 4.29
iTunes importing preferences.

75

> **TIP**
>
> **Item-Level Rendering:** We'll look at rendering in greater detail later, but FCE has a feature that is worth mentioning here. Render settings in the application have the ability to render audio at the item level. This means you can render a piece of audio, such as 44.1 kHz CD music, into the correct sampling rate as a separate item. If you place an audio clip in the Timeline and render it out at item level, that render file will stay with the clip wherever you place that audio in your Timeline. It will remain fully rendered to the correct settings. It will have a blue indicator bar on the clip to tell you it's been rendered as an item and will not need to be rerendered. Unfortunately, as of this time, item-level rendering of MP3 audio files does not produce the best quality and should be avoided.

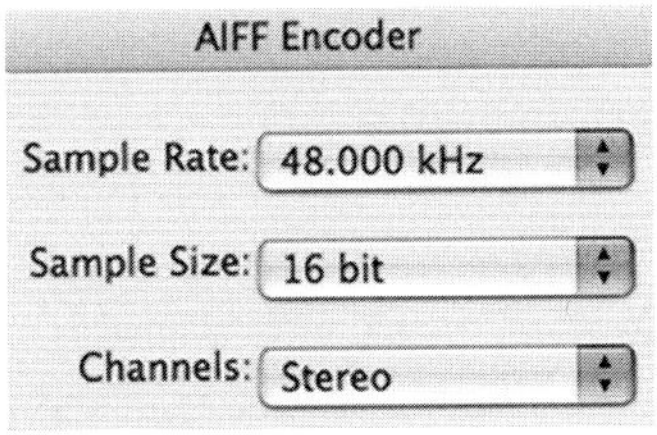

FIGURE 4.30
iTunes custom settings.

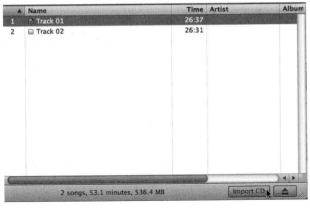

FIGURE 4.31
iTunes window.

FIGURE 4.32
Show Song File.

> **NOTE**
> *iTunes Music Store:* Music purchased from the iTunes music store will not work with FCE or any Apple Pro applications. The Digital Rights Management software attached to the file will prevent this. This music can be imported and will work with iMovie. It can also be exported from iMovie, and it can be burned onto a CD for your personal use.

it, or by holding down the **Command** key, move it to your media drive, and you're ready to import it into FCE.

SUMMARY

With these last two lessons, you have completed the process of correctly setting up your system and the application and gone through the ingest process, capturing from tape or transferring from hardware media. We are finally ready to begin the editing process. To start, I would suggest working with the tutorial media provided, or if you feel comfortable with the application, try working with your own ingested media.

LESSON 5

Cutting Up Those Shots

In this lesson we examine some video and cut it up. We've looked at the interface in detail, but now it's time to learn how to use FCE's tools. Final Cut Express has several different ways you can work with your video. The same function can be performed in many ways, so users can find the workflow with which they're the most comfortable.

LOADING THE LESSON

If you skipped directly to this lesson, first you must load the material from the DVD that accompanies this book.

1. Start by loading the DVD into your DVD drive and opening the disk.
2. Drag the *FCE_Media&Projects* folder onto your computer hard drive. This contains two folders called *Media* and *Projects*. After it has finished copying, eject the disc.
3. Inside the *FCE_Media&Projects* folder, open the *Projects* folder on your system hard drive and double-click the *Lesson 5* project to launch Final Cut Express.

The project is empty except for one sequence that is also blank. Notice that the Canvas is widescreen because this is an HD sequence, though we'll be working with DV material.

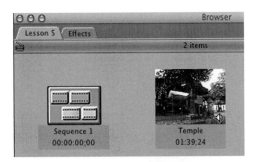

FIGURE 5.1
Clip in Browser.

Importing the Movie

Use **File>Import (Command-I)** to import the *Temple* file from the folder inside the *Media* folder on your hard drive. Or you can drag the clip directly from the *Media* folder into your Browser. It should look like Figure 5.1.

This is a *master clip*. Every time you import a clip or capture a clip or bring a new clip into the Browser, the first instance of that clip is always a master clip. A master clip can be cut up into smaller clips called *affiliate clips*. Any copy or portion of a master clip has an affiliate relationship to the master. All the pieces made from the master clip—all the affiliates and the master clip—must have the same name. If you change one, they all change.

MARKING IN AND OUT POINTS

Media can be long or short, but you'll usually want to use only a portion of it, cutting out the bit at the beginning where the camera's not steady or a section where someone steps in front of the lens. To do that, you mark In and Out points on a clip to define the sections you want to use—similar to the crop markers you may have used in iMovie HD.

1. Open *Temple* into the Viewer by double-clicking on it or by selecting it and pressing the **Return** key. You can also open it by dragging it into the Viewer or by right-clicking on it and selecting **Open in Viewer**.
2. Using the **I** key, mark an In point at the beginning of the clip.
3. Play through the clip or scrub through it until you find the last frame of the first shot. Use the **Left** and **Right** arrow keys to find the frame at 10;15.
4. Using the **O** key, mark an Out point.

Your Viewer will look like Figure 5.2. Notice the Out point mark in the upper right corner of the picture, indicating that the playhead is at the Out point. The best way to cut out this shot is by making it a subclip. Because a subclip is a master clip, you can rename the clip anything you want.

5. To make this shot a subclip, press **Command-U** or choose **Modify> Make Subclip**.
6. The clip will immediately appear in the Browser with its name highlighted, ready to be renamed.

7. Type in a name for the clip.

8. Switch back to Viewer (**Command-1**—that's the 1 above the QWERTY keyboard, not on the keypad), and you're ready to mark new In and Out points on the master clip to make the next subclip.

Although making a subclip does not create a separate QuickTime file, the subclip is treated as a separate piece of media, even though it really isn't. Working with subclips has several advantages. One is that it's easy to scrub the clip, running the mouse along the length of the media. Another is that it prevents you from inadvertently extending one shot into the adjacent shot during a transition, as we shall see in Lesson 8.

FIGURE 5.2
Viewer with In and Out points marked.

DV START/STOP DETECT

DV Start/Stop Detect is probably the best way to work with DV material in FCE. HDV and AVCHD material comes into the Browser already broken down into separate clips, but DV material often does not. The DV Start/Stop function uses the start/stop information from your camera to create markers on your video. This method works only if the clock on your camera is set. It doesn't have to be the right date or time, but it has to be set. No clock, no DV Start/Stop Detect. Once markers are set with DV Start/Stop Detect, they can be used to segment the master clip. Here's how it works:

> **NOTE**
> ***Return and Enter:***
> Remember that the Return key and the Enter key have different functions in the Browser. Return opens a clip, and Enter highlights the clip's name for you to rename it.

1. Bring your long clip of DV material into FCE, either by importing it, capturing it with the Clip method, or using Now.
2. Select the clip or clips. In this case, select the *Temple* clip you imported into your Browser.
3. From the **Mark** menu, select **DV Start/Stop Detect**.

You will immediately see the Scanning DV Movie(s) progress bar (see Figure 5.3). It can scan multiple clips at once or handle entire bins. It produces clips with markers at each camera start/stop.

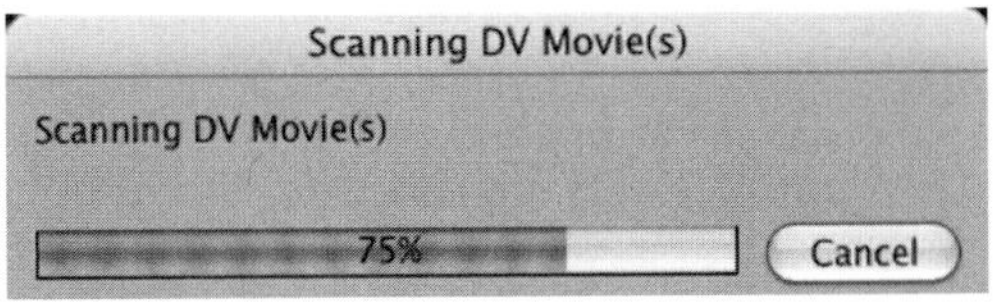

FIGURE 5.3
Scanning DV
Movie(s) progress bar.

After it's finished, it may look like nothing has changed, but it has. DV Start/Stop Detect adds markers at every shot change based on that date/time stamp. *Temple* should still be open in the Viewer; if it's not, double-click it in the Browser. In Figure 5.4, notice that the marked In and Out points are still there and that the playhead in the Viewer is sitting on the first marker, *Segment 1*. Each of the other markers appears in the scrubber bar at the bottom of the Viewer.

FIGURE 5.4
Master Clip with segments
in the Viewer.

Once the segment markers have been added to the material, it's easy enough to change the separate segments into shots:

FIGURE 5.5
List View button.

1. Change the Browser into List view, either from the **View> Browser Items>as List**, by using **Shift-H** to toggle through the Browser views, or by clicking the List view button in the upper right corner of the Browser, as shown in Figure 5.5.

2. Twirl open the disclosure triangle in the Browser, and marquee-drag through all of the markers, as shown in Figure 5.6.

3. Then select from the menu **Modify>Make Subclip**, or use the keyboard shortcut **Command-U**.

Before I do that, I often move the master clip into a bin that is appropriate for its content. To create a new bin, either use **File>New>Bin** or right-click in the Browser, and from the shortcut menu, choose **New Bin**, or use the keyboard shortcut **Command-B**. This way, when I make the subclips from *Temple*, they're already placed in the right bin.

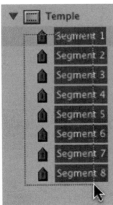

FIGURE 5.6
Marquee-dragging before
making subclips.

> **NOTE**
> ***Marker Shortcuts:*** You can easily move between markers
> in the Viewer with keyboard shortcuts:
> Shift-M (or Shift-Down arrow) takes you to the next marker.
> Option-M (or Shift-Up arrow) takes you to the previous marker.
> Command- (` key) will delete a marker under the playhead, as will the
> Delete button in the Marker dialog box. You can call this dialog box by
> pressing the M key while you're positioned on a marker.

A list of markers can be accessed by right-clicking in the current time indicator window in the upper right of either the Viewer or the Canvas (see Figure 5.7). This lets you jump from one marker to another.

> **TIP**
> ***Moving Shots Out of Bins:*** To move a shot out of the bin back to the top level of the Browser, drag the shot out of the bin and pull it onto the Name column header. That puts it at the top level of the project window.

The subclips appear in the Browser with the torn edges icon, as shown in Figure 5.8. All subclips are master clips, and though you can rename your subclips anything you want, be aware that the underlying media that remains on your hard drive is unchanged. Most important, its name is not changed. So if you ever need to reconnect the media or recapture it, FCE will want to do it under its original naming convention.

FIGURE 5.7
Markers in current time indicator box.

At this stage you're breaking down your material, organizing it, arranging it into bins, renaming clips, adding notes, and so on. This is critical if you're working on a project that's longer than ten minutes or so, or a project with a lot of material, regardless of its finished length. This process of viewing, logging, and organizing should not be skimped on, rushed, or dismissed as drudge work. It is crucial to the editing process.

USING MARKERS

If you're working with DV material without camera breaks, material captured from an analog-to-digital converter, or material that was dubbed to DV or HDV, you can still cut up your material using subclips. You can do that in a few different ways.

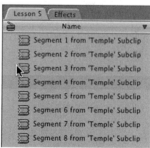

FIGURE 5.8
Subclips in Browser.

One way is by adding markers to the clip, similar to the way DV Start/Stop Detect worked. Open your long capture into the Viewer, and add markers as you play the clip—on the fly if you like—by tapping the **M** key or the grave (`) key. You can create markers with more precision, as well as set up extended markers to segment your material. Try this with *Temple*:

1. First, marquee-drag through any segment markers that may already be in the clip.
2. With the segment markers selected, hit the **Delete** key to wipe them out.

81

FIGURE 5.9
Edit Marker dialog box.

3. Double-click *Temple* to open it into the Viewer.

4. If there any In and Out points are in the clip, remove them by pressing **Option-X**.

5. Set a marker at the beginning of the clip. Do this by moving the playhead to the beginning of the clip with the **Home** key and pressing either the **M** key or the ` key.

If you wish, you can label the marker. Press the **M** (or `) key again while sitting over the marker. This brings up the dialog window in Figure 5.9. Change the name of the marker, and add comments if you wish.

This name will carry over into the name of the subclip. In this case, the subclip would be called *WS with memorials from "Temple" subclip*. The marker information and comments will display in the Viewer. This stays with *Temple* and will appear whenever the playhead is over the marker.

6. Play through the clip either with the spacebar or by scrubbing in the scrubber bar until you find the shot change.

7. Use the **Left** and **Right** arrow keys to find the first frame of the next shot at 10;16.

8. Add another marker.

You can work your way through the clip, adding markers at each shot change. As with DV Start/Stop Detect, the markers can be turned quickly into subclips.

9. Marquee-drag to select the markers from *Temple* in List view and press **Command-U**.

> **TIP**
>
> *Scroll Wheel:* FCE allows you to use the scroll wheel of a multibutton mouse, like the Apple Mighty Mouse, to do a variety of tasks. It's quite a powerful tool. Not only can you scroll the Browser window, but you can also use the scroll wheel to scrub the playhead in the Viewer window, in the Timeline Ruler of the Timeline window, and when the cursor is over the Canvas. If the cursor is above one of FCE's sliders, it will move the slider, changing the values. Holding the Option key while you scroll will gear up the scrolling and make it go faster. In the Timeline window, Shift-scrolling will scroll the contents of the window. This is especially useful during playback in the Timeline, as the window does not move automatically with the playhead.

If you're working on narrative film, tightly scripted material, or material with excess content that can be removed, *extended markers* might be useful. When you capture large sections of material, unnecessary pieces often come with it, such as clapperboards, director's instructions, setting the camera, bad takes, and so forth. You can avoid adding these into your subclips by extending a marker:

1. Start by finding where you would like the subclip to begin.
2. Add the marker with the **M** or **`** key.
3. Play through the shot until the director shouts, "Cut!" or until you find the end of the piece you want to make into a subclip.
4. Now extend the marker from the menus by going to **Mark>Markers> Extend**, or extend it even more simply by using the keyboard shortcut **Option-`**.

The nice thing about this technique is that when you create your subclips by selecting them and pressing **Command-U** or using the **Modify** menu to **Make Subclip**, the subclips are only for the duration of the extended marker. By extending the markers, you have defined the limits of the media available for each shot and basically defined rough In and Out points.

In the *Temple* clip, for instance, some camera bobbles are present, such as right at the end of the second shot—the glass-fronted hut. The start of the third shot also has a reframing zoom. By using extended markers, you can cut out these areas so they don't appear unexpectedly during a transition. You might also choose not to subclip a shot (e.g., the fourth shot in *Temple*). Extend the previous marker to the end of the third shot, and don't add a marker for the fourth shot. This is why there are only seven markers or extended markers, as in Figure 5.10.

83

FIGURE 5.10
Extended markers.

TIP
Edit Marker: If you Shift-click the Marker button in the Viewer, it not only sets a marker on the clip, but it also opens the Edit Marker dialog box, where you can enter information. You can also use Command-Option-M to open the Edit Marker window for the nearest marker before the current position of the playhead. This works for markers in either the Viewer or the Timeline.

Do not extend markers or define subclips too tightly. This should be only a rough cut that covers the entire portion of usable media. FCE will treat the limits of the subclip like the limits of its media and will not allow you to extend the shot farther, so always make the ends of the subclips—the limits of the media—as far as you can without going into another shot or into some rough material, such as a swish pan or a quick zoom, that you don't want to see on the screen.

Markers are an excellent tool for entering information about clips, even if you're not using the markers to edit your material. Here you can add comments as well as create *chapter markers* to use with iDVD and *scoring markers* to carry over to Apple's music-creation and audio editing application, Soundtrack, if you have it from an earlier version of Final Cut Express. It's important to note that these specialized markers should always be added only to the Timeline. None of these markers, if added to clips, will carry over into other applications. Markers are also searchable within a sequence, as we shall see.

NOTE
Removing Subclip Limits: Creating a subclip limits the available media to the length of the shot. If you ever need the rest of the captured material within the original shot, select the clip or clips in either the Browser or the Timeline and use Modify>Remove Subclip Limits. You will then be able to open the shot in the Viewer and access the whole length of the clip.

SLICING YOUR CLIPS

All of the methods described so far have been based on creating subclips. You can also work by making clips and turning them into master clips so that they can be renamed.

Slice 1

This can be done in a few different ways. Let's do this first in the Viewer:

1. Open *Temple* from the Browser into the Viewer.
2. It will probably have an In and Out point marked. You need to clear those.
3. Right-click on the scrubber bar at the bottom of the Viewer to evoke a shortcut menu, and select **Clear In and Out**. This will (surprise!) clear

the In and Out points (see Figure 5.11). You can also use the keyboard shortcut **Option-X**.

4. Let's begin with the second shot in *Temple*. Find the shot change at 10;16.

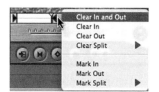

FIGURE 5.11
Clearing In and Out points in the Viewer.

5. Mark an In point by pressing the **I** key.

6. Press the **spacebar** to play *Temple*. Use the **Left** and **Right** arrow keys to find the end of the shot: the last frame of the thatched hut at 18;29.

7. Mark an Out point with the O key.

8. Create a new bin (**Command-B**) in the Browser and name it *Clips*.

9. Drag the marked clip of *Temple* from the Viewer and drop it into the *Clips* bin. Do not rename this clip because it would also rename *Temple*. The new clip still has an affiliate clip relationship to the master clip.

10. Go back to the Viewer and repeat the process, marking new In and Out points for each shot and dragging each into the *Clips* bin in turn.

You still cannot rename the clips because they are still affiliate clips. However, the next feature gets around this problem.

11. Select all the clips you've created in the *Clips* bin by marquee-dragging through them or by double-clicking on the bin to open it and then using **Command-A** to **Select All**.

12. With the clips selected from the **Modify** menu, go to **Modify>Make Master Clip**.

This will turn all of the clips into master clips, allowing you to rename them and organize your material.

NOTE
Clearing from the Browser Only: You can clear the In and Out points for a clip that's been opened from the Browser, but you can't clear the In and Out points from a clip that's been opened from the Timeline. A clip that's in a Timeline must by definition have an In and Out point—a start and end frame—even if it's the first and last frame of the clip.

NOTE

Edit Points: The shot change between edits takes place between the frames. In other words, you see one frame, and the next frame you see is the first frame of a different shot. So when you're marking In and Out points, you should know where the shot change is taking place. If you mark the In point for a frame that you're looking at in the Viewer, that will be the first frame of the new clip. The edit will take place in the space before that frame. If you mark the frame you're looking at as an Out point, that will be the last frame in the clip, and the edit will take place after that frame.

Conforming Sequences

A great new feature in Final Cut Express 4 is that a sequence can make its settings conform to the first clip placed in it. Let's see how this works.

1. Open *Temple* from the Browser into the Viewer.

It will probably have an In and Out point marked. We need to clear those.

2. Right-click on the scrubber bar at the bottom of the Viewer to select **Clear In and Out**, or use the shortcut **Option-X**.
3. If it's not already open, open the empty Timeline by double-clicking on *Sequence 1* in the Browser.
4. Drag *Temple* into it, dropping the clip on VI.

When you go to place the clip in the Timeline, you will immediately get the dialog box in Figure 5.12. When you are editing a clip into the Timeline, this gives you the option to conform the Timeline to match the clip properties. In this instance, the sequence is in HD, but the clip is standard definition DV. By clicking **Yes** in the dialog box, the sequence will immediately be changed to the correct settings for the media, so that's what you should do. Any subsequent clips that you edit into the Timeline—HD clips, for instance—will be scaled to

FIGURE 5.12
Change sequence settings dialog box.

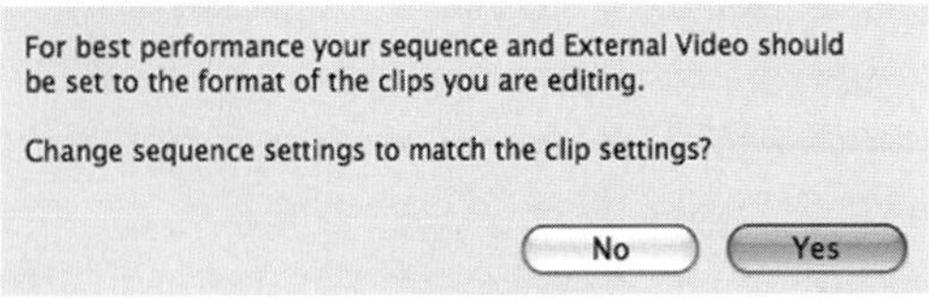

For best performance your sequence and External Video should be set to the format of the clips you are editing.

Change sequence settings to match the clip settings?

No   Yes

match the DV settings. If we clicked on **No**, the DV clip would be scaled up to match the HD sequence, keeping the HD settings in the Timeline, and the clip would appear in the Canvas with pillarboxing, black bands on the left and right, as in Figure 5.13. The DV clip is in standard 4:3, and the sequence, as all HD material, is in widescreen.

The *Editing* panel of *User Preferences*, which we saw in Lesson 3, contains a preference for how this dialog box behaves. You can have it **Ask** what to do, which is what happened here, or you can set to automatically **Always** conform the sequence or to **Never** conform the sequence. Ask is probably the best option. The great advantage of this feature is that it prevents you from accidentally editing in a sequence with the wrong settings and ending up in a great deal of trouble.

FIGURE 5.13
Pillarboxing in Canvas.

In this version of FCE, material that is placed in a sequence that doesn't match its settings—for instance, the DV that was placed and pillarboxed in the HD sequence—is scaled to fit the Canvas. In this instance, the file is scaled to 225 percent, which is a huge increase and will soften and degrade the image. To return it to normal, open the clip into the Viewer and reset the Scale value in the Motion tab. This will, of course, turn this clip into a small image in a very large frame. Final Cut Express's new behavior of always scaling to match the sequence should be used carefully, especially when working with still images that are smaller than the sequence frame size. This default behavior can be switched off in the *Editing* panel of *User Preferences*, right next to conform preferences.

87

NOTE
Only Standard Sizes: FCE4 will make sequences conform only to standard formats with which it works and that can be selected in the presets. You cannot, for example, take an MPEG-4 movie that's 640×480 running at 15 frames per second and expect FCE to conform the sequence and change it to those settings. It won't. Your material will simply be placed in the sequence, and the sequence settings will be unchanged. FCE will conform sequences only to clips that are in its standard settings.

Slice 2

The second Slice method is in the Timeline. This is where you really are slicing with a digital razor blade! When you place a clip in the Timeline, the playhead automatically jumps to the end of the clip, ready for you to place another clip in position. But in this case, we don't want it to do that.

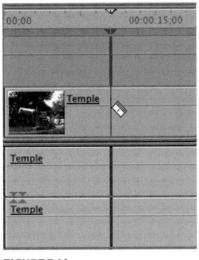

5. Click in the Timeline window to make it active (or use **Command**-3), and press the **Home** key to take you back to the beginning of the Timeline.

6. To make it easier to work in the Timeline, press **Shift-Z** (**Fit to Window**) to fit the contents of the Timeline into the window.

7. Press the **spacebar** to play *Temple*. The video plays in the Canvas.

8. Use the **spacebar** to stop and the **Left** and **Right** arrow keys to find the start of the shot of the glass-fronted hut at 00:00:10;16.

9. Make sure Snapping is turned on. Check the indicator in the upper right corner of the Timeline window. (We saw this in Lesson 2 on page 39.) Toggle it on and off with the N key.

FIGURE 5.14
Blade tool in the Timeline.

10. Select the Blade tool from the Tools palette, or call it up with the **B** key, and move it along the Timeline to the playhead line.

As you move along the clip in the Timeline, your cursor will show the Blade tool rather than the Selector (see Figure 5.14). You'll see dark triangles at the top and bottom of the playhead line, indicating that the cursor has snapped to the playhead.

11. Click with the Blade tool to cut the clip at the playhead.

This will cut the video and audio on the clip as though you were cutting it with a knife or a razor blade, which is how film and audiotape used to be cut when it was first edited. This is the digital equivalent for the same process.

12. Go to the end of the shot and use the **Left** and **Right** arrow keys to find the first frame of the next shot.

13. Click the Blade tool again, or use the keyboard shortcut **Control-V**.

14. Now that you've made one cut, find the next shot. Its first frame starts with the quick zoom at 00:00:19;00. Again, use **Control-V** or the Blade tool to cut the shot.

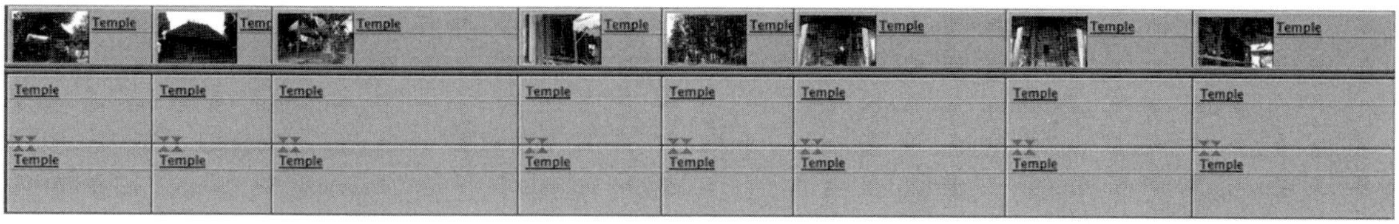

FIGURE 5.15
Cut clips in the Timeline.

15. Go through the Timeline and slice more clips by using **Control-V** to cut at the first frame of every new shot (see Figure 5.15).

16. After you've cut out the clips you want from the long shot in the Timeline, go to the Browser and select *Sequence 1*.

17. From the **Modify** menu, select **Modify>Make Sequence Clips Independent**.

18. If you've been using the Blade tool, you need to switch back to the standard Selection tool. To switch to it, you can click on the tool at the top of the Tools palette or press the **A** key. (Think A for Arrow.)

19. Drag the clips into a bin in the Browser.

These clips are all master clips and can be renamed, reedited, and organized. They will have the same master/affiliate relationship as a captured clip, an imported clip, or a subclip.

These *Temple* shots come into the Browser with In and Out points marked, and if you open the clips, you'll find that each contains all of the video that's in the original master shot called *Temple*. The upside of this is obvious. Because a sliced clip is a copy of the master clip, you can now access any shot in the reel from inside any sliced clip. That's the upside; the downside is scrubbing. The master clip is made up of a long length of material, perhaps even a whole reel

NOTE

Edit Points Redux: We talked about where the cut takes place when you're editing—that the In point cuts the space *before* the frame you're looking at, and the Out point cuts *after* the frame you're looking at. The Blade always cuts on the gap in front of the frame you're seeing in the Canvas. So to get the last frame of *Temple* when slicing in the Timeline, you have to be looking at the first frame of the shot after it. If you press Control-V on the last frame of the memorials shot, the thatched hut shot will have one frame of the memorials at its head.

of tape, although I would advise against this. It's now difficult to scrub in the Viewer because even a tiny movement will move the playhead a long way up and down the scrubber bar.

Slice 3

With the Slice 2 method, you're cutting the pieces you want to keep and moving them into the Browser. Let's look at another method that works almost exclusively in the Timeline. Here we'll cut away the pieces we don't want to use and leave behind in the Timeline the shots that contain the good material.

1. Begin by deleting everything in *Sequence 1*. **Command-A** will Select All, and the **Delete** key will remove everything.
2. Make sure there aren't any In and Out points marked in the master clip *Temple*, and bring a fresh copy into the sequence by dragging it into the Timeline.
3. Press the **Home** key to return to the start of the sequence.
4. Play forward until you reach the beginning of the second shot at 00:00:10;16. We want to remove the second shot from the sequence because we don't need it.
5. Mark an In point in the sequence by pressing the **I** key.
6. Play forward through the second shot and through the zoom at the beginning of the third shot, until about 00:00:21;02. We will cut out everything from the first frame of the second shot up to and including the frame where the playhead is parked, just as we mark In and Out points in the Viewer.
7. Press the **O** key to enter an Out point in the Timeline, which should look like Figure 5.16.

FIGURE 5.16
In and Out marked in the Timeline with Auto Select functions.

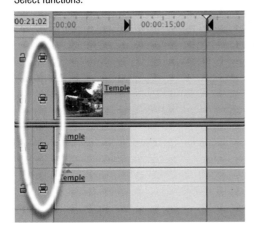

Notice the highlighted area in the tracks. This is the Auto Select function in Final Cut. Tracks can have their selections toggled on and off with the buttons circled on the left in Figure 5.16. This allows you to select only certain tracks. If you do not see the highlighted areas, it's probably because the clip or something in the Timeline is selected. It is critical that nothing is selected in the sequence when you use this technique. Anything that is selected (e.g., clip, audio, title) will be ripple-deleted instead of the marked In and Out section. The simplest way to avoid this is to press **Command-Shift-A** to **Deselect All**, the opposite of **Command-A**, **Select**

All. This drops anything that's been selected. A good habit to get into before you execute this technique is to always make sure the Timeline is the active window and press **Command-Shift-A**, or if you really like the menus, use **Edit>Deselect All**.

8. Now that we have the area we want selected, press **Shift-Delete** to execute a ripple-delete, removing that section of the video. You can also use the **Forward Delete** key on an extended keyboard to do this.

> **NOTE**
> ***Browser and Timeline Clips:*** This might be a good time to explain the relationship between the clips in the Browser and the clips in the Timeline. Quite simply, there isn't one—or at least no direct, linked relationship. They are separate, distinct items. They may be copies of each other, but they are separate clips that share the same media. So in the first Slice method, when you mark up the master clip with In and Out points, you are marking one clip and making copies of it in the *Clips* bin. When you drag the master clip from the Browser and place it in a Timeline, you are placing a copy of the master clip. So when you razorblade and ripple-delete the clip in the Timeline, you are not in any way affecting the master clip that remains untouched in your Browser.

91

This method of cutting away the bad material in the Timeline is a fast and efficient way to edit material. You end up with the shots you want to keep in the Timeline. This is a good method for working on something like a television news story, where a fast turnaround and quick cutting is necessary, and you're not concerned with storage, organization, or logging your material carefully.

If you do want to organize and rename your material again, choosing **Modify> Make Sequence Clips Independent** will separate the clips in the Timeline from their master/affiliate relationship. Now you can pull them into bins and rename them if you wish.

Slicing, whether in the Viewer or the Timeline, has the advantage of quickly and easily accessing all of your material while still cutting it up into shots for editing. However, it does have a couple of disadvantages. It can be difficult to scrub in the Viewer when the shot is very long, and you can accidentally extend the transition into another shot, which will look like a flash on the screen. This can never happen with properly made subclips.

92

TIP

Auto Select Shortcuts: Some keyboard shortcuts use the keypad of the extended keyboard to toggle off and on the Auto Select functions. Command-1, -2, -3, -4, and so on will toggle tracks V1, V2, V3, V4, and so on. Option-1, -2, -3, -4, and so on will toggle audio tracks A1, A2, A3, A4, and so on. Option-clicking on the Auto Select button for a video track will toggle soloing for just that one track. Option-clicking on the Auto Select for an audio track will do the same there.

Range Clipping

Another way to slice or make subclips is with the **Range** tool in the Timeline. Some people prefer this method because it offers a visual display of the In and Out points as you work. Let's try it.

Range Selection Tool - ggg

FIGURE 5.17
Range tool.

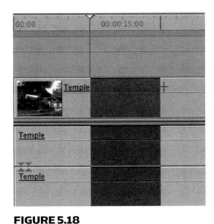

FIGURE 5.18
Range tool in the Timeline.

1. Again, delete any clips from the Timeline, and make sure there are no In and Out points in the master clip *Temple* before dragging it into an empty *Sequence 1*.

2. Select the Range tool from the tools. It's under the second icon from the top. You can also call it up by keying **GGG** (see Figure 5.17).

3. Position the playhead in the Timeline where you want the clip selection to begin.

4. With the Range tool, stroke one section of the clip (see Figure 5.18).

As you stroke the clip to make the selection, the Canvas will give you a two-up display that shows you the start and end frames as well as the timecode in the Timeline (see Figure 5.19).

5. Grab the selection from the Timeline, and drag it to the Browser, where it can be changed into a master clip if you wish.

FIGURE 5.19
Range selection
two-up display
in the Canvas.

ORGANIZING THE CLIPS

Once you have your material diced up, you should spend some time putting it away so you can find it again. There are no firm rules about this, and each project tends to dictate its own organizational structure. Usually I begin with one bin that holds all of the master shots, which are usually pretty big chunks of video: 10, 20, 30 minutes, usually not smaller. If the media is HD and has already been broken up into clips, I still keep the master shots in one bin. Making copies of clips in other bins for organizing doesn't duplicate the media on the hard drive and doesn't take up more space. From the master shots, clips are separated into bins. Keeping the master shots has the advantage that you can go back to the material in bulk to look through it again. I like to do this toward the end of the project to make sure I haven't overlooked or discarded anything, which can be useful in light of the way the material gets cut together.

The separate bins can be organized in a variety of ways. Narrative projects tend to have material broken down into scene bins, with sub-bins for different types of shots or characters, depending on how complex the scene is. Documentary projects tend to break the material down into subject matter: a bin for all of the forest shots, another for logging scenes, another for road work, another for weather, another for all of the interviews, another for sound, another for narration tracks, another for music, another for graphics. As I said, there are no hard-and-fast rules on how material is organized.

The real trick is to break down your material into enough bins so that your material is organized, but not so many bins that it becomes difficult to find material. As you copy clips into bins, add notes—lots of them. The more information you include on the clips, the easier it will be to find them.

Cutting up your shots and organizing them into bins is critical to working efficiently, particularly for long-form work projects longer than 20 minutes or so,

TIP

Reassembling Your Tape: Sometimes it's useful to skim through your media in the order in which it was shot. For DV material that comes in as long clips this is not a problem, but for HD material, where your clips are broken down as they're captured, there is a simple solution. After your material has been captured and placed in your master clips bin, make a new sequence in the bin, one for each tape, and lay all the shots for one tape in reel order in the sequence. You can then scrub through your material quickly. You can also copy and paste from these master sequences into editing sequences.

or short projects with a lot of material, or projects that may go on for a longer period of time. I know people who are working on projects that they envisage will take eight years or more to complete. The longer the project, the more tapes you have, the more sequences, the more complex everything becomes. Having your material well organized is crucial. If projects become very large, if the project file size itself gets large, approximately 50 MB, it's time to split up the project. Work in multiple projects for different sections. You can have multiple projects open at once and can move material, clips, and sequences from one project to another.

To help you organize your material FCE has provided some tools such as the comments and logging information that we saw in the previous lesson. Final

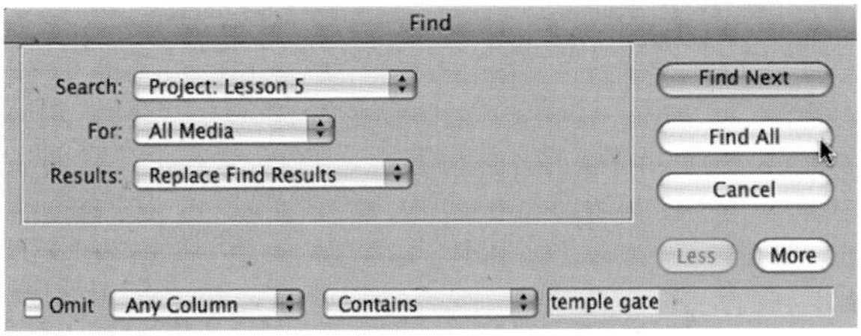

FIGURE 5.20
Find dialog box.

Cut's search tool is called the Finder. To search for something in a project, use the same keyboard shortcut as the Desktop Finder: **Command-F**. This brings up the **Find** window (see Figure 5.20). The first pop-up menu lets you search (1) the open project, (2) all open projects, and (3) the *Effects* tab. It searches anything tabbed into the Browser.

The second pop-up menu selects **All Media** or a choice of **Used** or **Unused Media**, and the third pop-up menu lets you replace or add to existing results. The two pop-ups at the bottom define parameters. The left one sets where it's going to look. Unless you have a pretty good idea where the information is (e.g., if you're looking for a specific type of file), just leave it on the default Any Column. The right pop-up menu lets you limit the search parameters to speed up the process by limiting the number of results.

The search function for Used or Unused is of mixed benefit. It's not a very useful feature for most people working in DV who capture large chunks of video, often whole one-hour tapes. If any part of that media file is used FCE will treat it as used. Even if you make a subclip from the media, the application will still look at the media file and if any portion of it is used, even a few frames, will mark it as used. It's more helpful for HDV and AVCHD users as their media gets broken into clips at each shot change. So if a shot is unused FCE can find it. But again if any piece of a clip is used the whole media file and anything associated with it is marked as used.

FIGURE 5.21
Finder results window.

If you click the **Find All** button rather than the default **Find Next**, the requested clips appear in a new Browser window (see Figure 5.21). Note the two buttons at the bottom that let you (1) show a selected item in the regular Browser bins and (2) remove selected items from a project.

95

> **TIP**
> **_Using Find to Keep Track:_** Because FCE doesn't keep track of shots that are taken from the Browser and put in a sequence, the Find window is one way to do this. By selecting the Unused pop-up menu, you can find the material and then use the check mark in the Good column to mark the unused clips. This technique is especially useful with HD material that's already broken up as you capture.

An important point about this Finder is that all the items it locates are directly related to the items in the Browser. Unlike FCE's usual behavior, where clips in sequences and bins can be copies of each other, here the found clips are directly linked to the clips in the Browser. Highlight a clip here, and it's highlighted in the Browser. Delete a clip here, and it's deleted from the Browser.

> **TIP**
> **_Other Searches:_** The search engine isn't only for finding shots. You can search for anything in FCE. You might want to find a filter or a transition. You can search for those as well.

LOOK BEFORE YOU CUT

Whatever way you work your video into clips or subclips, you're really looking through your material. You should watch for relationships—shots that can easily be cut together. Getting familiar with the material is an important part of the editing process, learning what you have to work with and looking for cutting points.

Look through the master shot *Temple*. It's quite short, but it shows a few shots that have obvious relationships. The same woman in the white woolen hat appears in four of them:

- In the third shot, as she bows before an incense bowl
- The shot from behind her that looks a little blue, in which she is walking up the stairs
- Another, in quick succession to the previous one, also from behind as she goes up the steps
- In medium shot from the side as she bows and prays

These shots can obviously be cut together to make a little sequence. You might want to put in a cutaway between the shot of her bowing at the bowl and from behind her walking up the steps or already at the top of the steps. From either of those two shots, a direct cut to her bowing would work without a problem.

Searching for these relationships between shots is critical as you look through your material. Some editors like to immediately create small sequences and group them together, not finely honed but roughly laid out so that first important impression is preserved. You may not use it in your final project, but assembling

> **NOTE**
>
> *The Cutaway:* Any editor will tell you that cutaways are the most useful shots. You can never have too many, and you never seem to have enough. No editor will ever complain that you have shot too many cutaways. A cutaway shot shows a subsidiary action or reaction that you can use to bridge an edit, like the shot of the interviewer nodding in response to an answer. The cutaway allows you to bridge a portion of the interviewee's answer where the person has stumbled over the words or has digressed into something pointless. A wide shot that shows the whole scene can often be used as a cutaway. Make note of these useful shots as you're watching your material.

related shots quickly into a sequence is an efficient way to make notes about your material. We'll look at assembling material into sequences in our next lesson.

You can have multiple sequences open at the same time. Timelines normally tab together into one Timeline window, but you can pull the timelines apart so you have two sequences open on the screen at the same time. You can pull shots from one sequence into another. By doing this, you're copying the shot from one sequence into the new sequence.

SUMMARY

In this lesson, we covered cutting our material, working with markers and using DV Start/Stop Detect, creating subclips, and slicing up our clips, as well as organizing our material so we can work efficiently. In the next lesson, we will look at putting our shots together in a sequence. We'll look at more precise ways of editing into sequences, moving your clips into the Timeline, and trimming them with some advanced editing tools.

LESSON 6

Editing Basics: Placing Your Shots

Now that you've marked up your material in Final Cut Express, you can go on to put them into the Timeline. FCE has several different ways, usually three or four, to do most of the editing functions. You can edit directly into the Timeline with the mouse, in the Viewer with buttons, or with keyboard short-cuts, which is probably the most efficient way to edit in most instances.

LOADING THE LESSON

If you haven't already transferred the *Media* and *Projects* folders to your computer, you should do so now (see the beginning of Lesson 2). Let's begin by opening the *Projects* folder on your hard drive and double-clicking the project file, *Lesson 6*, to launch the application. As in Lesson 2, before the project finishes loading, you may be greeted with the **Reconnect** dialog box. Do the following:

1. Click on the **Reconnect** button in the Offline Files dialog (see Figure 6.1). Do not click **Continue**.
2. In the next window that comes up, check the box to specify the drive where your media is located (see Figure 6.2).
3. Click the **Search** button.
4. FCE will find one of the items. If it's the correct item, make sure it's selected, and click the **Choose** button in the dialog box (see Figure 6.3). If it doesn't find it, use the **Locate** button to find it manually. It should find the other file as well.
5. The two files should then have been moved to the bottom of the Reconnect Files dialog box. Click the **Connect** button to reconnect the files (see Figure 6.4).

FIGURE 6.1
Offline Files dialog.

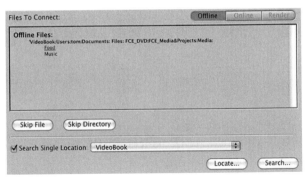

FIGURE 6.2
Reconnect Files dialog box.

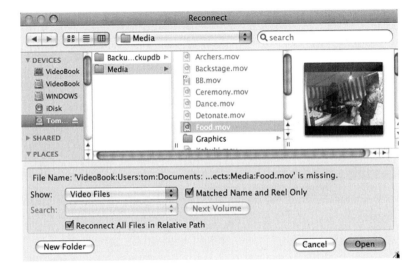

FIGURE 6.3
Reconnect Files dialog box.

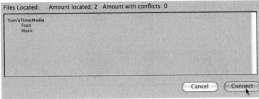

FIGURE 6.4
Items ready to be reconnected.

You may have to do this for each of the projects from this book that you open. If one of the lesson projects you're working on ever gets corrupted, you should retrieve a fresh copy from your DVD, move it to your hard drive, and reconnect it as we have just done.

Setting Up the Project

Inside the Browser of your copy of *Lesson 6*, you'll see an empty *Sequence 1*. Also in the Browser is an audio file called *Music.aif* and the master clip, *Food*, together with a bin called *Clips*. Open the *Clips* bin, and you'll see that the shots from *Food* have been cut up into subclips.

WORKING WITH THE CLIPS

To start, let's look at where we're coming from and the material we have to work with:

1. The empty *Sequence 1* should already be open; if it is not, double-click on it.
2. Open the *Clips* bin, and double-click on the shot called *Food1*, which is 6;01 long—six seconds and one frame.
3. Play the shot. Let it pan from left to right across the trays of food, let the pan end, give it a beat, and then stop.
4. Enter an Out point by pressing the **O** key or the Out point button in the Viewer.

FIGURE 6.5
Dragging into the Timeline.

This will probably be around 4;12—about four and one-half seconds long.

Try it a few times until you're comfortable with the pacing of the movement. You might find that the more times you try it, the more you're shaving off the shot. Perhaps you'll feel that the front needs to be shortened as well. Instead of beginning right at the start of the shot, enter an In point just before the camera pans right. When you have it the way you want, you're ready to move it into the Timeline. You can do this in four ways:

FIGURE 6.6
Edit Overlay.

1. Drag it there. Grab the image from the Viewer and pull it directly into the Timeline, dropping it onto V1 as shown in Figure 6.5.
2. Drag the clip from the Viewer to the Canvas, and the visual dialog box called the Edit Overlay (see Figure 6.6) immediately appears. Drop the clip on Overwrite.
3. Use the Overwrite keyboard shortcut, **F10**. If your keyboard shortcuts don't work properly, see the section on Exposé and Spaces in the Lesson 1 section on Optimizing Your System.
4. If you added the Editing Workshop buttons (see the Tip "Edit Buttons"), you can click on the red Overwrite button as in Figure 6.7.

FIGURE 6.7
Editing Workshop button in the Canvas.

You can execute the edit any way you like. Most people prefer to drag to the Timeline, but you must be careful because it's easy to drop the clip into the wrong track or to do an Insert instead of an Overwrite. (I personally

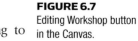

101

prefer the accuracy and exactness of dragging to Overwrite or using the keyboard shortcut.)

TIP
Edit Buttons: Although there are no edit buttons in the Canvas, you can make your own buttons for the primary edit functions that we'll be looking at in this chapter. I have created a button list for these functions that you can use. You'll find it in the *Extras* folder of the DVD. In addition to the edit functions, a couple of other buttons are useful, which appear over the Browser. To load the buttons, right-click in one of the coffee bean button holders and choose Load Main Button Bars from the shortcut menu. Navigate to the *Button Bars* folder of the *Extras* folder on the DVD and select *Editing Workshop Button Bars* to add the buttons to the windows. You will also see the *Default Button Bars*. To restore all the default buttons, you must reset them in each window, or you can use the saved *Default Button Bars* set to revert to the standard buttons.

Overwrite

Let's look at the Edit Overlay (Figure 6.6), which offers seven different editing options. The most commonly used are the **Overwrite** and **Insert** commands.

1. Drag the clip from the Viewer until the box marked Overwrite highlights.
2. Drop the clip.

It will overwrite whatever is in the Timeline, beginning where the playhead is parked. When you drag a clip onto the Edit Overlay or use a keyboard shortcut to execute an edit, the clip is placed in the Timeline on the designated destination tracks—in this case, V1 and A1/A2. These are the default destination tracks set in the patch panel at the head of the Timeline (see Figure 6.8).

The number of tracks and the types available as destination tracks are controlled by what is loaded in the Viewer. For instance, if you have a still image in the Viewer, only one destination track for video will be available. Similarly, if you have a piece of stereo music loaded in the Viewer, only two tracks of audio will be available as destinations, and no video track will be available, as in Figure 6.9.

FIGURE 6.8
Patch panel.

To get an idea of the functionality offered in the Edit Overlay, let's quickly drag a few shots into the Timeline to see how they work.

1. If you haven't already done so, drag *Food1* from the Viewer and drop it on Overwrite.
2. Select clips *Food2* and *Food3* in the Browser and drag them directly to the Overwrite box in the Edit Overlay.

The clips will appear in the Timeline following *Food1* in their bin order. Every time you place a clip in the Timeline, the playhead automatically leaps to the end of the clip, ready for the next edit event.

FIGURE 6.9
Patch panel with stereo music only.

TIP

Dropped Frames: One of the most common causes of dropped frames, especially for FCE users with slower computers, is that their viewing window is not fit to the video. If you look at your video in a small frame while the material is set to full size, you expect the computer to display only a portion of the video while playing it back. If this doesn't produce dropped frames on playback, it may display as stuttering video on your computer monitor. You can always tell if the image is too large for the viewing window when you see scroll bars on the sides, as in Figure 6.10. To correct this, select Fit to Window from the Viewer's Zoom pop-up menu, the left of the two pop-up menus at the top of the Canvas, or use the keyboard shortcut Shift-Z. Shift-Z is also used in the Timeline to fit the contents into the window.

103

TIP

Timeline In Point: You can also define the In point in the Timeline to be a different point from the playhead. Go to the Canvas or the Timeline window and press the I key to mark an In point (see Figure 6.11) at the playhead. This will be the In point for the next edit, regardless of where you move the Timeline playhead to, and when you drag the clip from the Viewer to the Canvas or press F10, the clip will drop at the marked In point and not at the playhead's current position.

FIGURE 6.10
Fit to Window.

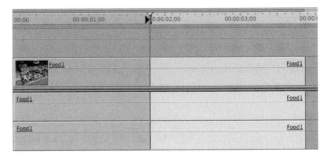

FIGURE 6.11
In point mark in the Timeline.

FIGURE 6.12
Snap markings.

NOTE

Overwrite Constraint:

Note that although you can drag a clip directly from the Browser to the Edit Overlay, F10 does not overwrite directly from the Browser. F10 works only when overwriting from the Viewer. If the Viewer is closed, F10 will simply put in a slug, which is a long section of black with a stereo audio track.

As you move the playhead onto the edit point, it should snap strongly to the join and display on the tracks the marks in Figure 6.12. If you don't see the snap marks, that means **Snapping** is turned off.

Insert

If Overwrite is the most commonly used of the Edit Overlay features, then the second most used must be **Insert**, which is where a nonlinear editing system shows its power.

1. Move the playhead to the edit between *Food1* and *Food2*.

2. Press the **N** key. Try it several times, toggling the Snapping function on and off.

The **N** key may become the one you use the most in Final Cut Express. You'll probably be changing from one mode to the other often.

Now with Snapping on, you should have the playhead parked between the clips.

3. Grab *Food5* directly from the Browser, and drag it to the Canvas, calling up the Edit Overlay.

4. Drop it on Overwrite to see what happens.

5. *Food5* wipes out all of *Food2* and some of *Food3*.
6. Quickly undo that with **Command-Z**.
7. This time, instead of dragging *Food5* onto Overwrite, drag it onto Insert.

> **TIP**
> ***The Magic Frame:*** If the playhead moves to the end of the
> last clip in a sequence, the Canvas displays the last frame of the clip with a blue
> bar down the right side. This is the Magic Frame, because the playhead is
> actually sitting on the next frame of video, the blank, empty frame, but the
> display shows the previous frame.

Immediately, the Timeline rearranges itself. *Food5* drops into the Timeline, appears between *Food1* and *Food2*, and pushes everything farther down in the Timeline, as shown in Figure 6.13.

FIGURE 6.13
The Insert edit.

Insert will move everything down the track regardless of a clip's position. So if you insert into the middle of the clip, the clip will be cut, and everything on all of the tracks will be pushed out of the way. This applies to all tracks, including music or narration, which you may not want to cut.

Track locks are useful in these circumstances. For instance, to prevent an insert from slicing into a music track, lock the track or tracks. All of the other tracks will move, but the locked tracks will remain stationary. Let's try this and see what happens:

1. Undo the Insert edit that you made when moving *Food5* into the Timeline.
2. The Browser contains an audio track called *Music.aif*. Grab the icon and drag it directly into the Timeline, and then place it on tracks A3/A4. Make sure you have a downward-pointing arrow when you place it on the tracks.

It takes up two tracks of audio because a stereo pair has left and right channels, one channel of audio on each track.

3. Again, move the playhead back between _Food1_ and _Food2_.

4. Execute the Insert edit with _Food5_. Or use the keyboard shortcut **F9**. Or, if you've added the Editing Workshop buttons, use the yellow Insert button.

Immediately, you'll notice that not only is the video being inserted into the sequence, but the music track is also being cut with the insert.

5. Undo that edit with **Command-Z**.

6. Click on the track locks (see Figure 6.14) at the head of each track. Remember that you need to lock or unlock both tracks of a stereo pair.

7. Redo the Insert edit, and you'll see that although the video moves to accommodate the clip, the music tracks do not.

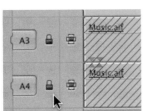

FIGURE 6.14
Track locks.

Before we go any further, let's undo the Insert edit and remove the audio on A3/A4, bringing the Timeline back to just three clips: _Food1_, _Food2_, and _Food3_. You can also remove the inserted shot by ripple-deleting it with **Shift-Delete**. You can also ripple-delete using the **Forward Delete** key on an extended keyboard, which is sometimes marked as **Del**.

Alternative Overwrite and Insert

Overwrite and Insert are the primary functions in the Edit Overlay, but let's look at another way to do them. Drag _Food5_ directly from the Browser to the Timeline. As you drag it onto the edit point between _Food1_ and _Food2_, a little arrow appears, indicating how the edit will be performed. If the arrow is pointing downward, as in Figure 6.15, the edit will overwrite. If the little arrow is pointing to the right, as in Figure 6.16, you will be doing an insert edit, which

FIGURE 6.15
Overwrite arrow.

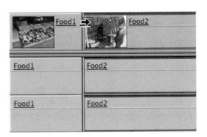

FIGURE 6.16
Insert arrow.

will ripple the sequence, pushing the other material in the Timeline out of the way. Notice as you do this how the two-up display in the Canvas changes. In Figure 6.17 the video is being overwritten, beginning at the end of *Food1* and wiping out all of *Food2* and most of *Food3*. In Figure 6.18 the shot is being inserted between *Food1* and *Food2*.

You'll also notice that as you work in the application, in addition to the arrow indicators, the clip colors change. In Overwrite, the track color changes to the highlighted brown color. In Insert, the track has an outline box.

107

FIGURE 6.17
Overwrite two-up Canvas display.

FIGURE 6.18
Insert two-up Canvas display.

The point at which the arrows switch from Insert to Overwrite is indicated by the faint line running horizontally through the clips in the Timeline about one-third of the way from the top. When you drop the clip, if the cursor is in the upper third, the edit will be an Insert. If it's in the lower two-thirds, the edit will be an Overwrite. It's the faint horizontal line you see running through the clips in Figures 6.15 and 6.16.

Replace

We'll cover Overwrite with Transition and Insert with Transition in Lesson 8, which deals with transitions. Right now, we will look at Replace, Fit to Fill, and Superimpose.

Replace is remarkably sophisticated. It will replace a clip in the Timeline with another clip either from the Viewer or dragged from the Browser to the Canvas. The important thing to understand about Replace is that it works precisely from the point at which the playhead is positioned. Let's do a Replace edit:

1. Start with your base three shots in the Timeline: *Food1*, *Food2*, and *Food3*.
2. Place the playhead at the edit point between *Food1* and *Food2* so we're at the beginning of *Food2*.
3. Open *Food5* into the Viewer, and make sure the playhead there is close to the beginning of the clip.
4. Drag it into Replace in the Canvas, or use the keyboard shortcut **F11**. *Food5* will immediately replace *Food2* in the Timeline. If you have loaded the Editing Workshop buttons, you can also use the blue Replace button.

The Viewer and the Canvas will show the same frame because Final Cut has taken the frame that was in the Viewer and placed it in exactly the same frame position as the shot it's replacing in the Timeline. It has extended the shot forward and backward from that point to exactly fill the duration of the shot it's replacing.

Take a look at the clips in Figure 6.19. The clip in the Timeline, *Food2*, has the playhead parked toward the end of the shot. Say we want to replace it with the clip *Food5*. In the Viewer, *Food5* has the playhead parked near the beginning of the shot. The current position of the playhead in *Food5* is indicated, but you can't replace *Food2* with *Food5* even though the new clip is much longer than the clip it's replacing. Why? Because FCE calculates the Replace edit from the position of the playhead. There just aren't enough frames in front of the

Viewer Playhead

Timeline Playhead

FIGURE 6.19
One clip trying to
replace another.

current position of the playhead in *Food5* in the Viewer to replace all the frames
in front of the current position of the playhead in *Food2* in the sequence. If you
tried to do a Replace edit to *Food5* in place of *Food2* in the Timeline, you would
get an "Insufficient content for edit" error message.

TIP
Alternative Replace: Another way to do a replace
function is to use Overwrite after first defining the limits of the shot you
want to replace. That's easy to do in FCE. With the playhead parked over the shot,
press the X key. This sets In and Out points on the Timeline that are exactly
the length of the clip, as in Figure 6.20. If you now do an Overwrite edit, it will
replace the shot in the Timeline. What gets selected and highlighted
in the Timeline is controlled by the Auto Select
buttons at the head of the tracks.

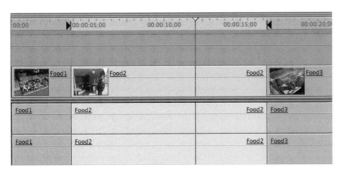

FIGURE 6.20
Ins and Outs in the Timeline.

Fit to Fill

Fit to Fill functions like Replace, except it's never hampered by a lack of media. Fit to Fill adjusts the speed of the clip to match the area it needs to occupy. This is a great tool for putting in still images or titles that you want to be a specific length. Because they aren't real video, Final Cut will produce the images very quickly and accurately. It's a little more problematic when using it with video where it can raise some problems.

1. To see how this functions, delete everything that you may already have in the Timeline and make sure the playhead is at the beginning of the Timeline.

2. Grab *Food4*, *Food5*, and *Food6*, and drag them to Overwrite in the Edit Overlay to move them into the Timeline.

3. Move the playhead in the Timeline so it's sitting over *Food5*, the middle of the three clips in the Timeline. Open the clip *Food1* into the Viewer.

4. Press **Option-X** to clear any In and Out points that might be marked on the clip.

You can see by the duration in the upper left corner of the Viewer that *Food1* is quite a bit shorter than *Food5*. *Food1* is 6:01, whereas *Food5* is 17:09.

5. Drag the *Food1* clip from the Viewer to the Edit Overlay, and drop it on the Fit to Fill box. Or use the keyboard shortcut **Shift-F11**. Or if you have the Editing Workshop buttons loaded, click the green Fit to Fill button.

The clip will immediately drop into the Timeline, and unless it is exactly the same size as the clip it's replacing, a colored render line will appear at the top of the Timeline—red if your system is not capable of playing back a speed change in real time and green if it is. The red or green render line indicates that the section of the Timeline needs to be rendered at some point before output. If the line is red, the clip will have to be rendered immediately to be viewed; if it's green, you will have a real-time preview. This section must be rendered because of the speed change to *Food1*, which is now in slow motion to accommodate the Fit to Fill edit. The clip in the sequence shows the speed change—in this case, 35 percent of real speed (see Figure 6.21). You will also see a green line at the top of the audio portion of the clip, indicating that it, too, because the sound is also slowed down, must be rendered before outputting.

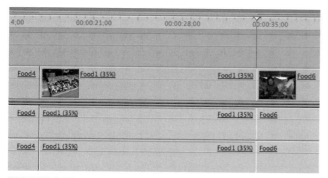

FIGURE 6.21
Slow-motion clip in the Timeline.

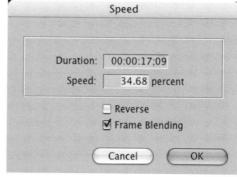

FIGURE 6.22
Speed dialog box.

The 35 percent shown in the Timeline, however, is not quite true. Let's check the speed. Select the clip *Food1* in the Timeline, and press **Command-J**, which calls up the **Speed** dialog box (see Figure 6.22). In this case, the speed is 34.68 percent. The real problem with speed changes is that it is difficult to create smooth motion, particularly at odd speeds such as 34.68 percent. At full-size, interlaced DV, you can get some nasty stuttering effects, particularly if the clips are speeded up. If you want to do slow or fast motion, it is better to use simple multiples: 50, 150, 25, or 200 percent. These are much easier to calculate and generally produce better results. Fit to Fill calculates an absolute number and, as you can see, usually a bizarre one.

Modify>Speed (Command-J) is where all clip speed changes are made. It is unfortunately not possible to ramp speed up or down so it accelerates and decelerates, at least not without outside help (see the *Time Remapping* tip). Frame blending can help, but it will slow down render time. The default is to have Frame Blending turned on. With Frame Blending off, FCE merely duplicates or drops frames as necessary to make up the right speed. For slow motion, you usually want to have Frame Blending turned on, but for clips being speeded up, it works better to have it switched off.

If you're slowing down the material, there is another way to do a Fit to Fill that will usually produce better results. With the playhead in the Timeline at the start of the clip, use **Command-Option-F** to match back to a new copy of the clip from your hard drive. This is not the clip in the Browser, which you can match frame to with the **F** key, but a new copy of the media called up from your hard drive. Now mark an In point on the new clip. Execute the speed change with **Command-J**—say, to 50 percent—and drag the clip to Replace. The slomo will be the duration of the clip it's replacing without rippling the sequence (see the tip "Changing to Slow Motion").

TIP
Time Remapping: Although the Time Remapping function—
the ability to change speed gradually—is only available in Final Cut Pro, you can
get a filter that will allow you to do this. Piero Fiorani has produced a number of excellent
plug-ins for FCE that you can download from his website http://web.mac.com/
piero.fiorani/PieroF_FCE_Effect/Welcome.html. Aside from being
excellent filters, they're also free.

TIP
Changing to Slow Motion: When a speed change is done in
a sequence, a Ripple edit is performed (i.e., the contents of the Timeline shift,
based on the new length of the clip). This is usually a good thing, but sometimes you don't
want that to happen. If you speed up a clip, the sequence will get shorter, and if you
slow down a clip, the sequence will get longer. Either way, everything after the
clip will move to accommodate the speed change.

112

Superimpose

Superimpose is used primarily to place titles on the track above the video. It again works a bit like Replace. The clip you're superimposing takes its duration from the clip you're placing it above. Drag the clip on Superimpose, and it will be placed above the clip that the playhead is sitting on.

FIGURE 6.23
Superimpose.

1. Let's ripple-delete the Fit to Fill shot, the middle of the three in the Timeline, so that we're left with only *Food4* and *Food6*. Select it and press **Shift-Delete**.
2. Place the playhead somewhere over the middle of *Food6*.
3. Drag *Food5* from the Browser to the Canvas, and drop it on the Superimpose box, or use the keyboard shortcut **F12**. If you have the Editing Workshop buttons loaded, you can click the purple Superimpose button in the Canvas.

The clip appears in the Timeline above the clip on the destination track, above *Food6* in this case, as in Figure 6.23. Notice how the audio track has gone onto A3 and A4, the tracks below the destination tracks.

NOTE

Superimpose: The term *superimpose* is often misunderstood. In FCE it means placing a clip on the track above the current destination track. It does not mean what many people expect: that the superimposed image will appear partially transparent and that the underlying image will still be visible beneath it. You can do that by adjusting the opacity of the clip on the upper track, which we'll look at later.

SUMMARY

In this lesson you've learned how to use the editing tools that moved clips into the Timeline: Overwrite, Insert, Fit to Fill, Replace, and Superimpose. We used drag and drop to the Canvas Edit Overlay, the keyboard shortcuts for each, and the Editing Workshop buttons. Now that we've looked at how to edit your shots and at the editing tools available in FCE, we'll proceed to putting a sequence together using these shots.

113

TIP

Different In Point: If you want to superimpose at some point other than right over a clip, you can do this by entering an In point in the Timeline. Go to the Canvas or the Timeline window and press the I key to mark an In point. This will be the In point for the next edit, and when you drag the clip from Viewer to Canvas to Superimpose, the clip will drop at the marked In point and not at the playhead's current position. Also note then when using the Superimpose function, the In point is not removed after you do the edit but remains in the Timeline. This is the only edit function that behaves this way.

LESSON 7

Editing Basics: Building Your Sequence

Now that you've cut up your material in Final Cut Express, it's time to put it all together. There is no right or wrong way to edit a scene or a sequence or even a whole film or video; there are only bad ways, good ways, and better ways.

LOADING THE LESSON

Let's begin by opening the *Projects* folder on your hard drive and double-clicking the project file, *Lesson 7*, to launch the application. As in Lesson 2, before the project finishes loading, you may be greeted with the Reconnect dialog box. Follow the steps in the previous lessons to reconnect:

1. Click on the **Reconnect** button in the Offline Files dialog.
2. In the next window that comes up, check the box to specify the drive where your media is located.
3. Click the **Search** button.
4. FCE will find one of the items. If it's the correct item, make sure it's selected, and click the **Choose** button in the dialog box. If it doesn't find it, use the **Locate** button to find it manually. It should find the rest of the files as well.

MAKING THE SEQUENCE

Inside the Browser of your copy of *Lesson 5*, you'll see four sequences:

- *Food Sequence*
- *Rough Cut*
- *Sequence 1*
- *Slip & Slide*

The Browser also contains the master clip, *Food*, together with the *Clips* bin, as in the previous lesson. *Sequence 1* is empty, and we'll look at *Slip & Slide* later in the lesson. *Rough Cut* is the first part of the edited sequence made up for you. Before we begin, however, let's take a quick look at *Food Sequence*, which is where we're going.

Now that we've gone through the principal means of going from Viewer to Canvas, let's edit our sequence together into the Timeline and then look at how to trim, adjust, and rearrange our clips. To start, we'll edit together a quickly paced sequence of shots. I like to begin by looking at the material I'm going to use for the sequence. Open the master clip *Food* in the Viewer and look through the material the way it was shot. Let's start working with the subclips that have already been prepared for you:

1. Double-click on *Food1* in the *Clips* bin to open it into the Viewer.
2. Scrub through to the point where the camera starts moving from left to right.
3. Find the beginning of the movement and mark the In point.
4. Now find the end of the movement and mark the Out point. We can leave the shots a little loose at this stage.

TIP

Marking Edit Points: Many editors like to mark their Out points on the fly. This allows you to judge the pace of the shot and the sequence—doing it almost tactilely—to feel the rhythm of the shot. After a few tries, you'll probably find that you're hitting the Out point consistently on the same frame. If you're not, perhaps it isn't the right shot to be using, or perhaps you should look again at the pace the sequence is imposing on you. It's possible the shot doesn't work where it is. Marking the In point is a little different because often you want to mark the edit point before an action begins, but judging how far in front of the action to begin on the fly is difficult. Many editors like to mark the In point while the video is playing backward. By playing it backward, you see where the action begins, and you get to judge the pace of how far before the action you want the edit to occur.

5. After you've marked the In and Out points, drag the clip to Overwrite or press **F10**.

I'm not sure which part of the second shot, *Food2*, I'll use at this stage, but I'll probably use something, so I'll cut a long piece.

6. Open *Food2* into the Viewer, and take the shot from just before the zoom starts. Let it run almost to the end, including the part with the hands turning the skewers.

7. Again, Overwrite to the Timeline.

Food3 is a little more complex. I want to use more than one part of the shot.

8. Start by marking the In point at the beginning of the shot.

9. Mark the Out point just before the short zoom out.

10. Overwrite the clip.

Ins and Outs

By putting the shot in the Timeline, I made a copy of the shot that's currently loaded in the Viewer. So now I can set new In and Out points for the clip that's still in the Viewer without affecting what I've already done to the shot in the sequence:

1. Set a new In point in the Viewer just before the pan left begins.

2. Let the shot carry over to the steaming kettle, until about the 8;18 mark.

3. Add an Out point, and add that to the Timeline.

4. Take a third section from that clip, from just before the camera tilts up until shortly before the shot ends, and add that to the Timeline.

Food4 might fit nicely before the close-up of the steaming tray.

5. Position the Timeline playhead between *Food2* and *Food3* in sequence.

6. Mark an In point at the beginning of *Food4* and an Out point just before the pan to the right, around 2;28.

7. Drag the clip to Insert or use the shortcut **F9**.

We might be able to get another piece out of *Food4*.

8. Mark an In point around 5;15, just at the beginning of the static portion of the shot of the man hunched over his soup.

9. Mark an Out point just before the camera pans left around 9;09.

10. Move the playhead in the Timeline in front of the first portion of *Food4*, to the edit point that separates *Food2* and *Food4*.

11. Execute an Insert edit to move the shot from the Viewer into the Timeline.

Bookends

Let's look at *Food5*. It's the most human part of the material: the little girl at the food stall. My thought is to use it as bookends, with the little girl at both the beginning and the end of the sequence.

117

1. Make the first part of the shot one clip, basically until after she hands the vendor her money. Mark an In point near the beginning of the shot and an Out point around 6;12.
2. Make sure the playhead is at the start of the Timeline, and then drag to Insert or **F9**.
3. Make the second part of *Food5* begin shortly before the vendor reaches for the biscuit, around 7;27. Mark an In point there and let it go until just before the end.
4. Move the playhead to the end of the Timeline with the **End** key.
5. Drag the second half of *Food5* from the Viewer to Overwrite, or press **F10**.

We want *Food6* to go just before the last shot.

6. Open *Food6* in the Viewer and play it.
7. Set the In point near the beginning.
8. Set the Out point before the second move with the biscuits, around 3;16.
9. In the Timeline, the playhead is probably at the end of the material. Use the **Up** arrow to move backward one edit.
10. Now drag the clip from Viewer to Insert, or use **F9**.

TIP
Timecode Location: To go to a specific timecode point in either the Canvas, the Viewer, or the Timeline, tap out the number on your keypad. (In the case of working with *Food6*, type in 316 and press Return.) The playhead will immediately move to that point.

The duration of this little sequence should be about 45 seconds, depending on how tightly you cut the shots. Looking through the clips, it obvious the sequence needs to be tightened up, as well as have the order rearranged. Your Timeline should look like Figure 7.1. The sequence called *Rough Cut* is made up of the edits up to this point for you to use if you wish.

REARRANGING THE SEQUENCE

FCE has several tools for refining your edit, fine-tuning, and rearranging the sequence. Let's look at some of those, working with the shots that we have edited together into the Timeline.

FIGURE 7.1
Timeline after first cuts.

FIGURE 7.2
Shuffle Edit arrow in the Timeline.

Shuffle Edit

The sequence contains three pieces of *Food3*. Let's begin by moving *Food1*, which is now the second shot in the sequence, between the first two pieces of *Food3* in the Timeline. This is called a *Shuffle edit*, or perhaps more commonly a *swap edit*, which is the term it was know by for many years.

1. Grab the *Food1* shot, and pull it along the Timeline to where you want to place it.

2. Make sure the head of *Food1* snaps to the edit point between the first two cuts of *Food3*.

3. When you get to where you want it to go, before you release the mouse, hold down the **Option** key.

The cursor will change into a downward hooked arrow on the clip (see Figure 7.2). You'll also see a number displayed. This tells you how far in the sequence you have moved the clip.

4. With the **Option** key down and the clip at the edit point, release the mouse to drop the clip between the two shots.

If you look at the Timeline, you'll see that you've done an insert edit as well as a ripple-delete. You've removed the clip from one point on the timeline, placed it somewhere else in the Timeline, and pushed

TIP
Shuffle Edit Limit: The Shuffle Edit function that lets you move clips will only work on one clip at a time. Unfortunately, you can't grab a couple of clips or a small section of clips and do the same thing. It also works best if you have Snapping turned on to avoid slicing off a little bit of a shot by accident.

119

FIGURE 7.3
After using Shuffle Edit.

FIGURE 7.4
Timeline after Paste
Insert.

everything out of the way to make room for it. Figure 7.3 shows the sequence after the Shuffle edit.

Ripple Cut and Paste Insert

Although you can move only one shot at a time when you do a Shuffle, there is a handy way to move groups of clips. Look at the two pieces of *Food4* followed by the first part of *Food3*. These three shots should be moved together right after *Food5* at the head of the Timeline. This would make them the second, third, and fourth shots in the sequence. I could just move *Food2* after them, but let me show you a way to move groups of clips.

1. Start by selecting the clips. It's simplest to marquee-drag through them or to select the first clip and **Shift**-select the third clip.
2. Next, cut them out, not with the usual **Command-X** but with **Shift-X**.

Using **Command-X** would create what's called a **Lift** edit but leave a gap in the sequence. Sometimes you do want to do this, but in this instance, we use **Shift-X**, which performs a **Ripple Cut** instead of the simple Lift. This not only cuts the clips out of the Timeline but also closes the gap the missing clips leave behind.

3. Now move the playhead to the edit at the end of *Food5*, between *Food5* and *Food2*. This is where you want to place the clips. Press **Shift-V**, which will paste the clips as a Paste Insert edit. **Command-V** would also paste but as an Overwrite edit.

Your Timeline should be laid out something like Figure 7.4.

> **TIP**
> *Closing Gaps:* FCE defines a gap as a space in the
> Timeline that extends across all tracks. So if you have a music track on
> A3 and A4, for instance, FCE will not see the space between the shots on the
> video tracks as a gap. This is where the ability to lock tracks really helps.
> If you lock those music tracks, you can then close the gap. Or use Option-click to
> lock all other tracks, and again you can close the gap. There are several ways to
> close a gap: Right-click in the gap and from the shortcut menu choose Close
> Gap. With the playhead over the gap, press Control-G. Click on the
> gap to select it and then press the Delete key.

Let's look through the sequence again. It's getting better, but there are still a few edits I don't like and quite a few shots that need trimming. We'll get to trimming in a moment, but let's rearrange a few more shots.

Add Edits

In the first shot, I like the way the camera moves around the girl at the beginning, and I like the way she hands over her money with her fingers splayed out. I'd like to lengthen the effect of this scene by basically making it take more time than it actually did. I'd like to move *Food2* right into the middle of that first shot, although I know *Food2* is too long; we'll trim it shortly.

1. Scrub or play through the beginning of the Timeline to find the point just after the camera moves around the girl and the vendor picks up the bag, around 2;15 into the sequence.

2. Make sure nothing is selected in the sequence, and use **Control-V** to slice the clip in the sequence.

3. Play or scrub forward in the Timeline to find the point just before the vendor reaches his hand out for the money, around 2;21.

4. Press **Control-V** again. You have now isolated a short section to cut out.

5. Ripple-delete it by selecting it and pressing **Shift-Delete** or the **Forward Delete** key. (You can no longer use the shortcut menu on the clip in the Timeline as you could in earlier versions of FCE.)

> **TIP**
> *Moving the Playhead:* Shift-Left or
> Right-arrow will move the playhead forward or
> backward in one-second increments.

121

Instead of using the Add Edit function with **Control-V**, you could also have done this by marking an In and Out point in the Timeline, as we did in the previous lesson, and ripple-deleting the short section. Although the keyboard shortcut is more efficient, you can also make an add edit with the Blade tool.

Range Clipping

Another way to do this would be to use the Range tool (**GGG**), which we saw in the previous lesson. You can use this feature to select a portion of the clip to ripple-delete (see Figure 7.5). You may have to switch off Snapping to make such a short edit. While you're dragging with the Range tool, you'll see a two-up display in the Canvas that shows you the start and end points of the edit (see Figure 7.6). The timecode display in the Canvas is that of the clip, beginning from the clip's start time of 00:00:00;00.

FIGURE 7.5
Range tool selection in the Timeline.

FIGURE 7.6
Two-up Canvas display.

FIGURE 7.7
Food sequence beginning.

Moving More Clips

Obviously the sequence now has a jump cut. So let's take *Food2*, which we moved earlier and should now be the sixth shot in the sequence, and do a Shuffle edit.

1. Drag and then hold the **Option** key to drop *Food2* between the two halves of *Food5* at the beginning of the sequence.

The beginning of the Timeline should look like Figure 7.7.

JUMP CUTS

The sequence as we've laid it out so far has the most obvious form of jump cut, which is any abrupt edit that jars the viewer. This is generally considered bad editing. The most common cause is having side-by-side shots, such as the two halves of *Food5*, that are very similar but not the same. You get this disconcerting little jump, as if you blacked out for a fraction of a second. It suddenly pulls the viewers out from the content of the video as they say to themselves, or perhaps even out loud, "What was that?" You can also get a jump cut if you put together two very different shots, such as the shot of a long street with the small figure of a person in the distance, cutting to a tight close-up. It's disorienting because the viewer has no reference that the close-up belongs to the person seen in the far distance in the previous shot. These are jump cuts, and you should try to avoid them. Or you could use them so often that it becomes your own personal style. Then it's art.

As you go through the sequence, you'll see another jump cut between two parts of *Food3*. The camera pans right from the cooking tray to the steaming kettle and then in a separate shot tilts up from the kettle to the cook. I would remove the first of these shots, taking out the pan. I've seen that cooking tray already, but the kettle and the chef are new.

The arrangement is almost right, but there is a problem with the very last shot. Just after the vendor puts the biscuit in the bag, the camera jiggles. I'd like to remove this, so we'll do it in the Timeline:

2. Scrub or play through *Food5*, the last shot in the sequence, to the frame when the biscuit just disappears into the bag behind the counter.
3. Use **I** to mark the In point in the Timeline. Right after this, the camera is jostled.
4. Move further down to where the vendor is about to reach forward with the bag, just before his hands separate.
5. Mark the Out point with the **O** key and ripple-delete the middle portion.

Now we have the same problem we had in the first shot. This time we're going to move *Food3* from its earlier position. This is the shot of the tilt from kettle to cook.

6. Drag and then add the **Option** key before you drop it between the two halves of *Food5* that you just split.

If you look through the sequence, you'll see that the shots are in the order we want, but we still need to tighten it up, trimming the shots to make to make the sequence faster-paced.

123

Storyboarding

Another way to lay out your sequences is by building storyboards in bins. Some editors like to do this. In Large or Medium Icon mode, you can do the following:

- Trim and set the clips
- Set the Poster frame
- Arrange the layout order of the shots in the Browser

To set the Poster frame of a clip when you're in Icon view, do either of the following:

- Open the clip into the Viewer, find the frame, and use **Mark**>**Set Poster** Frame (**Control-P**), or
- Press **Control-Shift** while you click on the icon in the bin. This will let you scrub the clip. Hold down the two modifier keys and release the mouse over the clip where you want to set the Poster frame.

Storyboarding is a fast, easy way to move around the order of the shots, to try different arrangements and sequences. Although you can't play back the clips as a sequence, you can make a quick arrangement of shots in your bin. Then marquee through the shots and drag them into the Timeline (see Figure 7.8).

The shots will appear in the sequence in the order they are in the bin. Notice that the shots in the Timeline in Figure 7.8 follow the bin order as they are laid out, left to right, top to bottom. Be careful with the row heights: Clips that are placed higher up in the bin will appear earlier.

TIP

Timeline Scaling: You can change the scale of the Timeline to zoom in and out with the tabbed slider at the bottom of the window. Pulling either end of the tab will change the scale of the Timeline window. At the bottom left is a little slider that will adjust the scale (see Figure 7.9). My favorite way is to use the keyboard shortcuts Option-= (think Option-+) to zoom in and Option – (that's Option-minus) to zoom out. What's nice about using the keyboard shortcuts is that it leaves the playhead centered in the Timeline as you zoom in and out. Just be careful a clip isn't selected in the Timeline because the scaling will take place around that rather than around the playhead. You can use Command-+ and Command—to scale in other windows, but Option-+ and – will always scale the Timeline even if the Viewer or the Canvas is the active window.

FIGURE 7.8
Storyboarded bin and
shots in the Timeline.

FIGURE 7.9
Scaling slider and
tabbed slider

THE TRIM TOOLS

Roll and **Ripple**, and **Slip** and **Slide** trim tools in the Tool palette (see Figure 7.10). The trim tools are clustered in the fourth and fifth buttons. Ripple and Roll change the duration of clips, and Slip and Slide leave the clip duration intact.

A *Ripple* edit moves an edit point up and down the Timeline by pushing or pulling all of the material on the track, shortening or lengthening the whole sequence. In a Ripple edit, only one clip changes duration, getting longer or shorter. Everything else that comes after it in the track adjusts to accommodate it. In Figure 7.11, the edit is rippled to the left, and everything after it moves left to accompany it, just as in a ripple delete.

A *Roll* edit moves an edit point up and down the Timeline between two adjacent shots. Only those two shots have their durations changed. One gets longer, and the adjacent shot gets shorter to accommodate it. The overall length of the sequence remains unchanged. In Figure 7.12, the edit point can be moved either left or right.

A *Slip* edit changes the In and Out points of a single clip. The duration of the clip remains the same, and all of the clips around it remain the same. Only the In and Out of the slipped clip change. If more frames are added on the front, the same amount of frames is cut off the end, and vice versa. If some are added to the end, an equal amount is removed from the beginning. In Figure 7.13, the contents of the shot change by changing In and Out points, but neither its position in the Timeline nor either of the adjacent shots is affected.

FIGURE 7.10
The Tool palette.

125

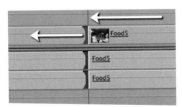

FIGURE 7.11
Ripple edit left.

FIGURE 7.12
Roll edit directions.

FIGURE 7.13
Slip edit directions.

FIGURE 7.14
Slide edit directions.

FIGURE 7.15
The Ripple tool.

FIGURE 7.16
Ripple tool right.

FIGURE 7.17
Ripple tool left.

A *Slide* edit moves a clip forward or backward along the Timeline. The clip itself, its duration, and its In and Out points remain unchanged. Only its position on the Timeline, earlier or later, shortens and lengthens the adjacent shots as it slides up and down the track. In Figure 7.14, the shot *Food6* can slide up and down the Timeline. The shot doesn't change, only the two adjacent shots.

The Ripple Tool

We're going to work with the Ripple tool first. Press the fourth button and extend the pop-out to select the tool as in Figure 7.15. You can also call it up by pressing **RR** (the **R** key twice). Let's use it on some of the shots we want to work on. Start with the edit between shots *Food4* and *Food3*. Take the tool and place it near the edit. Notice that it changes direction as you move it across the edit as in Figures 7.16 and 7.17.

When the tool is on the right side, it will ripple the second shot, and when it's on the left side, it will ripple the first shot. In this case, we want to ripple the second shot. The edit almost works, but it can perhaps be improved a little by tightening it up. The little pause at the beginning of *Food3* before the ladle moves makes the edit look awkward. You can ripple right in the Timeline. As you grab the clip, you will get a small two-up display in the Canvas.

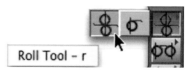

FIGURE 7.18
The Roll tool.

A word of caution about rippling: If you're working with material that's cut to narration or music, rippling will easily upset the timing of the sequence because it's pulling and pushing the entire track and its sync sound. So what's working for you at this moment in the edit may be ruining something else further down the Timeline. In these cases, the Roll tool may work better for you.

FIGURE 7.19
The Roll tool in the Timeline.

The Roll Tool

The Roll tool is also under the fourth button in the Tools, shown in Figure 7.18. It can be evoked with the **R** key. It is controlled similarly to Ripple and can be used in the Timeline as in Figure 7.19. The Roll tool acts on both shots, extending one shot while shortening the other. Although the Ripple tool changes the overall length of the sequence by moving everything up and down the line, the Roll tool affects only the two adjacent shots. Using Roll and Ripple, tighten up some of the shots in the sequence. I rippled the zoom into the skewers in *Food2* until all you see are the hands turning over the sticks on the grill.

127

Extend Edit

Final Cut's **Extend Edit** is another nice way to perform a Roll edit. It's a simple way to move an edit point, even one with a transition.

1. Select an edit by clicking on it or by using the **V** key.
2. Move the playhead in the Timeline a few frames before or after the edit point to where you want to move the edit. Press **E** or select **Sequence> Extend Edit**.

If the selection is dimmed in the menu or you hear a system warning, it means you don't have enough media to perform the Extend edit.

3. Undo that edit when you're done.

TIP

Ripple and Roll Shortcuts: You can also use the Ripple and Roll tools incrementally with keyboard shortcuts in the Timeline. Select the edit point by moving the playhead over it and pressing the V key. Now, by using the U key, you can toggle through Ripple Right, Ripple Left, and Roll. Whichever edit you have selected, you can now move incrementally with the left bracket ([) and the right bracket (]). Each tap will move the edit one frame left or right in the direction the bracket is pointed. Shift-[and Shift-] will move the edit whatever duration you have set for Multi-Frame Trimming in your User Preferences in the Editing panel of User Preferences. The default is five frames, but if you'd rather have three frames or ten frames, you can change it (see Figure 7.20). This also works if you select a clip in the Timeline and then choose either the Slip or Slide tool.

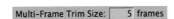

FIGURE 7.20
Multi-Frame trim size setting.

FIGURE 7.21
The Slip tool.

FIGURE 7.22
The Slip tool in the Timeline.

The Slip Tool

Let's look at Slip and Slide next. Slip works in the Timeline and the Viewer, whereas Slide works in the Timeline only. They do pretty much what their names imply. Slip is one of my favorite tools. It is especially useful for making small adjustments to a clip in the Timeline. You can select the Slip tool from the fifth button in the Tools, as shown in Figure 7.21, or call it with the **S** key.

I've created the *Slip & Slide Sequence* to help explain these two tools. Open the sequence by double-clicking it in the Browser. Use the Slip tool to grab the middle clip in the sequence. Move the clip from side to side, and you'll see the Timeline display as in Figure 7.22. What you're doing is slipping the media

FIGURE 7.23
Canvas two-up display using the Slip tool.

for the clip up and down its length. The overall duration of the clip remains unchanged, but the section of media for that duration is adjusted.

The Canvas again shows you a two-up display: the first and the last frames of the video. The shot in the sequence begins at 3;00 and ends at 4;29, a two-second shot. By dragging to the right, we are slipping the clip 10 frames as we see in Figure 7.23, the shot will now start at 2;20, ten frames earlier, and end at 4;19, keeping the same duration. It starts earlier, so it will end earlier. If the shot slipped in the other direction, it would start later in time but also end later. The two-up display will prevent you from slipping the clip too far into some unwanted material. If you're working without subclipping your material, as we discussed in the last lesson, you can see if you're slipping into the next shot.

It is also possible to slip in the Viewer, which can be especially beneficial when you're adjusting a clip before you bring it into the Timeline:

1. Return to the Selection tool with the **A** key, and double-click the clip to load it into the Viewer.
2. Hold down the **Shift** key as you grab either the In point or the Out point and drag. This way you will drag both points together and maintain a constant duration.

This is *slipping*, and what you see in the display (see Figure 7.24) is the start frame in the Viewer and the end frame in the Canvas. It doesn't matter which end you grab to pull; the display is always the same: Start in the Viewer, end in the Canvas.

The Slide Tool

Let's look at the last trimming tool, the Slide tool, which is also in the fifth Tools button (see Figure 7.25). The Slide tool can be brought out with **SS**. Like the Slip tool, it also works in the Timeline but not in the Viewer. The Slide tool

129

FIGURE 7.24
Slipping in the Viewer
with the Canvas display.

FIGURE 7.25
The Slide tool.

FIGURE 7.26
The Slide tool in the
Timeline.

130

doesn't change anything in the clip you're working on; it grabs the clip and pulls it forward or backward along the Timeline, wiping out material on one side and extending the material on the other side, as shown in Figure 7.26. Notice that you're not only moving the clip but also affecting the two adjacent clips, which is why they're highlighted with boxes.

The Canvas display (see Figure 7.27) is unlike the other two-up displays. You don't see the clip you're moving at all. What are displayed are the two adjacent shots:

- On the left, the end of the shot in front of the one you're moving
- On the right, the beginning of the shot after the one you're moving

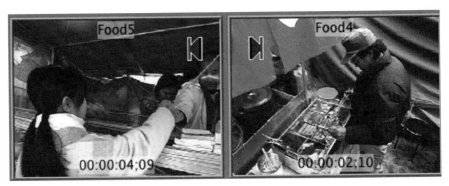

FIGURE 7.27
The Slide tool Canvas
display.

In these figures, by moving the second clip, *Food1*, earlier in time, the first shot *Foot5* is being shortened by 20 frames, and the last shot *Food4* is being lengthened by 20 frames.

You are limited in how far you can slide a clip by the amount of media available in the adjacent shots. If you move to the end of the available media, the film sprocket overlay will appear in the two-up display.

HOW LONG IS LONG ENOUGH?

A static shot, either close-up or medium shot, must be on the screen a much shorter time than a long shot in which the audience is following a movement. A shot that has been seen before, a repeat, can be on the screen quite briefly for the audience to get the information. Though there is no hard-and-fast rule, generally, shots without dialog remain on the screen no more than six to eight seconds on television with its small screen. In feature films, shots can be held for a lot longer because the viewer's eye has a lot more traveling to do to take in the full scope of the image. This is probably why movies seem much slower on the television screen than they do in the theater. Although a close-up can be on the screen quite briefly, a long shot will often contain a great deal of information and needs to be held longer so viewers have time for their eyes to take it all in. You can often hold a moving shot such as a pan longer because the audience is basically looking at two shots, one at the beginning and the other at the end. If the movement is well shot—a fairly brisk move, no more than about five seconds—you can also cut it quite tightly. All you need to show is a brief glimpse of the static shot, the movement, and then cut out as soon as the camera settles at the end of the move.

131

Look at your finished sequence. It should look something like the sequence called *Food* in the Browser. I still wouldn't be very happy with the piece, principally because the audio is so abrupt and choppy, marking each cut. Work still must be done to smooth out the sound, perhaps extend sound from a single clip, or add some constant underlying sound from somewhere else. But that's a topic for another lesson.

SUMMARY

In this lesson we've learned how to assemble our sequence and trim our shots, using the following:

- Shuffle edit
- Ripple Cut
- Paste Insert
- Storyboarding

- Ripple tool
- Roll tool
- Extend edit
- Slip tool
- Slide tool

Now you know the basic tools of editing with Final Cut Express, cutting your clips, getting them into the Timeline, and trimming them. Before we look at some advanced editing techniques, we'll see now to add transitions to your sequence. When you want to smooth out cuts or mark a change between scenes, you might want to add transitions. That's what we're going to look at in the next lesson: how transitions work and how to use them.

LESSON 8
Adding Transitions

Transitions can add life to a sequence, transform a difficult edit into something smoother, or give you a way to mark a change of time or place. The traditional grammar of film that audiences still accept is that "dissolves" denote small changes, and a fade to black followed by a fade from black marks a longer passage of time. With the introduction of digital effects, every imaginable movement or contortion of the image to replace one with another quickly became possible, and was just as quickly applied everywhere, seemingly randomly, to every possible edit. They can be hideously inappropriate, garish, and ugly, but to each his own. Transitions can be used effectively, or they can look terribly hackneyed. Final Cut Express gives you the option to do either one or anything in between.

Let's look at the transitions FCE has to offer. There are quite a few of them, 60 to be exact, although there is redundancy in the transitions. Some people seem to think that just because Apple put all those transitions in there, you have to use them all. Remember that most movies use only cuts and the occasional dissolve. Most film and television programs are cuts only, with a fade in at the beginning and a fade out at the commercial breaks.

Many third-party transitions and effects can also be purchased online from plug-in providers such as CGM Online. Any transitions or effects created using Apple's FXScript or FxPlug code bases will work in Final Cut Express 4, but filters created using the After Effects plug-in structure will not work in Final Cut. In this lesson we'll look at adding transitions, controlling them, and adjusting the look of your transitions, using parameters.

133

LOADING THE LESSON

Let's begin by loading the material you need on the hard drive of your computer, if you have not done so already.

1. Open the DVD and drag the *Media* folder from the DVD to your computer. This contains the media needed for the projects.
2. You may also want to drag the folder called *Transitions* from the DVD onto your media drive. This contains samples of each of the 60 transitions available in Final Cut Express.
3. Also make sure you have the *Projects* folder on your system hard drive.
4. Eject the DVD and launch the *Lesson 8* project from the *Projects* folder on your hard drive.
5. Once again, you may have to go through the reconnect process as in the Loading the Lesson" section in Lesson 2. You will first get the Offline Files window. Click the **Reconnect** button.

Inside your copy of the project *Lesson 8*, you'll find in the Browser:

- An empty sequence called *Sequence 1*
- The sequence called *Transitions* that has a few shots laid out in it, waiting for transitions
- The master clip *Village*
- The bin called *Clips*
- A still image called *Gradient.pct*, which we'll use later

To see the basic settings for each of the 60 FCE transitions, use **File**>**Import**> **Folder** to bring into the application the *Transitions* folder you copied onto your hard drive. The folder contains bins with all of the transitions grouped in the same fashion as they are in the application.

APPLYING TRANSITIONS

In the Browser, usually behind the project window, is a tab called *Effects*. If you open it, you will see a window with a group of bins as in Figure 8.1. You'll notice more than transitions in this window. For the moment, we're going to concentrate on the *Video Transitions* bin.

One of the bins in the Effects window is *Favorites*. We'll look at *Favorites* later in the lesson. Here you can park your special transitions and effects. It's probably empty now. Double-click on *Video Transitions* to open the bin. It should look like Figure 8.2, depending on how your Browser is set. The *Video Transitions* window shows yet more bins, and these bins contain the available transitions grouped into categories. I'd be very surprised if anyone has ever used them seriously on real projects and not just played around with them to try them out. The *Transitions* bin you imported contains previews of each of the transitions available in FCE. We're going to try out some of them in this lesson.

The default transition in FCE is the Cross Dissolve with a default duration of one second. In the bins in the Effects window and in the menus, you may see some transitions highlighted in bold. These are real-time capable transitions, if your system is fast enough to support them. If your system isn't fast enough, then very few will be in bold.

You can apply a transition in Final Cut Express in several different ways:

- Drag the transition you want from the Effects panel of the Browser, and drop it on an edit point.
- Select the edit point. (Remember, **V** will select the nearest edit point.) Then use the **Effects>Video Transitions** menu, and choose one.
- Select the edit point, and apply the default transition with the keyboard shortcut **Command-T**.
- Select the edit point, and by right-clicking on the edit point, call up the default transition from the shortcut menu.

There are a couple of other ways that we skipped in Lesson 6, using the two items in the Edit Overlay:

- Insert with Transition
- Overwrite with Transition

The default transition will appear in your sequence when you select Insert with Transition (**Shift-F9**) or Overwrite with Transition (**Shift-F10**).

Checking the Media

Let's begin by opening *Sequence 1* if it's not already open.

1. Select the three clips in the *Clips* bin, and drag them directly to the sequence.
2. It might be helpful to use **Shift-Z** (Fit to Window) if the clips appear too small in the Timeline.

FIGURE 8.1
Effects window.

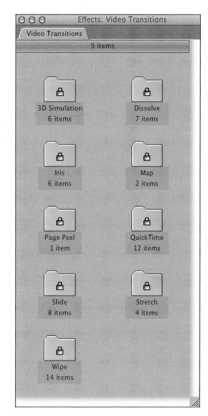

135

FIGURE 8.2
Video Transitions window.

Remember that these are all subclips, so each shot you just placed in the timeline contains the full extent of the media for that clip on the hard drive. Or at least Final Cut Express thinks so.

Let's try putting a transition onto the sequence we've laid out.

3. Grab the *Cross Dissolve* transition from the *Dissolve* bin, and drag it onto the edit point between *Village1* and *Village2*.

FIGURE 8.3
Transition error.

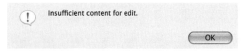

FIGURE 8.4
Insufficient content error.

You see that this isn't possible because you get the transition drag icon with a small X, as shown in Figure 8.3. If you try to perform the edit by using the keyboard shortcut **Command-T**, you'll get the error message in Figure 8.4. Why is this happening? The answer is simple: There isn't enough media in either clip beyond the edit point to perform the transition. The shots must overlap; frames from both shots must appear on the screen simultaneously. For a one-second transition, both shots must have one second of media that overlaps with the other shot. These frames come partly from inside the clip and partly from media beyond the edit point. The extra video frames, those beyond the edit point separating the two shots, are called *handles*.

1. Double-click *Village1* in the Timeline to open it into the Viewer.
2. Go to the end of the shot. Use **Shift-O** to take you to the Out point.

If Overlays are switched on in the View pop-up as they normally are, you'll see the telltale film sprocket hole indicator on the right edge of the frame (see Figure 8.5).

This overlay tells you that you're right at the end of the available media for that shot. There must be extra media available to create the overlap for the transition, as shown in Figure 8.6. The pale shot on the left has to overlap the dark shot on the right by half the length of the transition, and vice versa. If that media does not exist, you can't do the transition.

FIGURE 8.5
Film sprocket Overlay in the Viewer.

FCE usually assumes as a default that the transition takes place centered on the marked edit point, and not that it ends at the edit point. Therefore, to execute the default one-second transition, you need at least half a second, 15 frames, of available media after the Out point on the outgoing shot and 15 frames in front of the In point of the incoming shot. In this case, there is nothing, so you get error messages when you try to execute the transition. Unless you think of it ahead of time—and many times you don't—you'll have to deal with it when you're fine-tuning your edit. Often you'd rather not deal with transitions while you're laying out your sequence, leaving them until you've laid out the shot order.

If you know you have extra media in the original clip, you can always go back to extend the media. If this option is available, it's easy to do in FCE. Select **Remove Subclip Limits** from the **Modify** menu. In this case, however, extending the media will push it into another shot, producing a flash frame during the transition, something to be avoided. This is one of the benefits of subclipping: It prevents you from going beyond the shot when you're laying in a transition.

To be able to put in transitions, we'll have to trim the Out point of *Village1* and the In point of *Village2*. We could do this by dragging the ends of the shots to make them shorter, but that would leave a hole in the Timeline. Instead, we'll use the Ripple tool to shorten the shots.

1. Select the Ripple tool from the Tools palette, or use the keyboard short-cut **RR**.
2. With the Ripple tool, click just to the left of the edit point between *Village1* and *Village2*, as in Figure 8.7.
3. With Ripple active, type in −**15** for 15 frames. Notice the display that appears in the middle of the Timeline window (see Figure 8.8). Press the **Return** key.

137

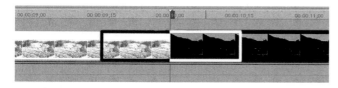

FIGURE 8.6
Overlapping video.

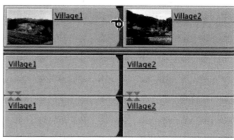

FIGURE 8.7
Ripple tool in the Timeline.

FIGURE 8.8
Ripple value in the Timeline.

We know this is the navigation shortcut for going backward half a second. Because we're in the Ripple tool, we're rippling it backward one-half second.

4. Click on the right side of the edit point at the start of *Village2*. Remember that you can use the **U** key to toggle from rippling one side, to roll edit, and to ripple the other side of an edit point.

5. This time type *15* (the plus is understood—that you want to move forward in time), and press **Return** to ripple the edit point half a second.

We've now rippled *Village2's* In point by half a second, half a second off the end of the first shot, and half a second off the beginning of the second. So we have removed a half second of material from both clips, leaving these as handles so there is enough room for the transition.

Over these three shots laid in the Timeline, if I ripple the Ins and Outs on both edits in the Timeline, taking 15 frames off the end and the beginning of each shot, I reduce the overall duration by two seconds. This will substantially change the timing of my sequence. If you plan to use transitions between shots, it's best to allow for the extra material within the shot before you lay it in the Timeline.

6. Once you've rippled the edits, go to the edit point in the sequence between *Village1* and *Village2*, and apply the transition.

138

Transition Alignment

FIGURE 8.9
Transition in the Timeline.

If you drag a transition from the *Transitions* bin to an edit point, it does not need to be dragged only to the center line. It can also be dragged to the Out clip so the transition ends at the edit point (the A side) or to the In clip so the transition begins at the start of the clip (the B side). This can be done only if there is sufficient material for this type of transition.

FIGURE 8.10
Clips overlapping in the transition editor.

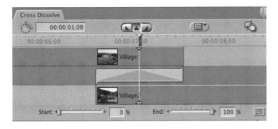

After you've applied a transition, if you double-click on the transition in the Timeline, it will open into the Viewer. Make sure you click on the transition area as in Figure 8.9, not on the edit point that divides the two shots. Here you can see how the video overlaps and why extra material handles are needed on either side of the edit point to create the effect (see Figure 8.10).

Once it's in the Timeline, the transition displays in one of three ways, depending on how it was

NOTE

Handles on One Side: If you only have video available for the transition overlap on one side of the edit, you should not try to execute the transition from the menu or with Command-T. These methods will usually execute the default Center on Edit transition. If one of the shots does not have enough material to do the transition, you'll get a one-frame transition. Just be careful, because it may seem that a transition has been entered into your sequence when there isn't anything there of value.

placed. Figure 8.9 shows the center position; the other two appear in Figures 8.11 and 8.12.

Making the transition to start or end on edit is useful if you have media available on only one side of the edit point, if you have a title or other clip on a track without any material adjacent to it, and at the beginning or end of your program.

Notice the sloping line indicators that show the type of alignment in each case. The last two transitions can be only half-second dissolves. When we rippled the sequence by 15 frames on each side of the edit point, only enough media was made available for a half-second Start or End on Edit transition. If the transition is to end on the edit point with the default duration, the incoming shot must be extended one whole second underneath the outgoing shot to accommodate it. Similarly, if you wanted to start the transition on the edit point with the default duration, the outgoing shot has to extend one second into the incoming shot, one second beyond the start of the edit point. If we made these changes, we could also easily change the type of transition alignment with the shortcut menu on the transition in the Timeline (see Figure 8.13).

FIGURE 8.11
End on Edit transition.

FIGURE 8.12
Start on Edit transition.

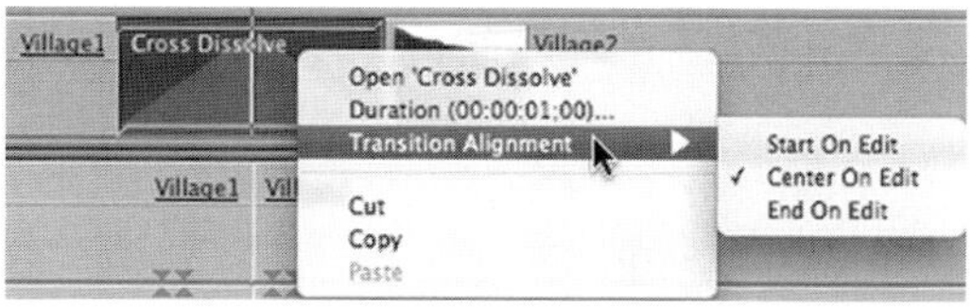

Using the Edit Overlay

Let's back up a bit to see another way to use the Canvas Edit Overlay to create transitions.

1. Delete everything in the Timeline.
2. Open *Village1* from the Browser into the Viewer.

FIGURE 8.13
Transition alignment shortcut menu.

139

Because this will be the first shot in the Timeline, I won't need to shorten the front of the clip.

3. Press the **End** key to take you to the end of the shot.
4. Press **Shift-left** arrow to move the playhead backward by one second.
5. Press **O** to enter the Out point and drag to the Edit Overlay Overwrite box, or press **F10** to overwrite it into the Timeline.
6. Open *Village2* in the Viewer from the Browser.

This clip we should shorten on both ends.

7. Go to the beginning of the clip, and press **Shift-right** arrow to move forward by one second, and enter an In point.
8. Then go to the end of the clip, and enter an Out point one second before the end (press **Shift-left arrow**, and then press **O**).
9. Drag *Village2* from the Viewer to Overwrite with Transition—*not* to Overwrite. Or use the keyboard shortcut **Shift-F10**.

The clip immediately drops into the Timeline after the first clip. The default transition has been added at the beginning of the clip, as well as a default audio cross fade. Adding the audio cross fade is a bonus that enhances the edit and helps smooth the transition (see Figure 8.14). If you use the shortcut menu to create a transition by right-clicking on an edit point in the Timeline and selecting **Add Transition 'Cross Dissolve'**, this will also add the audio cross fade.

RENDERING

Before we look at controlling our transitions, let's take a look at rendering, which will also apply to the work we do with animation and effects in later lessons. *Rendering* is creating media for a section of your sequence that doesn't exist on your hard drive. Sometimes your computer is fast enough to do this on the fly, just with its processor power and RAM, but other times it's not, and then a small QuickTime file must be created on your hard drive so you can play back the sequence. This is called a **render file**. Let's begin by adding a transition to your sequence:

FIGURE 8.14
Transition with audio cross fade.

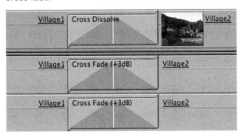

1. Double-click the *Transitions* sequence to open it into the Timeline window.
2. Click on the edit point between *Village1* and *Village2* to select it, or move the playhead to it and press the V key.
3. From the **Effects** menu, select **Video Transitions**>**3D Simulation**>**Zoom**.

With the transition applied in the sequence, you may have encountered for the first time the need for rendering. After you've entered a transition, you'll see that the narrow bar at the top of the Timeline has changed color from the normal medium gray shade. The bar inside the circled area in Figure 8.15 will have changed to red, green, yellow, or orange, depending on the type of transition you applied, your system capabilities, and your RT settings. If you are working with a system with no real-time capabilities, then a bright red line will appear over the transition, indicating that a portion of the sequence needs to be rendered.

FIGURE 8.15
Render indicator.

Rendering means that the application has to create media for which none exists. Most of the two shots are on your hard drive, but not the 30 frames that make up this one-second cross dissolve, during which one shot is changing into the other. The material of one shot mixed with another is not on your hard drive. All you have done is give the computer instructions to create that media. If you try to play across that part of the timeline with a non-real-time system, the Canvas will momentarily display the message in Figure 8.16.

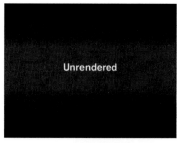

FIGURE 8.16
Unrendered warning.

Real-Time Preview

FCE's real-time preview can be seen only in the Canvas and only when the external viewing is switched off. It will not send a real-time DV signal out the FireWire cable. So you have a choice: either monitor through Fire Wire, but not in real time, or monitor on your desktop screen.

So if you think you have real-time capabilities and you're still seeing a red line in your sequence, it's probably because you have external viewing turned on. You can switch it off from the **View** menu by going down at the bottom to the **Video Out**. Here you can select either **Canvas Playback**, **Apple FireWire**, or **Digital Cinema Desktop** (see Figure 8.17). DCD allows you to see your video full screen on your computer. You can toggle this on and off with the keyboard shortcut **Command-F12**. Be careful with this, however, if you're working with DV material because it will scale up your material far past a size in which it should be seen. If you're working with HD material, though, this is a great way to work. All your keyboard shortcuts will work in DCD, **J**, **K**, **L**, **I**, and **O** will let you play and mark up clips and, of course, the Insert, Overwrite, and other shortcuts work as well. You can use DCD for clips in either the Viewer or when playing back the Canvas.

FIGURE 8.17
View>Video Out.

141

TIP

Full Size Viewing: Another way to see your material
at full size (if your monitor display has high enough resolution,
like a 24″ Apple Cinema Display) is to set your window arrangement to Two
Up and make sure your Viewer and Canvas as set at 100 percent. When they are
set to 100 percent, you are seeing the video as it actually is. At any other
setting, FCE will scale the image to accommodate the window, and
interlacing or other artifacts might not be visible.

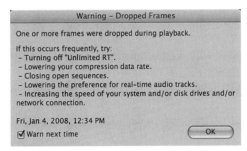

FIGURE 8.18
Unlimited RT dropped
frame warning.

Remember that this is real-time preview only. As soon as you revert to viewing your video externally or you want to output your material to tape, all those items that were in real time on your desktop a moment ago now have to be rendered out.

If you have your RT settings on Unlimited, which we discussed in Lesson 2, you may get a yellow or orange bar. The yellow bar indicates that playback is a proxy only; that is, if you've created a complex setting for your transition, only the default will be visible in real time. Orange indicates that you will likely get dropped frames when playing through this area. If you do play through, you may get the dropped frame warning message in Figure 8.18. If you switch this warning off in the lower left corner, you can then work in Unlimited RT without hindrance but with the occasional frame drop. To turn on the dropped frame warning, you'll have to go back to your User Preferences and switch it back on in the first tab.

FCE has the ability to do what's called **Dynamic RT**, which means that it will automatically, dynamically adjust the resolution of the image to preserve real-time playback. You'll see this when material with complex effects suddenly changes quality during playback. We'll see this more and more as our effects get more complex in the next lessons. Dynamic RT depends on the speed of the computer and the settings you use. With Safe RT, the render function will kick in if playback cannot be supported without dropped frames. With Unlimited RT, you can get playback with dropped frames, sort of a stuttering real-time playback of complex effects. With Dynamic, Unlimited RT, it will pretty much play through anything one way or the other. If the effect is too complex, or if the computer is less capable, you reach a point of diminishing returns, the point where it's just grabbing a few frames here and there for playback, and although it's real-time, it's hardly viewable, at which point it's better to use **Option-P**, I think. (See "Playing the Red.")

TIP
Playing the Red: By using Option-P, you can still play
through a red transition without rendering the sequence, not in real
time but in slow motion. This is a good way to see if the transition will play
smoothly—if there are any unforeseen flash frames or other unpleasant hiccups in
the effect. The faster your system, the faster it will play through the transition. More
complex effects that we will see later will only play slowly, even on the fastest computers.
What's nice is that FCE caches the playback, so the first time you play back using
Option-P, it might take quite a while, but if you playback again immediately using
Option-P, it will be considerably faster, often in real-time. Regular play with
the spacebar will still produce the unrendered message. You can also scrub
through a transition by switching Snapping off and mousing
down in the Timeline Ruler, slowly moving the
playhead through the transition area.

Render Commands

FCE's render commands are extremely flexible, if perhaps a bit confusing. What gets rendered is controlled by a complex combination of settings in the **Sequence** menu under **Render Selection**, **Render All**, and **Render Only**. To render a selection like a transition, you have to select it. You can click on the transition to select it. If you want to render a section of your Timeline, you can mark In and Out points in the Timeline and that area, controlled by the Auto Select buttons, will be your render selection.

The **Render Selection** menu (see Figure 8.19) controls rendering of a selection, either a clip, clips, or a segment of the Timeline marked with In and Out points. Normally, only the red **Needs Render** bar is checked for both video and audio. If you want to force a render on any of the other available items, select it. It will remain checked in the menu. Whenever you give the **Render Selection** command (see Table 8.1), those checked items would be included in the render.

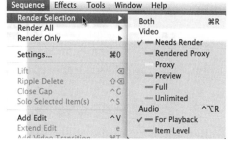

FIGURE 8.19
Sequence>Render
Selection.

The **Render All** menu (see Figure 8.20) gives you the same list, except many more items are checked by default. The **Render Only** menu (see Figure 8.21) is similar. It allows you to render selected items without changing the settings in **Render** and **Render All**. Note the inclusion in the **Render Only** menu of **Mixdown** for audio. This allows you to render out a mixed audio file of all your tracks, allowing easier playback. This is particularly important when outputting to tape.

143

Table 8.1 Render Commands	
Command	**Shortcut**
Render All	Option-R
Render Selection	Command-R
Render Audio Selection	Control-Option-R
Render Proxy	Command-Option-P
Render Preview	Control-R
Mixdown Audio	Command-Option-R
Item Level	Control-Option-R

FIGURE 8.20
Sequence>Render All.

FIGURE 8.21
Sequence>Render Only.

FCE has the ability to render audio at **Item Level**. This allows you to render a piece of sound, such as an MP3 file or a piece of 44.1 kHz CD music, into the correct sampling rate as a separate item. Wherever you place that audio in your Timeline, it will be fully rendered to the correct settings. It will have a blue indictor bar on it to tell you it's been rendered as an item and will not need to be rerendered. To render an audio selection, use the keyboard shortcut **Control-Option-R**.

The **Render Proxy** and **Render Preview** shortcuts allow you to force a render of material that is in proxy mode or real-time playback, which would not normally be rendered if you use **Render Selection**. You can render a selection that is proxy or real-time with the shortcuts or from the **Render Only** submenu.

Render Control

Normally, FCE will render to full resolution, but it is possible to adjust your render settings. Render settings are in the **Render Control** tab (see Figure 8.22) in **Sequence Settings**, which can be called up from the **Sequence** menu or with the keyboard shortcut **Command-0 (zero)**. Here you can set what you want to render, as well as control your render quality with the **Frame Rate** and **Resolution** pop-up menus. Setting these two pop-up menus to lower numbers will greatly speed up your rendering process.

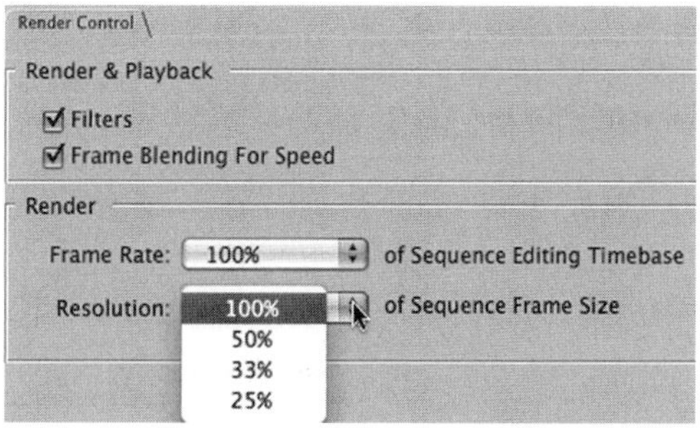

FIGURE 8.22
Render Control.

In FCE, you can switch between render settings at any time, which means that you can have material in various render resolutions throughout your sequence simultaneously. This can be a useful feature because it allows you to render complex material at lower resolution to speed up your workflow and to switch to full resolution for easier material. The feature does create one substantial problem, which we shall look at more in Lesson 19.

Render Management

Render files are stored in the *Render Files* folder and the *Audio Render Files* folder of your designated scratch disk. The renders are stored in separate folders according to the project name, one folder for each project. FCE keeps track of the renders required for the output of each sequence. It keeps all of the renders it generates for each session so you can step back through those 32 levels of undo and not lose your renders. As you keep rendering and changing and rerendering, FCE holds onto all of those renders it creates while the application is open. When you quit the application, it dumps any render files it no longer needs to play back any of the sequences in the project. It will hold onto any renders it needs for playback. All of these render files will start to pile up after a while. If you delete a project, its render files won't go with it. They'll just sit on your hard drive taking up space in the folder with the project's name.

It's a good idea to weed out the old files in your render folders, video more than audio because the files are much larger. Sometimes it might be as simple as discarding an old project folder and throwing out all the renders associated with it. Sometimes, for long-form projects that go on for a long time, managing your render files requires you to go in and dig out these old files. The simplest way to do this is to open up the Render Files folder for that project and switch the window to List view, as shown in Figure 8.23. List view will show you not only the file names, which are pretty meaningless, but also the date modified. By clicking on the **Date Modified** column, you can sort the renders by when they where created, giving you a clue about which ones are worth keeping and which aren't.

If you're uncertain, select the render file and switch to **Column** view, where you can use the preview window to look at the little QuickTime file that the render

145

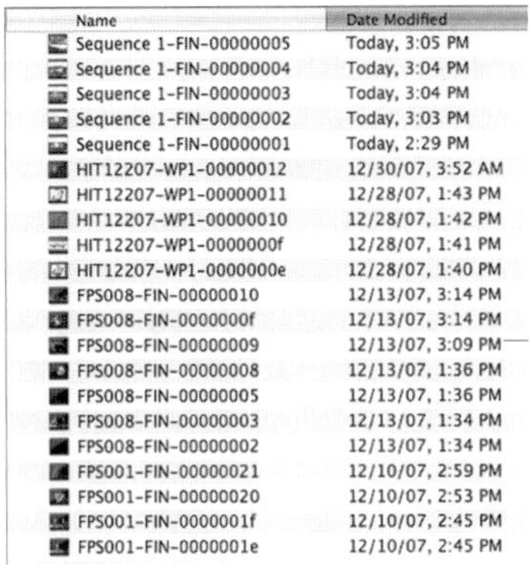

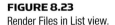

FIGURE 8.23
Render Files in List view.

FIGURE 8.24
Render Files and preview window.

generates (see Figure 8.24). Move the files you think you don't need into the trash, and run the project. If the project needs some of the render files, you'll get the **Reconnect** dialog box. That will give you a chance to move the missing items back into the *Render Files* folder.

CONTROLLING TRANSITIONS

Once you've played back your transition with **Option-P** a couple of times or rendered it and looked at it, you may discover that it isn't quite the way you'd want it to be. You may want to shorten or lengthen it or shift the actual edit point. Assuming you have material available for this, it is easiest to do in the Timeline. To change the duration of the transition, grab one end of it and pull, as in Figure 8.25. It's a good idea to switch Snapping off (toggle with the **N** key) before you do this because it's very easy to snap the transition down to nothing. As you pull the transition, a little window displays the amount of change as well as the new duration of the transition. If you have an audio cross fade as well as a video transition, that will also change duration with your action. While you're dragging the transition end, you'll get the two-up display in the Canvas that shows you the frames at the edit point.

FIGURE 8.25
Lengthening a transition in the Timeline.

You can also reposition the edit point in the center of the transition. Move the Selector to the center of the edit, and it will change to the Roll tool, allowing you to move the edit point, together with the transition along the Timeline, left and right as desired (see Figure 8.26). You can also ripple either shot, but to do that, you must call up the Ripple tool (**RR**) and pull either shot left or

146

right, shortening or lengthening the sequence while not affecting the transition (see Figure 8.27). Again, the two-up display in the Canvas will show you the frames you're working on.

FIGURE 8.26
Rolling the transition edit point.

Transition in the Viewer

Final Cut gives you another way to fine-tune the transition in the Viewer (see Figure 8.28). I've replaced the Cube Spin transition with the Swing transition. To do that, select the transition in the Timeline, and from the menus, choose **Effects>Video Transitions>3D Simulation>Swing**. Double-click on the transition in the Timeline window to open it into the Viewer. The Viewer displays the transition as a separate track sitting between the two clips as if they are overlapping on two video tracks.

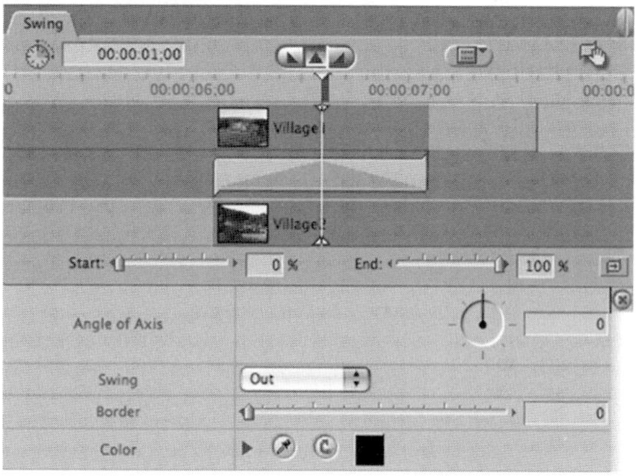

FIGURE 8.27
Rippling the transition edit point.

The Viewer allows you to control the transition. Some of the transitions, such as Swing in Figure 8.28, have quite a few controls. At the top in the center is a small group of three buttons. These let you align where the transition will occur. By default, the transition is placed in the Center on Edit position between the two clips, shown by the middle button. Using the left button lets you move the transition so it begins at the edit point. The right button moves the transition so it ends at the edit point.

147

FIGURE 8.28
Swing controls in the Viewer.

In the Viewer you can fine-tune the effect to shorten or lengthen it as needed. As in the Timeline, you can do this by dragging either end of the transition. The Canvas displays the end and start frames for the two shots. By grabbing the center of the transition, you evoke the Roll tool, which allows you to drag the transition forward and backward along the clips, provided that media is available.

You can also Ripple edit the end of either an outgoing or incoming clip by pulling it (see Figure 8.29). You don't have to call up the Ripple tool. By moving the cursor into position, it will change to the appropriate tool. As with all Ripple edits, you are changing the duration of the tracks involved and may be pulling the alignment of clips on different tracks out of kilter.

FIGURE 8.29
Alignment buttons.

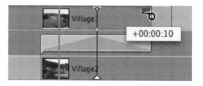

Notice the two sliders in the Viewer, one for Start and the other for End, each with percentage boxes adjacent. The transition starts at 0 percent completed and ends at 100 percent completed. You can adjust these sliders so the effect will pop in at more than zero to start or suddenly finish before the transition reaches completion. In most transitions, this produces a rather ugly effect. There is also a small arrow button to the right of the End slider. This will swap the effect for you, usually reversing the direction. Below that is a small circle with a red cross in it. This is the **Parameters Reset** button and is useful for more complex transitions. Note that the **Reset** button does not reset the Start and End sliders, nor the arrow, only the other parameters.

TIP

Dragging from the Viewer: The grab handle in the upper right corner lets you pull a transition from the Viewer onto an edit point in the Timeline. This is useful if you've opened the editor directly from the *Transitions* bin or if you want to apply the same transition to another edit point. This is the only way you can grab the transition. There is also a pop-up menu for recent clips in the Viewer. This is handy sometimes because you can't access all the standard features like the Generators and other tabs when you have a transition open in the Viewer.

USING TRANSITIONS

Now that we know how to add and trim transitions, let's look at the transitions themselves. To change the transition, we do the following:

- Drag the new transition from the transitions folder in the Effects window, and drop it on the existing transition in the timeline, *or*
- Select the transition in the Timeline by clicking on it and then select a new choice from the **Effects>Video Transitions** menu.

I'm not going to go through each of the transitions, although I would like to highlight a few of them because they will show you how the controls work in some of the other changeable transitions. To see all the transitions, look at the individual QuickTime movies in the *Transitions* folder on the DVD. Many of the transitions have lots of variables, such as colored borders and the direction in which a motion transition occurs, such as in Swing.

FIGURE 8.30
Page Peel.

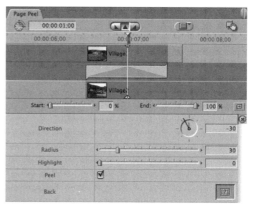

FIGURE 8.31
Page Peel controls.

Page Peel

Page Peel (see Figure 8.30) is often overused, but sometimes it is exactly the right effect. This transition gives us our first introduction to FCE's **Well**. Apply the transition from **Video Transitions>Page Peel>Page Peel**, and then double-click on it to open it into the Viewer (see Figure 8.31). The **Direction** dial changes the angle at which the page peels back. The default is −30 and pulls the lower right corner toward the upper center of the image.

The **Radius** slider sets the tightness of the peel. A small number will make it peel very tightly, and a high number will make the turn of the page quite loose. The **Highlight** slider puts a gleam of light on the back of the turning page. The farther to the left you move the Highlight slider, the more muted the shine becomes. There is no control of the width of the highlight area.

If you uncheck the **Peel** check box, the image will not only peel back but also curl in on itself. With a tight **Radius**, you'll get the image rolling up like it's a scroll. One of Page Peel's interesting features is the **Well**, which lets you use another image as part of an effect. The Well, the indented filmstrip icon that controls the **Back** function, lets you map another image onto the back of the Page Peel. The default is to place the same image, flopped, on the back of the page, but you can use any image in your project. To put a color on the back, as in Figure 8.30, use the **Generator** in the Viewer to create a color matte.

> **NOTE**
> ***Static Well:*** Unfortunately, the Well won't track an image or change if a video clip is used. The Well uses the In point of the video clip as its map. In the case of Page Peel, there is no movement on the backside of the page. Sorry!

FIGURE 8.32
Generators button.

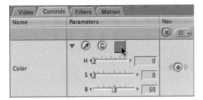

FIGURE 8.33
Color Matte Controls tab.

FIGURE 8.34
System color picker.

1. Open any clip into the Viewer, or call one up from the Recent Clips pop-up. The A with the Filmstrip icon in the lower left corner evokes the Generators (see Figure 8.32).

2. Select **Matte>Color**. The only difference between **Color** and **Color Solid** is that one is gray and the other blue by default, but either can be changed to whatever color you want.

3. Set the color in the Controls tab (see Figure 8.33). Click on the swatch to access the system color picker (see Figure 8.34).

Note the swatch tray at the bottom, which lets you move color selections from application to application, not just within FCE.

4. Switch back to the Video tab and drag the Color Matte from the Viewer into the Browser.

5. Reopen the Page Peel transition from the Timeline into the Viewer.

6. Pull the Color Matte from the Browser, and drop it into the Well, making it part of the transition.

> **TIP**
> **Selecting Color:** Whenever you need to select a color from anywhere on your desktop, click on the color swatch to open the color picker. If you click on the magnifying glass next to the color swatch, you can move around anywhere on the computer desktop.

Push Slide

The **Push Slide** transition (**Video Transitions>Slide>Push Slide**) is often used when making slide shows where one image pushes the other out of the frame and replaces it. The controls (see Figure 8.35) are pretty straightforward: an **Angle** dial and controls for adding a border. Angle defaults to straight up, but you can set it to any angle you want. At −90, the incoming image will slide in from the right and push the outgoing image off the left side of the screen.

The **Border** control can be quite useful. It not only helps in separating the images more clearly, but it also covers the black band that appears on the edge of some digitized images. This is normally in the blanking area under the television mask and not seen by the viewer. However, if the image is moved, as it is here

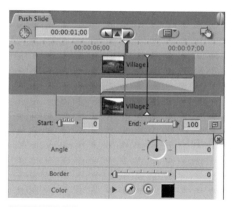

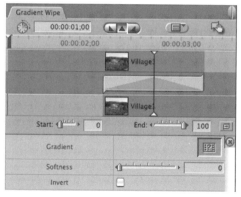

FIGURE 8.35
Push Slide controls.

FIGURE 8.36
Gradient Wipe controls.

and in other digital video effects, the black edge becomes visible. The Border will help disguise that, or at least make it a feature.

Gradient Wipe

The **Gradient Wipe** transition (**Video Transitions>Wipe>Gradient Wipe**) is a deceptively simple-looking filter with very few controls. Its real power lies in the Gradient Well (see Figure 8.36). In its default condition, it's nothing more than a simple wipe from left to right. In the Browser is an image called *Gradient.pct*. To see what it looks like, rather than open it into the Viewer where the transition is already loaded, right-click on it and select **Open in New Viewer** (see Figure 8.37). You'll see that it's a complex, grayscale checkerboard pattern. This is the basis of patterning in a gradient wipe. The image will be wiped on or off, based on the grayscale values of pattern image. The darkest parts of the pattern image will be where the incoming image will appear first, and the lightest parts will be where the image will appear last. In the gradient pattern that we have, some of the outside boxes will appear first, as in Figure 8.38. The lower left to upper right diagonal of the image will still be from the outgoing shot. To apply the gradient to the transition drag it into the Gradient Well in the Viewer.

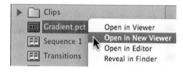

151

FIGURE 8.37
Open in New Viewer.

FIGURE 8.38
Gradient Wipe pattern.

There is no end to the variety of patterns you can get to manipulate this control. If you don't like a pattern, replace it with another. To really see the power of transition effects, you should look at the Softwipe effects from CGM. The demo versions are in the *Extras* folder of the DVD. You can download some great gradient patterns from CGM's website, and this will work not only with Softwipe but also with the Gradient Wipe transition. They add an important tool to Final Cut's transitions.

> **TIP**
> **Lens Flare Transition:** Also in the *Extras* folder on the DVD is a Lens Flare Transition that you can easily use. It requires a quick Cross Dissolve and a composite mode. The instructions are in the folder.

I like the Gradient Wipe because it is so infinitely variable, and you can always find some way to make it look just a little different and just right for the effect you want. A trick I've used in the past is to use a grayscale frame of either the outgoing shot or the incoming shot as the image for the Well. It makes the transition look like a slightly sharp-edged dissolve because the elements of the shot are affecting how the transition happens.

Favorites

Once you've started to make a few transitions that you like—maybe a special Page Peel with your logo on the back or a Gradient Wipe with a particular pattern—you might want to save these in your *Favorites* bin in the Effects tab behind your Browser.

1. To make this Gradient Wipe a favorite, grab the Gradient Wipe we just created, and drag the transition with the Grab Handle over to drop it into the *Favorites* bin. You can also drag a transition directly from the Timeline into *Favorites*.
2. Open *Favorites*, and switch it to List view as in Figure 8.39. Remember that **Shift-H** will toggle through the views.
3. In List view you can change the duration of the transition to your favorite length.

FIGURE 8.39
Favorites bin.

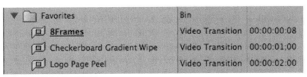

You could drag a cross dissolve from the *Dissolves* bin and change its duration to a favorite length you want to keep.

You may notice that the transition in the *Favorites* bin is a duplicate. The usual behavior when moving items from one bin to another is that the item is relocated. But when moving an element to *Favorites*, a copy is created. You can put any transitions, video or audio, any effect, or even a generator into *Favorites*. You can rename the transition or effect to anything you want. Note that although *8Frames*, which is an eight-frame dissolve, appears underlined, it is not the default transition. Only the standard cross dissolve with the standard one-second duration can be the default.

NOTE

Saving Favorites: It's important to note that Favorites are saved as part of your FCE preferences. If you trash your *Preferences* file, as you may need to do from time to time, your Favorites go with it. There is a simple solution to this: Drag the Favorites bin from the Effects panel and place it in your Browser. This is a copy of the Favorites bin in Effects and will remain with the project, even if the prefs are trashed. I keep a Favorites project and in it a bin with my favorite effects and filters, sometimes in stacks in separate folders. Whenever I want to access these effects, I open the Favorites project and drag the folder into the new project. I add new effects to it, and occasionally I burn the project onto a CD as a backup.

SUMMARY

That's it for transitions! Everybody has his or her favorites. Mine are fairly simple—mostly cross dissolves, occasionally a Gradient Wipe or a Push Slide. I've never used many of them. Many probably should never be used, and you'll probably never see most of them. Next we look at advanced editing techniques with the trim edit window and splitting edits.

LESSON 9

Advanced Editing: Trim Edit and Splitting Edits

Film and video are primarily visual media. Oddly enough, though, the moment an edit occurs is often driven as much by the sound as by the picture. So let's look at sound editing in Final Cut Express. How sound is used, where it comes in, and how long it lasts are key to good editing. With few exceptions, sound almost never cuts with the picture. Sometimes the sound comes first and then the picture, and sometimes the picture leads the sound. The principal reason video and audio are so often cut separately is that we see and hear quite differently. We see in cuts—for example, we look from one person to another, from one object to another, from the keyboard to the monitor. Though my head turns or my eyes travel across the room, I really only see the objects I'm interested in looking at. We hear, on the other hand, in fades. I walk into a room, the door closes behind me, and the sound of the other room fades away. As a car approaches, the sound gets louder. Screams, gunshots, and doors slamming being exceptions, our aural perception is based on smooth transitions from one to another. Sounds, especially background sounds such as the ambient noise in a room, generally need to overlap to smooth out the jarring abruptness of a hard cut.

To do this, we'll use some advanced trimming tools. First we'll look at the Trim Edit window, and then we'll see a few different ways to do Split edits so the sound and the picture do not cut in at the same point.

SETTING UP THE PROJECT

This is going to sound familiar, but it's worth repeating. Begin by loading the material you need on the media hard drive of your computer:

1. Launch the *Lesson 9* project from the *Projects* folder on your hard drive.

2. Once again, you may have to go through the reconnect process (see "Loading the Lesson" in Lesson 2). You will first get the Offline Files window. Click the Reconnect button.

You'll find in the project's Browser an empty sequence called *Sequence 1* and a *Rough Cut* sequence that we'll look at during this lesson. You will also see the master clip *Backstage* and the folder called *Clips*, which contains the subclips pulled from the master.

In this lesson we're going to look at backstage preparations for a Kabuki performance. Before beginning the lesson, it might be a good idea to look through the material, which is about three and one-half minutes long. You can start by double-clicking the shot *Backstage* to open it in the Viewer and then playing through the material.

THE TRIM EDIT WINDOW

Before we get into editing this material, we should look at FCE's Trim Edit window, which is a powerful tool for precisely editing your material and looking at edit points.

1. You open the Trim Edit window by double-clicking on an edit point or by moving the playhead to an edit point and using the menu **Sequence>Trim Edit** or the keyboard shortcut **Command-7**.
2. Let's bring a couple of shots into the Timeline. Select *Backstage01* and *Backstage02* in the *Clips* bin, and drag them directly to Overwrite in the Canvas.

FIGURE 9.1
Trim Edit window.

3. Double-click on the edit point between the shots in the Timeline. This will call up the window in Figure 9.1.

Notice the sprocket hole indicators on the inner edges of the frames. This overlay indicates that the clips are at the limits of their media, but we can still ripple this edit just as we did in the previous lesson when we had to ripple the two shots to create room for a transition.

The green bars over the frames in the Trim Edit window indicate what mode you're in. When a green bar appears over both sides, as in Figure 9.2, you're in Roll edit mode. By clicking on one side or the other, you can ripple either the outgoing shot, as in Figure 9.3, or the incoming shot, as in Figure 9.4. To get back to Roll edit, click on the space between the two frames.

Just as in the Timeline, you can toggle between the Ripple and Roll tools in the Trim Edit window with the **U** key. The way the **U** key cycles between Ripple Left, Ripple Right, and the Roll tool is also reflected in the way the edit point is selected in the Timeline (see Figures 9.5 to 9.7).

You can ripple and roll the edit points by dragging them in either window. When you're in Ripple mode, the cursor will change to the Ripple tool, and when you're in Roll mode, the cursor automatically becomes the Roll tool.

You can also use the little plus and minus buttons at the bottom of the window to make incremental edits on either side of the Trim Edit window. FCE allows

157

FIGURE 9.2
Roll edit indicator in Trim Edit.

FIGURE 9.3
Ripple Left indicator in Trim Edit.

FIGURE 9.4
Ripple Right indicator in Trim Edit.

FIGURE 9.5
Roll edit indicator in the Timeline.

FIGURE 9.6
Ripple Left indicator in the Timeline.

FIGURE 9.7
Ripple Right indicator in the Timeline.

you to move the edit point by one or five frames at a time with the buttons. The five-frame value can be changed anywhere from 2 to 99 in the preferences in User Preferences in Multi-Frame Trim Size. The top of the Trim Edit window contains a lot of useful timecode information about where the A side ends, where the B begins, the durations of the shot, and their place in the Timeline.

TIP
Trim Edit Shortcut: In the Trim Edit window, in addition to the trim buttons, you can use the keyboard shortcuts [and] to trim plus or minus one frame and Shift-[and Shift-] to trim plus or minus the multiframe trim size. As with the buttons, these will work on the fly while you're in looped Play-around mode.

- The number to the far left is the duration of the outgoing shot, *Backstage01* in this case (*A* in Figure 9.8).
- The next timecode number is the Out point of the outgoing shot (*B* in Figure 9.8).
- The center number under the track indicator is the current time in the sequence (*C* in Figure 9.8).
- The next number displayed is the duration of the incoming shot (*D* in Figure 9.8).
- On the far right of the window, the number is the current In point of the incoming shot, *Backstage02* (*E* in Figure 9.8).

Outgoing Clip: Backstage01		Track V1 ▾		Incoming Clip: Backstage02
00:00:13;08	00:00:13;07	00:00:13;08	00:00:16;28	00:00:00;00
A	**B**	**C**	**D**	**E**

FIGURE 9.8
Timecode display at the top of the Trim Edit window.

You can play either side of the Trim Edit window with the **J**, **K**, and **L** keys. The green bars at the top determine which side plays. If you're rippling the left side, that side will play; if you're rippling the right side, the incoming shot will play.

When you're in Roll mode, the green bar above both displays and the side that plays are determined by the position of the cursor. If the cursor is over the left or outgoing side, that side will play. If the cursor is over the right or incoming side, that side will play. To trim an edit, you modify the In or Out point with the **I** and **O** keys. Your change will be reflected in the edit, either as a ripple or as a roll, in the Timeline.

The **spacebar** serves an interesting function in the Trim Edit window. It acts in looped Play-around mode. It will play around the edit point again and again so that you can view it repeatedly. The amount of Play-around—how much before the edit and how far after the edit—is controlled in User Preferences under Preview Pre-Roll and Preview Post-Roll. The default is five seconds before the edit and two seconds after. I usually set it down to two or three seconds before and two after.

Final Cut Express has the ability to do *dynamic trimming* in the Trim Edit window. You'll see a little check box at the bottom of the window that activates this function, which can also be turned on in User Preferences. Dynamic trimming affects the control of the **J**, **K**, and **L** keys. Whenever you press the **K** key to pause, the edit will automatically execute. This will work in any edit mode: Roll, Ripple Left, or Ripple Right. As soon as you press the **K** key to pause, the edit will be executed. It's pretty slick. Try using the **J**, **K**, and **L** keys to dynamically trim.

159

1. Switch to ripple mode on either side. (We can't do a Roll edit because there isn't any available media until the shots have been trimmed.)

2. Use the **J** and **L** keys to play forward and backward.

3. If you want to stop playback without doing an edit, don't press the **K** key but use the **spacebar** to stop.

4. When you do want to do the ripple, simply press the **K** key, and the edit will be done.

NOTE
Moving Slowly in the Trim Window: You can move forward slowly by holding down the K and L keys together. To move backward slowly, hold down the K and J keys together. To go forward one frame, hold down the K key and tap L. To go backward one frame, hold down the K key and tap J.

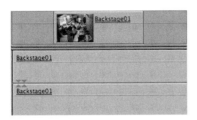

FIGURE 9.9
Split edit.

FIGURE 9.10
J-cut.

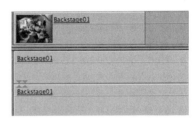

FIGURE 9.11
L-cut.

THE SPLIT EDIT

A common method of editing is to first lay down the shots in scene order entirely as straight cuts. Look at the sequence called *Rough Cut*, which is the edited material cut as straight edits. What's most striking as you play it is how abruptly the audio changes at each shot. But audio and video seldom cut in parallel in a finished video, so you will have to offset them.

When audio and video have separate In and Out points that aren't at the same time, the edit is called a split edit (see Figure 9.9), a J-cut (see Figure 9.10), or an L-cut (see Figure 9.11). Whatever you call it, the effect is the same. There are many ways to create these edits, which I lump together as split edits.

In the Timeline

Many instructors tell you to perform these edits in the Viewer, but I think the Viewer is the least flexible place to create them. Let's set up a split edit inside the Timeline. It's a much more logical and effective place to perform this type of work.

In making split edits, particularly in the Timeline, you will be frequently linking and unlinking clips, switching off the link between synced video and audio. You can do this with the little switch in the upper right corner of the Timeline window that toggles Linked Selection off and on (see Figure 9.12). When Linked Selection is turned on, the button is green, and when it's off, the icon is black.

FIGURE 9.12
Linked Selection
button.

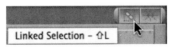

You might want to switch Linked Selection off if you want to move a lot of synced sound clips, splitting the audio and the video. In most cases, I don't think that this is ever a good idea. I think Linked Selection should be maintained at all times and toggled on and off only as needed for individual clips. You might get away with leaving it off most of the time, but one day it will leap up and bite you—hard! So for these lessons, let's leave Linked Selection turned on.

160

Before we begin working on the sequence, it is probably a good idea to duplicate the *Rough Cut* sequence. Select it and use **Edit**>**Duplicate** or the keyboard shortcut **Option-D**. This way you can also refer back to the original *Rough Cut* if you ever need to. Start by double-clicking the copy of *Rough Cut* and looking at the Timeline.

TIP

Disappearing Buttons: If your Linked Selection button or your Snapping button disappears from the Timeline window, right-click on the button holder, and from the shortcut menu choose Remove>All/Restore Default. Or choose Load All Buttons Bars, and pick your favorite configuration, the Default Button Bars set we created or the Editing Workshop Button Bars from the DVD.

The trick to smoothing out the audio for this type of sequence—or any sequence with abrupt sound changes at the edit points—is to overlap sounds and create sound beds that carry through other shots. Ideally, a wild track was shot on location sometimes called *room tone* when it's the ambient sound indoors. This is a long section of continuous sound from the scene, a minute or more, which can be used as a bed to which the sync sound is added as needed. Here there is no wild track as such, but some of the shots are lengthy enough to have a similar effect.

Before we get started, we want to change the type of audio that's used in the sequence. Double-click on the first shot, *Backstage01*, to bring it into the Viewer. Notice that at the top of the Viewer, there are two tabs for the two audio tracks Mono (a1) and Mono (a2). This is the default capture setting for FCE material. Unfortunately, it's more difficult to work with audio such as this because you have to adjust the two tracks separately. The best thing to do is to change your audio in the Timeline to a *stereo pair*, which is very simple to do:

1. Select everything in the Timeline, **Command-A**.
2. From the **Modify** menu, use **Stereo Pair** or the keyboard shortcut **Option-L**.

As soon as you do this, the clip that was in the Viewer will disappear. If you reopen it into the Viewer, you'll see only one audio tab marked Stereo (a1a2), and each of the clips in the Timeline has little inward-pointing pairs of green triangles on each of the tracks (see Figure 9.13). This indicates that these are grouped as stereo pairs. It's much easier to work with your audio when the tracks are stereo pairs because both channels will move in unison.

FIGURE 9.13
Stereo pairs indicators.

161

> **TIP**
> **Single-Track Audio:** Often you record audio on a single audio channel. Many cameras do this when you plug in an external microphone; only one of the stereo channels gets used. It's worth deleting the empty track. If the audio is a stereo pair, first change it to Mono (a1)(a2) from the Modify menu, or use the shortcut Option-L. Then Option-click to select the track you don't need and delete it. You can center the audio for the remaining track if you need to by selecting it and pressing Control-period. If you want to double the audio to fatten it, you can. Option-click on the remaining audio track to select it, and then Option-shift drag it to the empty audio track to duplicate it. Select the video and two audio tracks, and press Command-L to link them into a single clip.

Making Split Edits

1. Play through the first three or four shots in the *Rough Cut* copy sequence. The change between the first and second shot is quite noticeable, and even more so between the second and third.

2. Hold down the **Option** key, and select the audio portion of the second shot, *Backstage06*.

3. With the **Option** key still pressed, tap the **down** Arrow key twice. This will move the stereo pair of audio down two tracks. This can be done with any tracks, video or audio, as long as nothing is in the way, such as another clip.

4. Again, holding down the **Option** key, drag the head of the audio edit point toward the beginning of the Timeline (see Figure 9.14). While you drag it, a small box will appear. It gives you a time duration change for the edit you are making. It may be helpful to toggle Snapping off with the **N** key.

5. Repeat the process on the other side of the audio. Holding down the **Option** key, drag out the audio so that your sequence looks like Figure 9.15.

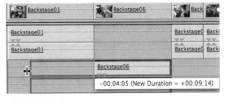

FIGURE 9.14
Dragging audio to create a split edit.

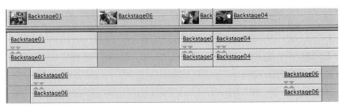

FIGURE 9.15
Timeline after making split edits.

You have now created two split edits for the clip *Backstage06*.

Adding Audio Transitions

We want the sound of the first shot, *Background01*, to fade out before it ends. The simplest way to do this is to apply an audio cross fade:

1. Select the edit point by clicking on it.
2. To Add the audio transition, use the menu **Effects> Audio Transitions>Cross Fade (0 dB)**. You could also drag the transition from the Effects tab of the Browser if you prefer.

Because the audio is not butted against anything, the application will by default create an End on Edit transition, as shown in Figure 9.16.

FIGURE 9.16
Cross fade (0 dB) applied.

163

> **TIP**
> ***Toggling Linking:*** Option-clicking the audio (or video) edit point will turn off Linked Selection if LS is turned on. If Linked Selection is off, Option-clicking the edit point will turn it on.

> **TIP**
> ***Linear or Logarithmic:*** FCE has two cross fades: the default +3 dB, which can be added with the keyboard shortcut Command-Option-T, and a 0 dB transition. The +3 dB cross fade, which the FCE calls an "equal power cross fade," is often used when cross-fading two sections of audio that are in line and butted up against each other like the video transitions we made in the previous lesson. This is generally preferred because it gives a logarithmic roll of sound, which is the way sound works. The 0 dB cross fade is a linear fade and is what should be used for a fade in or fade out when there is no sound in line that it is cross fading to. If it's used as a cross fade to another piece of sound, it will often produce an apparent dip in the audio level at the midpoint of the crossover between the audio clips.

In the Viewer

You can also create a split edit in the Viewer. Let's first set up a new sequence:

1. Begin by opening *Sequence 1* again. You should have two shots *Backstage01* and *Backstage02* in it.

FIGURE 9.17
Marking Split Audio In.

FIGURE 9.18
Split edit in the Viewer.

2. Delete the second shot so that only *Backstage01* is left. Let's make a split edit with a clip from the Browser.

3. Find the clip *Backstage06* in the *Clips* bin in the Browser.

4. Double-click on it to open it into the Viewer. Because we want to use all of the audio, begin by marking a split audio In point at the beginning of the clip. With the playhead at the very start of the shot, either right-click and from the shortcut menu choose **Mark Split**> **Audio In** (see Figure 9.17) or use the keyboard shortcut **Command-Option-I**.

5. Play through the clip until you find the In point for the edit at 4;10.

6. Instead of pressing **I** to enter the In point, press **Control-I**.

Next we'll make the split edit for the Out point.

7. Play forward until you get to the Out point at 9;18.

8. Instead of pressing **O** to enter the Out point, press **Control-O**.

Note the markings in the Viewer scrubber bar and on screen in Figure 9.18 that indicate the split edit.

Viewer to Timeline

The simplest way to work with the split edit in the Viewer is to drag and drop to the Timeline.

FIGURE 9.19
Setting destination tracks in the patch panel.

1. Reset the destination tracks in your Timeline by pulling the a2 button down to A4 and the a1 button down to A3 in the patch panel at the head of the tracks, as in Figure 9.19. Or use the keyboard shortcuts **F7-3** and **F8-4**—that's **F7** followed by the number **3** and **F8** followed by the number 4.

2. Make sure Snapping is turned on. If it isn't, press the **N** to switch it on.

3. With the playhead at the end of the shot in the Timeline, drag the clip from the Viewer to the Timeline, as in Figure 9.20.

The edit will be performed as in Figure 9.21. This seems to be strange behavior on the part of the application, but it has always done this for some reason. When this happens, grab the clip and slide it to butt up against the first shot, as shown in Figure 9.22.

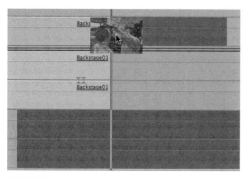

FIGURE 9.20
Dragging a split edit to the Timeline.

FIGURE 9.21
Displaced split edit in the Timeline.

FIGURE 9.22
Correctly placed split edit.

165

SUMMARY

In this brief lesson we've looked at using some advanced techniques, working with the Trim Edit window, and learning how to create split audio edits in the Timeline and in the Viewer. We'll stop at this stage and pick up work on this sequence in the next lesson, where we look more closely at how to adjust and control audio levels.

LESSON 10

Advanced Editing: Using Sound

We've started to work on the backstage sequence, and we've created a split edit in the Timeline and added an audio cross fade. Now we're going to adjust the sound levels for the sequence in the Viewer and in the Timeline.

SETTING UP THE PROJECT

From your hard drive, launch the *Lesson 10* project. Reconnect the media files if the Offline Files dialog appears. In the project's Browser, you'll find an empty sequence called *Sequence 1*, which you can use to work with if you wish, and a couple of other sequences, *Rough Cut* and *Final*. You will also see the master clip *Backstage* and a folder called *Clips*, which contains the subclips pulled from the master.

Look at the sequence called *Final*. The three and one-half minutes that is *Backstage* have been cut down to one minute and 23 seconds for the *Final* sequence. This is where we're going. Notice how the audio overlaps and the way it fades in and out.

CONTROLLING LEVELS

You can control the audio levels for clips in either the Timeline or the Viewer. It's easier and quicker in the Timeline, but the Viewer controls afford a great deal more precision.

In the Timeline

To work in the Timeline, let's start by duplicating the *Rough Cut* sequence, as we did in the last lesson:

1. Select *Rough Cut*, and press **Option-D** to duplicate it.

2. Then double-click the new *Rough Cut Copy* to open it.

To adjust the audio levels in the Timeline, you must first turn on the **Clip Overlays** button in the lower left corner of the Timeline window (see Figure 10.1), or you can use the keyboard shortcut **Option-W**. It's a good idea to leave the Clip Overlays turned off when you're not using them because it's easy to accidentally shift the level line while just trying to grab a clip to move it.

FIGURE 10.1
Clip Overlay button.

When the Clip Overlays are turned on, a thin pink line appears through the middle of the audio portion of the clips. This is the audio level control for the clips. Notice also the thin black line that appears at the top of the video. This controls the opacity for the video portion.

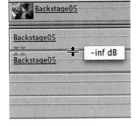

First play through the sequence to listen to it. Then play the audio for the third shot in the sequence, *Backstage05*. It's pretty low and adds nothing to the soundtrack except to muddy it a bit. To eliminate the audio, you can select the audio portion of the clip with the **Option** key and delete it. However, if you ever decide you want that audio or if you move the clip to a place where the audio is needed, it's a bit of a nuisance to get it back.

FIGURE 10.2
Dragging the level line.

A simpler way is to reduce the audio level to zero. With Clip Overlays turned on, move the cursor over the line. It will change to the Resizing tool. Grab the line and pull it down to the bottom of the clip as shown in Figure 10.2.

> **NOTE**
>
> ***What Is a Keyframe?*** We'll be talking more about keyframes as we get farther into the book. A keyframe is a way of defining the values for a clip at a specific moment in time, a specific frame of video. Here we're dealing with audio levels, so we're saying that at this frame we want the sound to be at a particular level. By then going to a different point in the clip and altering the levels, we will have created another keyframe that defines the sound level at that particular frame. The computer will figure out how quickly it needs to change the levels to get from one setting to the other. The closer together the keyframes are, the more quickly the levels will change; the farther apart they are, the more gradually the change will take place.

Fading Levels in the Timeline

You usually don't want to reduce the overall levels. More often you'll want to reduce the levels of portions of the sound, raise other portions, or fade in or out. For a simple fade, you could use one of the cross fade transitions that we saw in the previous lesson, or you can do it by fading the level line. To do this, you use the **Pen** tool, several of which are available at the bottom of the Tools palette (see Figure 10.3). You can also call up the Pen tool with the **P** key. Let's create a fade-in at the beginning of the second shot, *Backstage06*, which is on A3/A4.

1. Move the Pen over the pink level line in the clip. The cursor will change to a pen nib, allowing you to click on the line to create a point (see Figure 10.4). This adds a tiny diamond to the levels line called a keyframe.

2. Put a keyframe about one second from the beginning of the shot by clicking with the Pen tool on the level line.

3. As you move the cursor to the newly created keyframe, it will change into a crosshairs cursor. This lets you grab the keyframe and move it up or down. Pull the keyframe down to about −7 dB, as in Figure 10.5. Notice that because there are no other keyframes on the level line, the volume for the entire clip is reduced.

4. Take the Pen tool and grab the very left end of the level line. Pull it down to create a curved fade-up ramp (see Figure 10.6).

169

FIGURE 10.3
Pen tools.

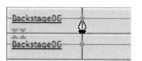

FIGURE 10.4
Adding a keyframe.

FIGURE 10.5
Lowering the keyframe level.

FIGURE 10.6
Fade-out in the Timeline.

TIP

No Switching Necessary: If you don't want to switch to the Pen tool from the standard Selector tool, then as you move the cursor to the level line and it changes to the Resizing tool, hold down the Option key, and the cursor will automatically change to the Pen tool. If you are working with the Pen tool and you want to switch to the straight-level line-moving Resizing tool, hold down the Command key.

We haven't finished with *Backstage06* yet. We still need to bring the sound up to full level as the shot is introduced and fade it out at the end.

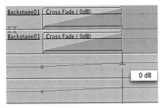

FIGURE 10.7
Ramping up the audio.

5. To bring the level back up, add a keyframe at about the point where the cross fade begins on A1/A2.

6. Next, add another keyframe at about the point where the cross fade on V1 ends.

7. Push the level line back up to 0 dB (see Figure 10.7). Because this is the last keyframe on the level line, everything after that point will come back up to full volume.

8. Finally, to finish *Backstage06*, we want to fade out the audio at the end. With the Pen tool, add a keyframe to the level line about two seconds before the end of the clip.

FIGURE 10.8
Slow fade-out.

9. Go to the end of the clip, and pull the end of the line all the way down to create a slow fade-out, as in Figure 10.8.

10. On A1/A2, it would be a good idea to add a cross-fade transition between the silent *Backstage05* and the next shot, *Backstage04*. Select the edit point and from the **Effects** menu choose **Audio Transitions**>**Cross Fade (0 dB)**.

Controlling Track Levels

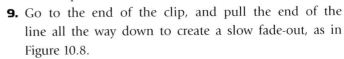

FIGURE 10.9
Track tools.

There may be occasions when you want to change the audio level for an entire track—say, of music—to give it a lower base level. This is especially true of CD music, which is often recorded and compressed at maximum audio levels, often too high for use with most digital video systems. You can do this by selecting the track you want with the Track tool, which is the first button in the third group in the Tools palette (see Figure 10.9).

You can select a single track, multiple tracks forward and backward, a single track forward and backward, or a whole track of audio and adjust its level globally. Select the items or the track with the Track tool (**T**). Once you have your track or clips selected, go to **Modify**>**Levels**, or use the keyboard shortcut **Command-Option-L**.

This command calls up a dialog box that allows you to adjust the audio levels of the clips (see Figure 10.10). The slider or the value box will change the gain setting for all of the clips selected. The Relative and Absolute pop-up menu sets how the gain is affected. Absolute will make the level you set affect all of the clips, eliminating any fades. Using the Relative setting will change the value of the levels relative to any current settings or fades. This global levels control works not only on audio but also on opacity on a title or on the video portion of a clip.

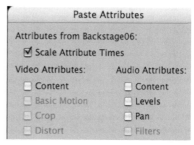

FIGURE 10.10
Level controls.

Another way to change the audio level of more than one clip is to change its attributes. You can copy an audio clip by selecting it and pressing **Command-C**. Select the clips you want by marqueeing or **Command**-clicking, and choose **Paste Attributes** from the **Edit** menu, or press **Option-V**. Then check the attributes you want to paste to the other clips' **Levels** or **Pan** values (see Figure 10.11).

FIGURE 10.11
Pasting audio attributes.

Notice the Scale Attributes Over Time check box at the top. It defaults to the on position. If you have keyframed the levels in the copied clips, that keyframing will be distributed proportionately onto the pasted clip, based on the relative durations of the clips. If the copied clip is longer, the key framing will be tightened up; if it is shorter, the keyframing will be spread out. If you want to paste the keyframes with the same duration as in the copied clip, uncheck **Scale Attributes Over Time**.

171

TIP
Changing a Range of Keyframes: You can also change the relative or absolute levels of a group of audio keyframes. Use the Range tool (GGG) to select the area that includes the audio keyframe (see Figure 10.12). If you then apply the Levels function, it will raise or lower the relative or absolute values of the keyframes in the selected area.

FIGURE 10.12
Range selection of audio keyframes.

NOTE

Waveform in the Timeline: When you're working in the Timeline, it may be beneficial to turn on the waveform display in the Timeline window (see Figure 10.13). Do this by going to the Timeline Options pop-up menu by clicking the tiny triangle in the bottom left of the Timeline window (see Figure 10.14), and select Show Audio Waveforms, or use the keyboard shortcut Command-Option-W. Wait a few moments for the waveforms to draw. Because displaying the audio waveform in the Timeline takes a good deal of processing power (prereading the audio and then displaying it), the redraw ability and video playback capabilities of the computer are markedly slowed down. So it's a good idea to toggle the waveform display on and off as needed with that handy keyboard shortcut.

172

FIGURE 10.13
Waveform in the Timeline.

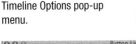

FIGURE 10.14
Timeline Options pop-up menu.

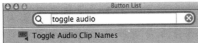

FIGURE 10.15
Button List search.

FIGURE 10.16
Toggle clip name buttons.

A new feature in FCE4 is the ability to switch off clip names for audio and video in the Timeline. This is useful because as you can see, the clip names obscure the waveform and make it hard to work with keyframes. Similarly, when we're working on the video's Opacity keyframes, the clip name can get in the way. To do this, you must use a button that you create.

1. Go to **Tools**>**Button List**, or press **Option-J**.
2. In the Search box, type in *toggle audio*, and a button will appear as in Figure 10.15.
3. Drag the button to the button holder in the Timeline window.
4. Next, in the search box, type in *toggle video*, and drag the Toggle Video Clip Names button next to the first in the Timeline window.

Or if you have the Editing Workshop Button Bars loaded, they will already be in the Timeline window (see Figure 10.16). When the clip names are toggled off, the clips will appear in the Timeline, as shown in Figure 10.17.

5. Click the **Toggle Audio Clip Names** button to switch off the audio clip names.

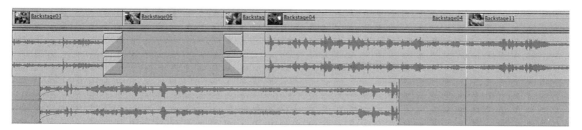

FIGURE 10.17
Timeline clips without
audio names.

FIGURE 10.18
Backstage11
overlapping clips.

173

More Fades

Before we look at how to control audio levels in the Viewer, let's do some more
work on the *Rough Cut Copy* sequence. Look at the fifth shot in the sequence
Backstage11. We need to overlap its audio underneath the adjacent clips.

1. With the **Option** key pressed, select the audio portion of the clip. Still
    holding down the **Option** key, tap the **Down** arrow key twice to move
    the stereo pair onto A3/A4.
2. Holding down the **Option** key again, drag out the front and end of the
    audio portion of *Backstage11* so it overlaps the adjacent clips, as shown
    in Figure 10.18.
3. The next step is to add a fade-out at the end of *Backstage04* on A1/
    A2. Select the edit point, and use the menus to select **Effects>Audio
    Transitions>Cross Fade (0 dB)** to put in an audio fade-out on the end
    of the clip.

Backstage17, which immediately follows *Backstage11*, is quite loud and has a
pronounced music track.

4. As you did with *Backstage05* earlier in the sequence, suppress the sound of *Background17* completely by dragging the level line down to the bottom.

For the next shot, *Backstage03*, I want to fade up the sound, but as so often happens when working with video, I want the fade to come up before the shot begins.

Use a Roll edit or Extend edit to move the audio portion of the shot earlier in the sequence.

FIGURE 10.19
Roll or Extend audio edit.

1. Again, hold down the **Option** key, and click on the edit point in the audio tracks between *Backstage17* and *Backstage03* on A1/A2.

2. Now, either use the Roll tool to move that audio edit about a second earlier or do an Extend edit, moving the playhead about one second earlier and pressing the E key to create a split edit that looks like Figure 10.19.

3. To complete the fade, with the edit still selected, press **Command-Option-T** to add the cross fade.

I would like to fade in the overlapping *Backstage11* a little earlier. To do this, I need to ripple the sequence to move the overlapping on A3/A4 so they butt up against each other. We'll do this with the Ripple tool.

FIGURE 10.20
Multitrack ripple edit.

4. With the Ripple tool, select the left side of the edit between *Backstage04* and *Backstage11*.

5. Hold down the **Command** key, and click just to the left of the audio portion of *Backstage11*, in the empty space between it and the previous shot (see Figure 10.20). You can now ripple the empty space together with *Backstage04*.

6. Pull the edit until the audio tracks collide on A3/A4.

In the Viewer

Let's add the fade at the beginning of *Background11* in the Viewer.

1. Switch back to the Selection tool with the **A** key, and double-click on the audio portion of the clip.

This opens the clip to the Viewer but with the Stereo (a1a2) tab in front (see Figure 10.21). Here, you can see the clip's audio waveform. Notice the pink line in the center of the audio track. As you move the cursor over the line, it changes to the Resizing tool we saw earlier, which allows you to raise and lower the audio level.

At the top of Figure 10.21, you'll notice the **Level** slider and the **Decibel Indicator** box. It's currently at 0, which is the level at which the audio was captured. You can raise and lower the audio levels with the slider if you wish. As you move the pink line up or down with the

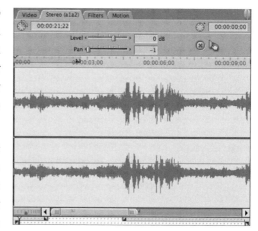

FIGURE 10.21
Stereo (a1a2) Viewer.

Resizing cursor, both the Level slider and the Decibel Indicator box at the top move. A small window appears in the waveform and shows the amount in decibels that you're changing the audio level (see Figure 10.22). Notice also that because this is a stereo pair, you are seeing two waveforms in this window and that they move together when you raise and lower the level of one track.

To add a keyframe, just as in the Timeline, either use the Pen tool or hold down the **Option** key as the cursor approaches the level line. The cursor changes into the Pen tool.

175

2. Press the **Home** key to take you back to the beginning of the shot in the Viewer, and then go forward about one second into the shot.

3. Add a keyframe with the Pen tool or the **Option** key.

4. Add another keyframe to the left of the first, and then drag it down and to the left so it's at the beginning of the shot.

5. Pull down the keyframe at the beginning of the shot so the audio fades up from the beginning of the shot (see Figure 10.23).

If you're wondering why you don't first try to add the keyframe right at the beginning, it's because if you're using the Selection tool, it's difficult to grab

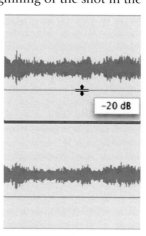

FIGURE 10.22
Decibel level change indicators.

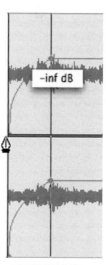

FIGURE 10.23
Audio fade-in.

the very beginning of the Level line because the cursor wants to change to the Resizing tool to grab the edge of the clip itself.

An audio keyframe can be deleted in several ways:

- Grab it and pull it down out of the audio timeline.
- If the Pen tool is active, hold down the **Option** key when you're over the keyframe. The cursor will change into the Pen Delete tool (see Figure 10.24).
- Use the shortcut menu by right-clicking on the keyframe and selecting **Clear**. To move the keyframe, grab it and slide it left and right along the line.

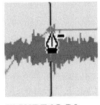

FIGURE 10.24
Pen Delete tool.

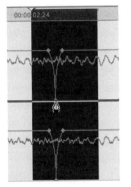

FIGURE 10.25
Zoom tool in the waveform with audio slice.

> **TIP**
> **Zoom a Marquee:** You can also use the Zoom tool to drag a marquee along a section of the waveform to zoom into just that portion of the display. This technique will work in the Viewer, the Canvas, and the Timeline.

One of the great features for editing sound in the Viewer is that you can do it with great precision, down to 1/100th of a frame (see Figure 10.25). To do this, you must zoom into the waveform, either with the scaling tab at the bottom of the Viewer window or with the Zoom tool, which you can call up with the Z key. To zoom out, hold down the **Option** key while you click on the waveform. You can also use **Command-=** to zoom in and **Command-−** to zoom out. The black band in Figure 10.25 represents one frame of video, and you can zoom in farther still. Notice the tiny slice of audio that has been cut out of the track, less than one video frame in length.

FCE has the ability to automatically record slider movements while playing back a clip in the Viewer. This is switched at the bottom of the **Editing** panel in the **User Preferences** by checking the box for **Record Audio Keyframes**.

Because the Viewer is a pretty cramped space, a nice trick is to pull your Stereo (a1a2) tab out of the Viewer and dock it into your Timeline, as shown in Figure 10.26. Then as you play back your audio, you can monitor it on the meters and ride the levels up and down as you like with the Slider or with your mouse's scroll when it's over the Slider. When you stop playback, the keyframes necessary to reproduce your level control will be added to the clip as in Figure 10.26.

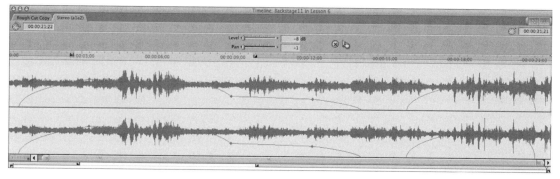

FIGURE 10.26
Stereo (a1a2) tab in the docked Timeline.

> **TIP**
> **Controlling Levels with Shortcuts:** A great way to adjust the levels of a clip is to do it while it's playing back. If you're working on a clip in the Viewer, or if you select a clip in the Timeline, you can raise and lower the audio levels with the keyboard shortcuts Control-[and Control-]. The first will lower the level by 3 dB, and the second will raise it 3 dB. Using Control-− (minus) and *Control-=*, you can lower and raise the audio by 1 dB. The great thing about these shortcuts is the audio can be adjusted during playback. There will be a brief pause while the level changes, but then playback continues. Try it. It's really useful. Note however, that you cannot record keyframes this way, only raise and lower the overall level.

177

NORMALIZATION

One of the great new features of FCE4 is Normalization. This is the ability to set the levels for a clip or multiple clips to a specific level. What this does is take the loudest point in the clip and set it to a specific level. This is great for sound that is overall too high or too low. Let's try it on *Background11*. There are some sharp peaks of sound that actually reach zero, and I would like to keep the loudest sound to around −6 dB.

1. Start by selecting the clip in the Timeline or by having the audio open in the Viewer.
2. From the **Modify** menu, select **Audio>Apply Normalization Gain**, or if you have the Editing Workshop Button Bars loaded, use the button in the Timeline, as in Figure 10.27.

FIGURE 10.27
Normalization button.

FIGURE 10.28
Gain filter controls.

3. In the dialog box that comes up, enter a value of −6 dBFS.

Nothing appears to have happened, but the audio has been adjusted, not with the level controls but with the **Gain** filter. If you have the clip open, go to the Filters tab in the Viewer, and you'll see the Gain filter has been applied to the clip. The Overall level of the clip has been reduced by −5.39 dB (see Figure 10.28) to keep the peak value at −6 dB. Notice the slider that let's you adjust the Gain level. The slider can be pushed way, way up to +96 dB, much higher than you would ever want to go.

One of the reasons this is a great new feature is that in previous versions of FCE you could not raise the audio level of a clip more than +12 dB. If you wanted to go higher, you had to double or even triple tracks to duplicate sound. Now that's no longer necessary. By the way, if you apply Normalization again, it will not add another Gain filter but will simply replace the existing values with your new settings.

FINISHING UP

Let's finish off the *Rough Cut Copy* sequence. We only have a few more levels to tweak. Farther along in the Timeline is another portion of *Backstage05*. This time we do want to use the sound.

1. Again with the **Option** key, select the audio portion of *Backstage05* and move the stereo pair down to A3/A4.

2. Extend the front of the sound until it butts up against *Backstage11*, also on A3/A4.

3. Extend the end of the sound as far as it will go, which isn't that far.

Between *Backstage03* and *05* are two shots, *Backstage09* and *10*, which are both quite loud.

4. Marquee-drag or **Command**-click to select them, and use **Modify> Levels** or **Command-Option-L** to reduce their levels to −9 dB.

5. To smooth the transition between *Backstage09* and *Backstage10*, we're going to add a cross fade, but because this is not a simple fade-up or fade-out but a real cross fade between two pieces of audio, we use the

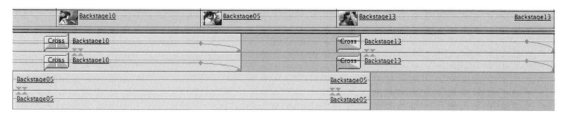

FIGURE 10.29
Middle portion of the
completed sequence.

default Cross Fade (+3 dB), the equal power fade, which smoothly blends the sounds together. Select the edit point, and use **Effects>Audio Transitions>Cross Fade (+3 dB)** or the keyboard shortcut **Command-Option-T**.

6. Next, extend the end of the audio on *Backstage10* so that it's underneath the following shot *Backstage05*.

7. With the Pen tool, make a slow fade-down on the audio of *Backstage10* that you extended under *Backstage05*. Or you could add a 0 dB cross-fade transition on the end and lengthen the transition.

8. Add a cross-fade transition to the beginning of *Backstage13* that follows *Backstage05*.

9. With the Pen tool, add a slow fade-out to the end of *Backstage13*.

The middle portion of the sequence should now look like Figure 10.29.

End of the Sequence

The ending portion of the sequence presents an interesting problem that will again require a Ripple edit of empty space.

1. Pull the audio tracks for *Backstage02* down onto A3/A4, and extend them front and end as far as you can.

2. There is one more stereo pair to pull down onto A3/A4: the last shot, *Background14*. Bring the audio down to A3/A4, and extend the front until it meets *Backstage02* on A3/A4.

I want to put a cross-fade transition between the two shots on A3/A4, but I can't because there isn't enough media available on the end of *Backstage02*. I need to ripple that shot back by 15 frames to create enough space for the overlap.

NOTE

Pan Values: In addition to the pink levels line in the Viewer, there is a purple pan line. In a stereo pair such as this material, the pan lines are defaulted to −1. This indicates that the left channel is going to the left speaker and the right channel to the right speaker. By moving the lines up toward zero as in Figure 10.30, the two tracks are centered between the speakers. Going to 1 will make the channels cross over and swap sides. You can also type in a value in the Pan slider box.

When you have a multitrack recording with separate Mono (a1) and Mono (a2) sound, the Viewer appears with separate tabs, one for each channel. Level and Pan values can then be set separately for each channel, one set to −1 and the other to 1. This allows you to move the audio from one side of the stereo speakers to the other. When you're working with separate channels using the pan line, you can shift the sound to come from either the left side or the right side. Moving the Pan slider to the left to −1 will move all of the sound to the left speaker, and moving the Pan slider all the way to the right to 1 will move the sound to the right speaker. As with Level, Pan values can be keyframed. The classic example is the racing car that approaches from the left (with all the sound coming from the left speaker), roars by, and disappears to the right while the sound sweeps past to the right speaker.

A little trick to quickly get the channels centered between the speakers is to select the clips in the Timeline and use the keyboard shortcut Control-period to center the tracks to the zero value.

FIGURE 10.30
Changing spread values.

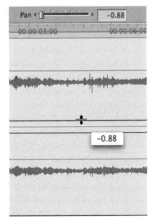

3. With the Ripple tool, select the left side of the edit at the end of *Backstage02*.

4. Holding down the **Command** key, click just to the left of the beginning of *Backstage16* tracks on A1/A2, as shown in Figure 10.31.

5. Pull the edit point to the left so that it moves 15 frames, or edit it numerically (Type −15 and press the **Return** key). As you type, a little box will appear at the top of the Timeline window telling you that you're rippling the edit as in Figure 10.31.

6. With the Selection tool, select the edit on the A3/A4 tracks between *Backstage02* and *Backstage14*, and apply the +3 dB cross fade with **Command-Option-T**.

7. Finally, select the audio edit on A1/A2 at the beginning of *Backstage16* and apply the 0 dB cross fade.

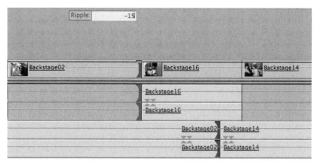

FIGURE 10.31
Selecting the Ripple edits and numerically editing.

FIGURE 10.32
Audio meters.

Audio CDs

For normal speech, it's probably best to keep the recording around −12 dB, perhaps a little higher for louder passages and a bit lower for softer ones. Many audio CDs are very heavily compressed, right up to the limits of digital audio. If you see your audio meters hitting the top of the scale, lighting up the two little orange indicators at the top, bring down your audio levels a few dB. You'll probably find you have to do this for most audio CD material. These are ideal for applying normalization. The sound is usually very compressed, has little range between high and low, and responds well to compression. Make

> **NOTE**
>
> ***Metering:*** Key tools for working with sound in Final Cut are its audio meters (see Figure 10.32). The standard audio level for digital audio is −12 dB. Unlike analog audio, which has quite a bit of headroom and allows you to record sound above 0 dB, in digital recording 0 dB is an absolute. Sound cannot be recorded at a higher level because it gets clipped off. Very often on playback of very loud levels, the recording will seem to drop out completely and become inaudible as the levels are crushed beyond the range of digital audio's capabilities.

181

sure when you monitor your tracks that you monitor not only single tracks but also your mixed track. Often a single track will not exceed peak level, but a mix of all your tracks may send your meters well into the red.

> **TIP**
>
> ***iMovie Sound Effects:*** It is possible to bring iMovie sound effects into Final Cut Express. The trick is to know where they are and to copy them to somewhere else. Do this very carefully.

1. Right-click on the iMovie application inside your *Applications* folder.
2. From the shortcut menu, select **Show Package Contents**.

3. Go inside the *Contents* folder to the *Resources* folder, and find the *iMovie '08 Sound Effects* folder.

The iMovie sound effects are MP3s and should be converted to AIFF using iTunes or the QuickTime Pro Player, if you have that.

VOICE OVER

Final Cut Express has a feature called **Voice Over**, which allows you to record narration or other audio tracks directly to your hard drive while playing back your Timeline. Voice Over is most valuable for making *scratch tracks*, test narrations used to try out pacing and content with pictures. It could be used for final recording, although you'd probably want to isolate the computer and other extraneous sounds from the recording artist. Many people prefer to record narrations before beginning final editing so the picture and sound can be controlled more tightly. Others feel that recording to the picture allows for a more spontaneous delivery from the narrator. However you use it, Voice Over is an important tool in the application.

Voice Over is found under the **Tools** menu. This brings up the window in Figure 10.33. Or better still, call it up from the menus under **Window>Arrange>Voice Over Recording**, which brings a three-up display: Viewer on the left, Voice Over in the center, Canvas on the right, and Browser and Timeline below.

The first steps you'll have to take are to configure your recording setup for your **Source, Input**, and **Sample Rate**. Source defines where the sound is coming from: the computer mic input, a USB device, a camcorder, or an installed digitizing card. Input controls the type of signal being received, whether it's line level, balanced audio in, digital audio, or whatever your source device is capable of handling.

FIGURE 10.33
Voice Over tool.

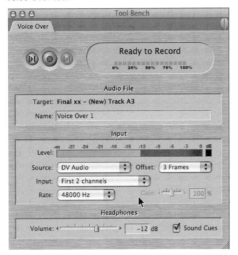

Let's look at some of the controls in this panel. The large red button, the middle of the three in the top portion of the window, is the **Record** button. It will also stop the recording, as will the **Escape** key. The button to its left is the **Preview/Review** button and will play the selected area of your sequence. The button to the right is the **Discard** button. Immediately after a recording or after aborting a recording, pressing the **Discard** button will bring up the warning shown in Figure 10.34.

183

> **TIP**
> ***More RAM for VO:*** Because Voice Over works in RAM, storing the sound before recording it to disk, you may need to put more RAM into your computer than the minimum requirements asked for by FCE because the audio is buffered in RAM as it's recorded. For example, 48 kHz audio consumes 6 MB per minute. So a half-hour track would take 180 MB. Once they are recorded, all of these recordings are stored in your *Capture Scratch* folder with the project name.

> **TIP**
> ***DV Input:*** If you're recording through a DV camcorder or other DV device, make sure that Video (at the bottom of the View menu) is switched to Canvas Playback. If it's set to Apple FireWire, the playback signal will be going out through the cable, which prevents you from recording from it. Two sets of signals going in opposite directions just won't work. If you have Apple FireWire selected in the View menu, you'll get an error message that the application is unable to open the device because it's in use. Also, make sure your camera is in camera mode and not in VCR mode. It must be in camera mode to get the input from the microphone.

Offset adjusts for the delay taken by the analog-to-digital conversion. USB devices typically take one frame. DV cameras can be three frames or more.

FIGURE 10.34
Discard warning dialog.

The Gain slider, next to the **Input** pop-up, allows you to control the recording level based on the horizontal LCD display meter. This is fine for scratch tracks, but for finished work, it is probably better to have a hardware mixer before the input for good mic level control.

The Headphones volume does just what it says. If there is nothing jacked into the headphone output of your computer, the sound will come out of the computer speaker. To avoid recording it or the sound cues, uncheck the **Sound Cues** box.

> **TIP**
>
> **Playback Levels:** Don't be fooled by FCE's vertical audio meters. These display the playback levels; they do not show the recording level.

FCE gives the recording artist elaborate sound cues, which are turned on with the little check box. Together with the aural sound cues in the headphones, there is visual cueing as well, which appears in the window to the right of the Record button. As the recording starts, a countdown begins, with cue tones as the display changes. It starts pale yellow and becomes darker and more orange until recording begins. Then the display changes to red. There is a cue tone at five seconds from the end of the recording as well as beeps counting down the last five seconds to the end of the recording. Recording begins during countdown and continues two seconds after the end of the recording during Finishing. Although this doesn't appear in the Timeline after the recording, you can drag out the front and end of the clip if the voice started early or overran the end.

I think the best way to work with Voice Over in the Timeline is to define In and Out points. If no points are defined, recording will begin at the point at which the playhead is parked and go until the end of the sequence or until you run out of available memory, whichever comes first. You can also simply define an In point and go from there or define an Out and go from the playhead until the Out is reached. Because the Timeline doesn't scroll as the sequence plays, it might be helpful to reduce the sequence to fit the Timeline window. **Shift-Z** will do this with a keystroke.

FIGURE 10.35
Mute/Solo buttons.

Sometimes during recording you don't want to hear certain tracks, or you just want to hear a single pair of tracks. FCE makes it simple to do this with the **Mute/Solo** buttons. You open them by clicking on the tiny speaker button in the far lower left corner of the Timeline window, which pops open the array of **Mute/Solo** buttons (see Figure 10.35). Clicking on the headphones will turn them red and solo that track, muting the others. You can turn on or off any combination of **Mute** and **Solo** buttons that you need. Notice the green **Visibility (Audibility)** buttons at the head of the Timeline. The difference between these and the **Mute/Solo** buttons is that when audibility is switched off, that track will not play out to tape. If a track is muted, it will still output, even though it can't be heard during playback in the Timeline.

Recording is always done to a destination track that has free space. Voice Over always records a mono track. It does not make a stereo recording and take up two tracks. If there is no free space within the defined area of the recording,

Voice Over will create a new track. So if you record multiple takes, they will record onto the next lower track or onto a new track. The Audio File window will give you the track information (see Figure 10.36). You can name the recording in the Audio File window, and each take will be numbered incrementally.

FIGURE 10.36
Audio File window.

After recording, the new Voice Over clip appears selected. You can play it back for review, but if you want to record further takes, use **Control-B** to switch off the clip audio so you don't hear it during playback of the next take.

After a discarded take, Voice Over will record to the previously assigned track with the previously assigned name. After a few takes, you may want to discard a previous take and reassign the targeted track so that Voice Over will work with the empty tracks you vacated. Also, you should be careful to switch off previous takes as you go so the talent doesn't hear the previous recording in the headphones while recording.

After a recording session with Voice Over, it would not be a bad idea to go into your hard drive and root out old tracks that aren't needed and may be filling up your drive. Any takes you recorded that you no longer want can be deleted from your sequence, but they aren't automatically deleted from your hard drive. Also remember that the recordings are only a part of your sequence and will not appear in your Browser at all, unless you put them there.

> **TIP**
> *No Timecode in Voice Over:* There is no timecode or other identifying information other than the assigned name with any Voice Over recording, in case you need to reconstruct your project at a later date. It may be a good idea to keep this recording preserved on tape or on disk if you want to use it again.

185

SUMMARY

In this lesson we looked at working with sound in Final Cut Express. We covered cutting with sound, overlapping and cross-fading tracks, transitions, normalization and gain, meters, and FCE's Voice Over tool. Sound is often overlooked because it doesn't seem to be that important, but it is crucial to making a sequence appear professionally edited. In the next lesson, we'll look at some of the titling options available in Final Cut Express.

LESSON 11

Adding Titles

Every program is enhanced with graphics, whether they are a simple opening title and closing credits or elaborate motion-graphics sequences illuminating some obscure point that can best be expressed in animation. This could be simply a map with a path snaking across it or a full-scale 3D animation explaining the details of how an airplane is built. Obviously, the latter is beyond the scope of both this book and of Final Cut Express alone, but many simpler graphics can be easily created within FCE. More advanced motion graphics can be done in FCE's companion application LiveType, but that would be the subject for another book. In this lesson, we look at typical titling problems and how to deal with them. As always, we begin by loading the project.

SETTING UP THE PROJECT

Let's begin by opening the FCE project that we'll be working on from your hard drive:

1. Double-click on the project file *Lesson 11* to launch the application.
2. If necessary, reconnect the media file as we have done before.

Inside the project in the Browser you'll find a *Basic Animation* sequence that we'll look at later. There is also an empty *Sequence 1* that is ready for you to use, the master clip, *Kabuki*, and the *Clips* bin.

3. Begin by opening *Sequence 1*.
4. We'll be working with only the picture here, so deselect the a1/a2 destination tracks in the patch panel by clicking on them.
5. Drag a clip—let's say *Kabuki1*—from the *Clips* bin and drop it onto Overwrite in the Edit Overlay.

TEXT GENERATOR

Now let's look at FCE's **Text generator**:

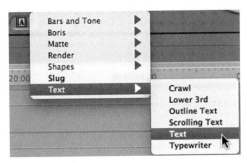

FIGURE 11.1
Text generator.

1. To get to it, click the small **A** in the lower right corner of the Viewer.

2. Go into the pop-up menu, drop down to **Text**, slide across, and pick **Text** again, as in Figure 11.1. Or use the keyboard shortcut **Control-X**.

In addition to Text, you will also see Lower Third, Outline Text, and the basic animations Scrolling Text, Crawl, and Typewriter. The most important text tools are in the Boris submenu: Title 3D and Title Crawl. We'll look at the Boris tools in the next lesson, but let's begin by looking at the way FCE's basic Text tool works.

> **TIP**
> **Scrolling Text, Crawl, and Outline Text:** Neither FCE's Scrolling Text nor Crawl should be used as a first choice. To create text animations for scrolling or rolling titles (vertical movement) or crawling titles (horizontal movement), you should use Title Crawl, which can be set to do either movement. This should always be the preferred tool. Do not use Outline Text. The primary text tools should always be Title 3D and Title Crawl.

Text

This is for very basic text graphics like simple on-screen words. The Text generator should be used only for very simple, quickly built text blocks like placeholders. Let's look at the Text generator because it has many of the typical text controls you can work with in FCE. When you select FCE's basic Text tool, it immediately loads a generic text generator into the Viewer (see Figure 11.2).

Notice that this generator has (1) a default duration of 10 seconds and (2) a default length of two minutes. You can designate any duration for a text file up to 12 hours. However, once the text file has been placed in a sequence, its duration can no longer be extended beyond the designated duration. So, for example, if I accept the default length and place the text file in a sequence, I can no longer make the duration go beyond two minutes. If you know you have to make a very long text file, change the duration *before* you place it in the sequence. You can always make it shorter but not longer. It's a good way to create a video bug—that little graphic that's always in the bottom right of your TV screen—or a warning that a tape is only a sample copy and not for distribution.

The first point to realize about this text generator is that at the moment, it exists only in the Viewer. Usually the next step I take is to put it somewhere useful, either into the Browser or the Timeline.

FIGURE 11.2
Generic sample text in the Viewer.

189

1. Put the playhead anywhere over the shot that's in the Timeline.
2. Drag the generic text generator from the Viewer to the Edit Overlay to Superimpose, or use the keyboard shortcut **F12**.

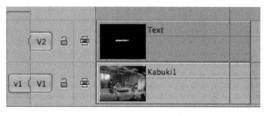

FIGURE 11.3
Supered text in the Timeline.

The text will appear above the shot, with the same duration as the shot (see Figure 11.3). Notice that the application ignores the marked Out point and takes its duration from the length of the shot underneath the playhead on V1, which is the designated destination track.

You can also drag and drop the generator into the Timeline onto an empty track or the space above the tracks. Whether you drag the generic text generator to the Timeline or the Browser, you are creating a copy of that generator. Be careful not to do anything to the generator in the Viewer. People often lay the generator in the Timeline, work in the Viewer, and then wonder why the text in the Canvas still says "Sample Text."

First, you should open the new generator that you created in the Timeline. I always leave the playhead in the Timeline parked over the middle of the clip with the text supered on it. That way, whatever I do in the Text controls appears a moment later supered on the clip in the Canvas.

3. Open it by double-clicking on the Text Generator in the Timeline window.

> **TIP**
>
> **Background:** If you place text in the Timeline over nothing, the blackness you see in the Canvas behind the clip is the emptiness of space. You can make it a variety of colors, including checkerboard under the View>Background menu, but this is only for viewing purposes. If you want an actual color layer, use the Generators to make a color matte. Make it any color you want, and place it on the layer below all other material.

The Viewer screen will look the same, except now you'll be working on the generator in the Timeline, which is what you want. The label area at the top of the Viewer will tell you where the text came from. Figure 11.4 shows the label for text generated in the Viewer. Figure 11.5 shows the label for text that's been opened from a sequence.

The other telltale sign that indicates whether a title or a clip has been opened from the Browser (or generated in the Viewer), or has been opened from a sequence, is in the scrubber bar at the bottom of the Viewer. In Figure 11.6, the clip has been opened from the Browser. The scrubber bar is plain. In Figure 11.7,

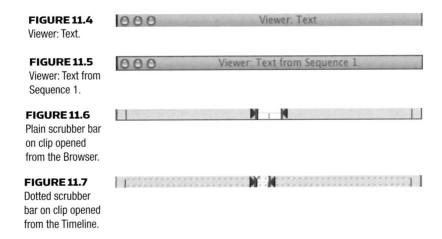

FIGURE 11.4
Viewer: Text.

FIGURE 11.5
Viewer: Text from Sequence 1.

FIGURE 11.6
Plain scrubber bar on clip opened from the Browser.

FIGURE 11.7
Dotted scrubber bar on clip opened from the Timeline.

the clip has been opened from the Timeline. The scrubber bar shows a double row of dots, like film sprocket holes.

Now we're ready to start making that graphic:

4. After you've opened the generator from the Timeline into the Viewer, click on the Controls tab at the top. You might also want to stretch down the Viewer to see all the controls (see Figure 11.8).

These are the default settings. At the top is the text input window in which you type whatever you want to appear on the screen.

5. Click on **SAMPLE TEXT**, and type in *Kabuki*, press **Return**, and type *Performance*.
6. Click out of the window or tab to the **Size** box. The default is 36 point, which is quite small for video display.
7. Type in a size of *72* and press **Return**, which loads the size setting.

Above the Size slider is the **Font** pop-up menu, in which you can pick whatever TrueType fonts you have loaded in your system. It defaults to Lucida Grande, which is a pretty good font to use with video. If you have fonts on your computer that are not showing up here, then they are probably PostScript fonts. Unfortunately, FCE's titling tools do not work with PostScript, only with TrueType fonts.

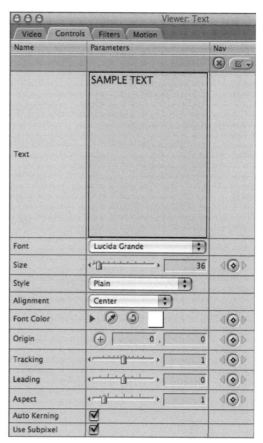

FIGURE 11.8
Text Control window.

Note that the **Font** pop-up menu and all the settings in the text block will change all the letters for everything in the text block. You cannot control individual letters, words, or lines of text. This applies to all of FCE's text generators except for Boris. Both **Title 3D** and **Title Crawl** have full text control, as we shall see.

The left and right alignments are not to the screen but to the Origin point, the way it works in Illustrator and Photoshop. So if you want left-justified text on the left side of the screen, you have to move the x value (horizontal) of the origin point about −300 or a little less to keep it in the Safe Title Area (STA) if you also set the Alignment to Left. This applies only in the Text tool. Other tools such as Scrolling Text align to the screen as you might expect, with left as the left edge of the STA and right as the right edge of the STA (see "Safe Areas").

TIP

Computer Display: Because much of FCE is real time, text will not require rendering on many computers. This means that as soon as the text is put into the Timeline, it is at render quality. The title is rendered into interlaced DV material, ready for display on a television set. That's what it is designed to do. It is not designed for display on a computer screen, which is why the text on your computer screen, and in these graphics, looks somewhat jagged and poorly rendered. You must judge your graphics output on a television set or video monitor. You cannot assess them properly on your computer monitor.

TIP

No Word Wrapping: FCE's titler is limited in many ways, and word wrapping is one of them. You have to put in the line breaks where appropriate, or your text is liable to run off the screen.

TIP

Sliders: If you have a three-button mouse with a scroll wheel, you can move any of the sliders, like the Size slider, with the scroll. Just position the cursor over it and move the wheel.

The **Style** pop-up menu lets you set text styles such as bold and italic. Below Style is the **Alignment** pop-up menu. A word of caution: Although the default setting is **Center**, the words in the text window are left-justified. Ignore that. The choice in the pop-up menu rules; the text window display isn't WYSIWYG.

Font Color includes a color picker and a color swatch as well as a disclosure triangle that twirls opens to show the **HSB** (Hue, Saturation, and Brightness) sliders and **Value** boxes. The small icon between the eyedropper and the color swatch allows you to change the direction in which the color moves if you animate it. The ability to animate the controls in FCE's Text tools allows for great creative possibilities. We'll do a basic text animation later in this lesson.

Because of the limitations of television's color and brightness capabilities, it's important that you try to keep your luminance and chrominance values within the correct range. Oversaturated colors or video levels that are too high will bloom and smear on a television set. Set the HSB value so that brightness is no more than 92 percent. This may look pale gray on the computer screen, but as far as NTSC video is concerned, it is white, and it will look white on a television screen.

This is often a problem with using artwork that hasn't been designed specifically for video. All sorts of issues affect images used in video: interlacing, limitation in how saturated a color can be and how bright it can be, the chrominance and

NOTE

Safe Areas: Televisions have a mask on the edge that cuts off some of the displayed picture area. What you see in the Viewer and the Canvas is not what you get and can vary substantially from television to television. That is why the Canvas and Viewer are thoughtfully marked with a Safe Action Area (SAA) and a smaller area that is defined as the Safe Title Area (STA)—the marked boxes seen in Figure 11.9. These are turned on with the View pop-up menu at the top of the Viewer and Canvas. Make sure that both Overlay and Title Safe are checked to see the SAA and STA. What's within the SAA will appear on every television set. Because television tubes used to be curved, and some older ones still are, a smaller area was defined as the STA in which text could appear without distortion if viewed at an angle. Titles should remain, if possible, within the STA. This is not important for graphics destined only for Web or computer display, but for anything that might be shown on a television within the course of its life, it would be best to maintain them. That said, you will often see titles that are well outside the STA and lying partially outside even the SAA.

luminance range limitations of NTSC, moiré patterns, and compression. Unless the artist makes the necessary adjustments while creating the work, it often looks unsatisfactory when incorporated into a video production.

You can set the **Origin** with a **Crosshair** button or with *x, y* values. You can use the crosshairs by clicking on the button and clicking wherever in the Canvas you want the center point of the text to be. The value windows are more precise. The first window is the horizontal, or *x* value; the second window is the vertical, or *y* value. The default is 0, 0, which is the center of the screen. This is centered on the baseline of the first line of text—in this case, somewhere under the **b** in **Kabuki**.

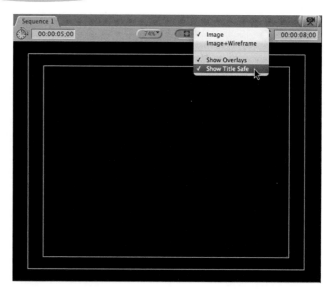

FIGURE 11.9
Safe Action and Safe Title Areas with View pop-up menu.

You can also position the text by moving it about the screen in the Canvas, but you should not do this. Whenever placing or animating text you should always place it with the Origin controls and animate the Origin values.

Tracking is the spacing distance between the letters in a word (not to be confused with kerning), which is the spacing between individual letter pairs. The higher the tracking value, the farther apart the letters will get. Small increases in tracking will have a surprisingly large impact on letter separation. As you move tracking below zero, the letters will scrunch together, and if you go low enough into negative values, the letters will flip over.

Leading (pronounced *ledding*, as in little bits of lead spacing used in hot-metal typesetting) is the spacing between lines. The default is zero. A setting of -100 moves the text up so that it's all on one line. A value of 100 moves the text down a whole line.

Aspect adjusts the vertical shape of the text. Low numbers such as 0.3 and 0.4 stretch text vertically, and higher numbers such as 2 and 3 will squeeze down the text significantly. Be careful with the Aspect control. Very little movement from the default of 1 will cause ugly antialiasing (stair-stepped edges) to appear

TIP

Fonts and Size: Not all fonts are equally good for video. You can't just pick something you fancy and hope it will work for you. One of the main problems with video is its interlacing. Video is made up of thin lines of information. Each line is switching on and off 60 times per second. If you happen to place a thin horizontal line on your video that falls on one of those lines but not the adjacent line, that thin horizontal line will be switching on and off at a very rapid rate, appearing to flicker. The problem with text is that a lot of fonts have thin horizontal lines called serifs, the little footer that some letters sit on (see Figure 11.10).

Unless you're going to make text fairly large, it's best to avoid serif fonts. You should probably avoid small fonts as well. Video resolution is not very high—the print equivalent of 72 dpi. You can read this book in 10-point type comfortably, but a 10-point line of text on television would be an illegible smear. I generally don't use font sizes smaller than 24 point and prefer to use something larger if possible.

FIGURE 11.10
Serif fonts.

around the text. **Auto Kerning** adjusts the letter spacing based on the letters' shapes rather than absolute values.

Lower Thirds

A lower third is the graphic you often see near the bottom of the screen, such as those identifying a speaker or location that you always see in news broadcasts. They are simple to create in Final Cut, although they are fairly limited. If you want to create something more exciting or stylish, you'll probably find it easier to do in Photoshop, Title 3D, or LiveType, which has animated lower thirds templates. Because Lower Third is so limited, it's quick and easy to use. Figure 11.11 shows the simple **Lower Third** that FCE generates. It's set down in the lower left corner of the Safe Title Area.

You can create the graphic in the Viewer before you move it to the Timeline, but remember that once you've moved it to the Timeline, what's there is now a copy. I like to move the graphic to the Timeline, and, as before, you can put the playhead over it and quickly see what you're doing in the Canvas. Let's start by putting a new clip into the Timeline and adding the Lower Third to it:

1. Move the Timeline playhead to the end of the sequence by pressing the **End** key.
2. Double-click on *Kabuki2* from the *Clips* bin and Overwrite it into the Timeline.
3. Put the playhead over *Kabuki2* in the Timeline.
4. Click on the **Generators** button in the Viewer, and in the menu drop down to **Text>Lower Third**.
5. Use the Superimpose function to put the Lower Third over the clip in the Timeline.
6. Double-click on the Lower Third in the Timeline, and go to the Controls tab in the Viewer (see Figure 11.12).

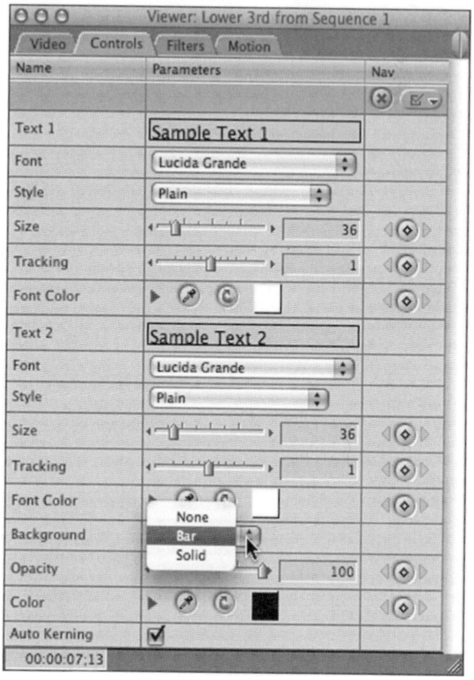

You'll see that the Controls are quite different for lower thirds. You have some new parameters, and you are missing a property as well. There is no Alignment pop-up menu.

TIP
Tracking: If the Auto Kerning check box near the bottom of the controls is not checked, Tracking will not function.

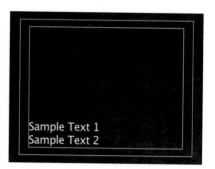

FIGURE 11.11
Lower Third.

FIGURE 11.12
Lower Third controls.

195

TIP

Flickering Text: Interlace flickering caused by serifs and other fine lines can be alleviated somewhat by smearing the image across the interlace lines. It is easiest to do this with text created in Photoshop, where you can apply a one-pixel vertical motion blur. You don't have to soften the whole image like this. If there are particular portions that appear to flicker, you can select them with a marquee or lasso, slightly feathered, and apply the vertical motion blur to just that portion of the image.
Or you can duplicate the Text Generator in the sequence and stack one on top of the other. Apply a slight Blur or Antialias filter to the bottom copy. Only the slightly blurred edge that sticks out from underneath the unblurred copy will be visible, smearing the edge. You can also darken the lower copy to give the text a slightly harder edge.

You have two lines of text. Unlike the regular text window, each of the two text boxes here can only hold one line of text. Each text box can be set to any font, size, or color. You can make a line as long as you want, but if you make it too long, it will run off the screen. At the bottom of the controls, you have the ability to create a background for the text and to adjust the opacity of the background.

196

Bar appears as a line between the text blocks. Although it has an opacity of 100 percent, it will show some of the underlying video through it. **Solid** is a block of color that appears behind the two text blocks. You can apply one or the other but not both. You could, however, add another Lower Third beneath it, with no text, just the background, as shown in Figure 11.13. The size of the background area is fixed and controlled by the size of the text above it.

FIGURE 11.13
Lower Third with bar
and background.

Drop Shadow

Drop shadows are important to give the image some depth and separation. It would be quite useful for our text where the white of the letters is over the bright highlights on the image below (see Figure 11.14). You can add a drop shadow to your text in the Motion tab of the Viewer.

You must activate the Drop Shadow with the check box on the left side of the controls. The control panel, once twirled open, shows all the expected features: **Offset, Angle** of offset, **Shadow Color, Softness,** and **Opacity** (see Figure 11.15).

FIGURE 11.14
Drop shadowed text.

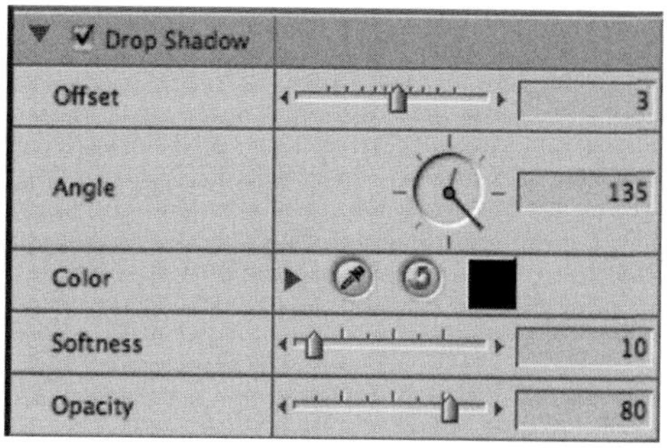

FIGURE 11.15
Drop shadow controls.

Offset controls how far from the image the shadow appears. When using Drop Shadow with the text tools, you'll want to use a value in the 2 to 5 range. The **Angle** dial will point your shadow in whatever direction you want. The default direction, falling off to the lower right, is the most commonly used drop shadow angle. **Softness** lets you control the amount of blurring on the edges of the shadow. The **Opacity** slider defaults to 50 percent, which is probably too low for use with text. You might want to push up Drop Shadow's Opacity to 90 to 100 percent and use the Softness slider to take the edge off it.

BASIC ANIMATION

Final Cut Express allows you to create many different types of animation for both motion and filters. Many of the text parameters, for instance, in the Text Controls tab can be animated. To make an animation, you have to understand the concept of keyframes. When you change the properties of an image—in text, for instance—you define how it looks. When you apply a keyframe, you define how it looks at a particular moment in time, at a specific frame of your video. If you then go to another point in time, some other frame of video—say, five seconds farther into your video—and change the values for the image, the application will automatically create another keyframe, which defines how it looks at that point in time. The computer will then figure out—it will *tween*—what each of the intervening frames of video would look like over that five seconds. We've already done some animations when we animated audio levels. Now let's do a simple motion animation. We'll animate the leading and the color for the text.

1. Start by making sure the playhead is at the beginning of the Timeline, over the first stack, *Kabuki1*, and the basic text is on top of it.
2. Open the *Text* clip in Viewer and go to the Controls tab. Either grab the Leading slider and pull it down to −40, or dial in −40 in the value box. The lines of text should look scrunched together as in Figure 11.16.
3. Click on the color swatch and set the color to a pale yellow.

197

FIGURE 11.16
Text Leading at −40.

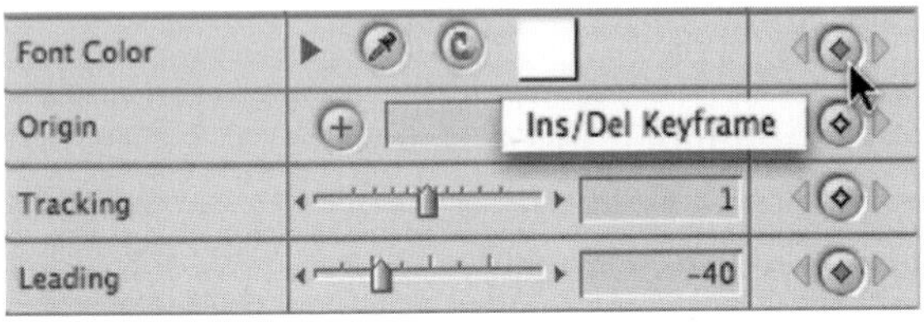

FIGURE 11.17
Leading and Color
keyframes set.

FIGURE 11.18
Text with Leading at 25
and color change.

4. Now click on the empty diamond keyframe buttons next to the Leading value and the Font Color (see Figure 11.17). The little buttons will go green to indicate that you've added a keyframe and are on the keyframe.

5. Press **Shift-O** to move the playhead to the last frame of the clip.

6. Change the Leading value to 25. You do not have to add another keyframe; one will be added for you automatically because the value has changed.

7. Click on the color swatch and change the color value to a darker yellow. The Canvas will show the text spread out as in Figure 11.18.

8. Scrub the Timeline Ruler to see the animation in the Canvas. You may have to render it for real-time playback.

That's it! You've done your first basic video animation. We'll do a lot more in the lessons ahead. To see the finished version of our little animation, open the *Basic Animation* sequence.

SUMMARY

In this lesson we looked at FCE's basic text tools and did a simple animation. In the next lesson, we will look at the considerably more powerful Boris Calligraphy and explore some of the animation capabilities it opens up.

LESSON 12

Boris Calligraphy and Advanced Titling

In the previous lesson, we looked at FCE's text tools. Now we're going to look at Boris Calligraphy, which is made up of two elements: Title 3D and Title Crawl. This is actually a plug-in to FCE's Generators created for Apple by Boris FX. These supersede the FCE text tools and should be the title tool of choice for most of the work you do. These generators give the user great control and flexibility with text.

SETTING UP THE PROJECT

Let's begin by opening up the *Lesson 12* project from your hard drive, and, if necessary, going through the reconnect process. Inside the project in the Browser, you'll find some sequences, which we shall look at in the course of this lesson. One of the sequences, *Sequence 1*, is empty and ready for you to use. You will also see the master clip, *Kabuki*, and the *Clips* bin.

1. Begin by opening *Sequence 1* if it's not already open.
2. We'll be working with only the picture here, so as in the previous lesson, deselect the a1/a2 destination tracks in the patch panel by clicking on them.
3. Drag a clip—let's say *Kabuki3*—from the *Clips* bin, and drop it onto Overwrite in the Edit Overlay.

TITLE 3D

Title 3D is a feature-packed tool, an application in itself, with complex animation capabilities that are beyond the scope of this book. I'm going to show you some of its principal tools, but for a thorough look at its capabilities, consult the excellent PDF in the *Boris Calligraphy Docs* folder inside the *Extras* folder on the Final Cut installation disc.

1. Call up Title 3D from the Generators pop-up menu in the Viewer.
2. Go to the submenu **Boris**, and select **Title 3D**. Though it looks as if nothing happened, the Viewer has changed.

3. Go to the Controls tab in the Viewer, and click on the **Title 3D click for options button** (see Figure 12.1). This will launch a separate titling window that is part of the Boris interface (see Figure 12.2).

FIGURE 12.1
Title 3D click for options button.

This is the first of five tabbed windows that give you access to Title 3D's powerful and complex tools. In fact, Title 3D has so many controls that there seem to be controls for the controls.

The window for the first tab on the left side is obviously the text window where you set up your text, font, style, size, alignment, and even justification. Unlike the FCE text box, it is truly WYSIWYG. Most important, each control can be applied to each letter or group of letters separately. So now, with little trouble, you can make a garish combination of colors and fonts, such as I have done in the sequence *Calligraphy*.

FIGURE 12.2
Title 3D interface.

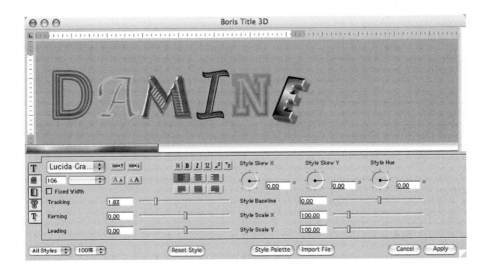

FIGURE 12.3
Word wrapping.

FIGURE 12.4
ІText window ruler.

Before you do anything in this window, you may want to click on the second tab and change the default **No Wrap** to **Wrap** (see Figure 12.3). You can leave the wrap default at 512 where you get a word wrapping that will fit inside a standard 720 video image's Safe Title Area. You can set whatever margins you want in this window, just as in a word processor (see Figure 12.4). In fact, many of Title 3D's controls are similar to word processors and other graphics applications, such as Adobe Illustrator. The **Top-down Text** and **Right-to-left Reading** check boxes at the bottom of the same tab are great if you want vertical text or if you're doing Hebrew or Arabic text.

> **TIP**
> **Text Control Shortcuts:** If the Kerning, Tracking, or Leading value box is active, you can make the values go up or down by holding down the Option key and tapping the Up and Down arrow keys to raise and lower the values. With the text selected and holding down the Option key, you can tap the Left and Right arrow keys to increase the tracking. Or with the cursor positioned between letters and holding the Option key, you can adjust the kerning of individual letter pairs.

201

After you've set word wrapping and any margins you want, go back to the text window to enter your text, and set your font and alignment specifications. The top portion of the window allows you to enter and select text, which you can adjust with the controls at the bottom part of the window.

At the top of the text window is a ruler that allows you to set tabs for precise positioning of text elements (see Figure 12.4). The white area seen in the ruler is the active text part of the screen, and the gray area is beyond the word wrapping. Use the **Tab** key to navigate from one tab indent to the next. After you've set a tab, you can double-click on it to toggle between left-justified, right-justified, and

									Style Skew X		Style Skew Y		Style Hue	

Arial Black · 36 36 · Fixed Width N B I U .3 ·3 Style Skew X 0.00° Style Skew Y 0.00° Style Hue 0.00°

Tracking	0.00	Style Baseline	0.00
Kerning	0.00	Style Scale X	100.00
Leading	0.00	Style Scale Y	100.00

FIGURE 12.5
Text controls.

center-justified. This tool is especially useful when making long scrolls, such as movie credits, which often use columns and indents for different sections.

Let's look at some of the phenomenal text control in Calligraphy. In the bottom portion of the first tab (see Figure 12.5), the first pop-up menu obviously sets the font. The two buttons to the right will move you up and down through your font list. Below the **Font** pop-up is a **Point Size** value box. The two buttons to the right will incrementally raise and lower your point size. To the right of the font controls are six buttons that let you set the following attributes:

- Normal
- Bold
- Italic
- Underline
- Superscript
- Subscript

Below that, three Paragraph buttons let you set alignment: Left, Center, and Right. Below that are three buttons that set justification, spreading the letters uniformly across the screen the way the text on this page is justified. The **Tracking** slider adjusts the letter spacing globally, across all the letters.

Kerning adjusts the spacing between individual pairs or groups of letters, as opposed to tracking, which controls the whole block of words. Kerning is important for many fonts, especially when you are writing words such as HAVE, and you want to tuck the A and V closer together than fonts normally place them.

FIGURE 12.6
Skewed, Scaled, and
Baseline-shifted letters.

The **Style** controls allow you to skew the text on the *x* and *y* axis. **Style Baseline** lets you to raise and lower letters separately, but **Style Scale X** and **Style Scale Y** let you scale individual characters on the *x* and/or *y* axis independently from each other, allowing you to create interesting and unusual letter arrangements, as shown in Figure 12.6.

The buttons and pop-up menus along the bottom of the window (see Figure 12.7) have a variety of functions. The **All Styles** pop-up menu at the far left lets

FIGURE 12.7
Pop-up menus and
buttons in the Title 3D
window.

you change to **Basic Style** or **Draft Typing**. All Styles lets you create any kind of styling with edges, drop shadows, and bevels, but it can be slow to both draw in the Title 3D window and render. Basic Style displays only simple color and text positioning while you work. Draft typing, on the other hand, lets you draw the text properly in the window, but when you start to type, it switches to a simple text display to make it easier to see and to speed up the text display while you're typing.

The **Percentage** pop-up menu lets you change the display size of the text window, a useful feature if you have a lot of text and want to quickly move around in it. The **Reset Style** button resets all of the parameters for the words in the text window. It does not, however, reset wrapping, tabs, justification, or margins. The **Style Palette** is a great

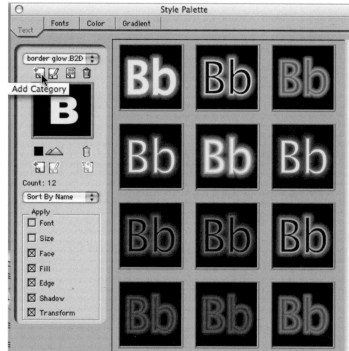

FIGURE 12.8
Style palette.

tool (see Figure 12.8). It allows you to create your own text style and to name and save it. This way you can replicate styles from file to file, and even project to project, simply and efficiently. The Style Palette comes with prebuilt text styles, which are all customizable, a tab to save favorite fonts, useful complementary color groups, and even prebuilt color gradients. To save a style you've created, click on the **Add Category** button, or add to an existing category, and then click on the **Add Style** button, which is just above the word *Count* in Figure 12.8.

The **Import File** button allows you to bring into the Text window a previously created plain text file or RTF (Rich Text Format) file. All of the justification and styles applied there will be honored in Title 3D. **Cancel** and **Apply** are self-explanatory.

Because Title 3Ds are *vector-based graphics*, you can scale the text, twisting and skewing the letters, and you won't get antialiasing or stair-stepping on the edges of the letters. When a bitmapped graphic is created, such as the FCE Text tool,

203

FIGURE 12.9
Left: Bitmapped text;
Right: Vector-based
text.

the color and position of each pixel in the image are defined. If you scale that image, you have to scale the pixels, trying to create pixels where none previously existed. When a vector graphic is created, no pixels are defined, only the shape is. So if you scale a vector graphic with its scaling functions, you're just redefining the shape; no pixels need to be created until the image is displayed on the screen.

Figure 12.9 shows what happens when a bitmapped text file (Helvetica 72 point) is scaled 300 percent and when a vector-based text file is scaled the same amount. It's essential that the scaling for the vector graphic be done within Title 3D and not by using the Scale slider in the Motion tab.

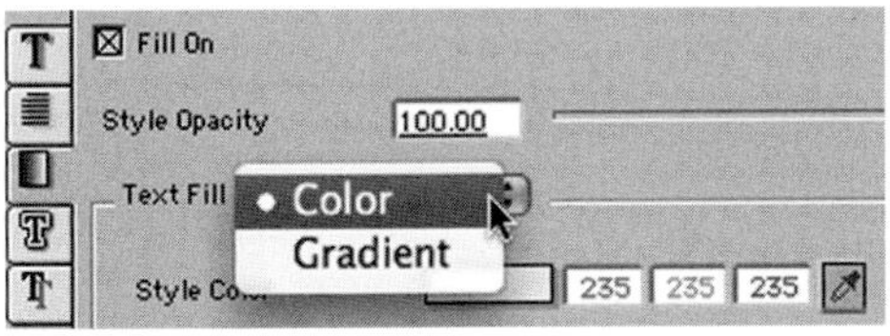

FIGURE 12.10
Text color.

These are only the first two tabs in Title 3D. Before we go further, let's add some text to the text window:

1. You should already have wrapping turned on, so start by making sure the alignment is set to Center.
2. Type in **Kabuki Performance**.
3. Select the text. This is important because each character can be different, so, like a word processor, the text must be selected before making changes.
4. Set the font to Arial Black, which is perhaps the most commonly used font in video.
5. Set the point size to 72, and the text will automatically wrap to find the screen.

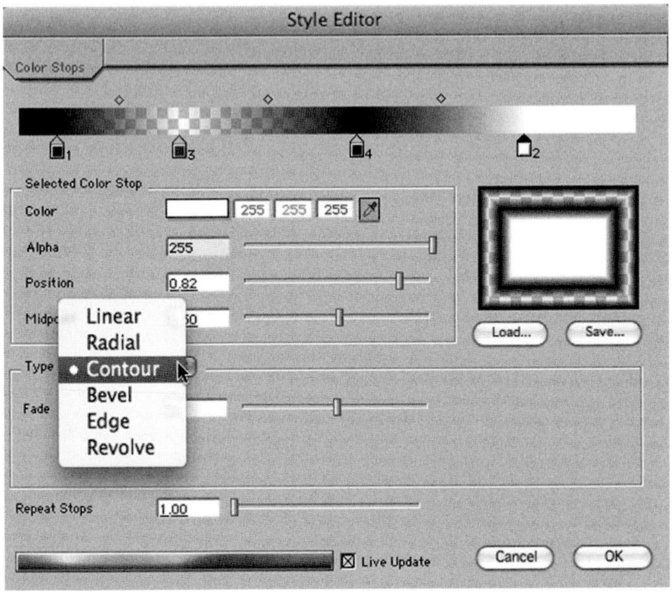

The third tabbed panel, **Text Color**, lets you set the text fill and opacity (see Figure 12.10). Notice the little check box in the upper left corner that lets you turn off the fill, so you only have the text outline if you want it. The **Text Fill** pop-up menu lets you choose to fill the text with a color or a gradient. If you choose **Color**, the Style Color swatch allows access to

FIGURE 12.11
Gradient style editor.

the system color picker that we saw earlier. If you choose **Gradient**, you will get access to an incredibly powerful gradient editor (see Figure 12.11). The gradient

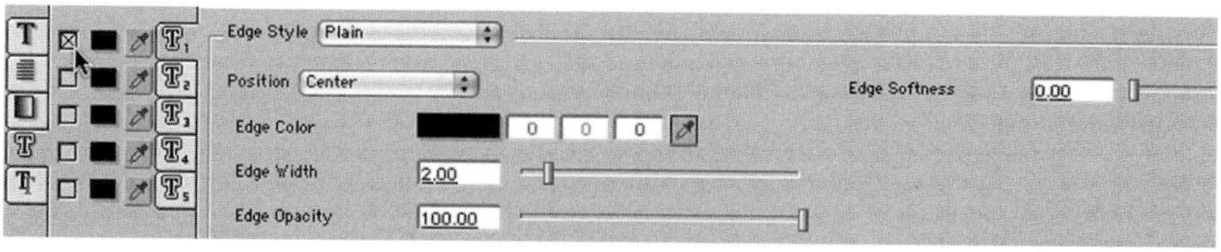

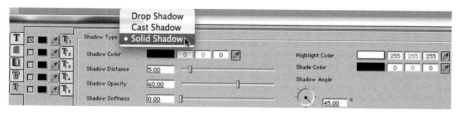

FIGURE 12.12
Text Edge.

FIGURE 12.13
Drop Shadow.

style editor allows multiple color points as well as transparency. To add color stops, click below the gradient-bar display. Notice the useful little check box for **Live Update**, which will show your gradient on your text in the text window as you make changes.

The fourth tabbed window lets you set the width and opacity for the **Text Edge**, and not just a single edge but up to five separate edges for each letter (see Figure 12.12). Each edge can be Plain, Bevel, or Glow, and can be Center, Inside, or Outside. The slider on the right controls the softening blur for each edge. The variations possible with five edges are almost infinite—definitely more than anyone could need. To turn on an edge, you have to make sure that the check box for the panel you're working in is switched on. There are two color swatches, one in the body of the body and one next to the check box. What's nice about this second check box is that it allows you to set the color and color pick with an eyedropper for a text edge that you're not working with at the moment—a very useful feature in the software.

The fifth panel sets up to five separate **Drop Shadows** (see Figure 12.13). These can be a standard **Drop**; a **Cast** shadow, which slopes away from the text; or a **Solid** shadow with sides, which creates a kind of extruded text look. Drop and Cast shadows don't have Highlight or Shade color, but they have a Softness control that appears when the shadow pop-up menu is changed. Each shadow also has controls for color, distance, opacity, and angle. As with edges, make sure you turn on the check box for each of the shadows you want to include.

One major drawback of working with Boris Calligraphy is that while you're working in Title 3D, you cannot see the text composited on top of the image.

1. So before we start working further on the title, press the **Apply** button to create your title in the Viewer.

205

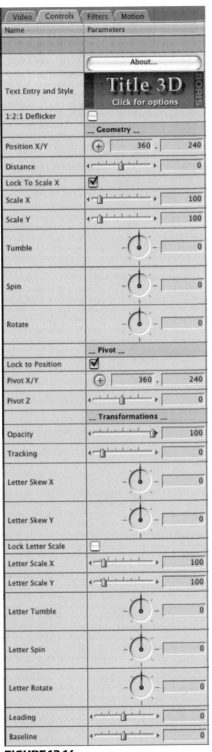

2. Once you've created your text, switch back to the Video tab and drag it to the Timeline or Superimpose it over the clip that's already there.

3. We're going to enhance it further, so double-click the Title 3D file in the Timeline to open it into the Viewer.

4. Then click on the Controls tab to open all the controls for Title 3D. Figure 12.14 shows some of the controls for animating this tool.

5. We'll create a couple of easy animations, but first click on the Title 3D logo at the top of the controls panel to access the text again.

6. Select the text, and remove any fancy edges, gradients, and drop shadows. Keep it just a simple text with a pale color.

Look at the controls panel and the sliders and dials that let you change the geometry and position of the text. Although **Position** places the text in the screen, **Distance** makes the text appear nearer or farther away. The **Scale** value in this panel will allow you to get clean, large fonts. When working with Title 3D, scale your text here in this panel, not with Scale in the Motion tab.

Tumble, **Spin**, and **Rotate** turn the entire text block around on the *x*, *y*, and *z* axes, respectively. A nice thing about Calligraphy is that if you have a real-time capable system, most of these motion settings, including drop shadow, will preview in real time.

The **Pivot** section controls the point around which the text tumbles, spins, and rotates. If the **Lock to Position** box is checked, the controls have no effect. With the box unchecked, the text will rotate around the selected pivot point, which can be set with numeric values or with the crosshairs button. Neither the **Tumble** nor **Spin** controls function with the X/Y controls, but their movement is affected when the Z slider is activated. The **Transformation** sections affect all of the letters in the text block, but affect each character individually.

FIGURE 12.14
Title 3D controls.

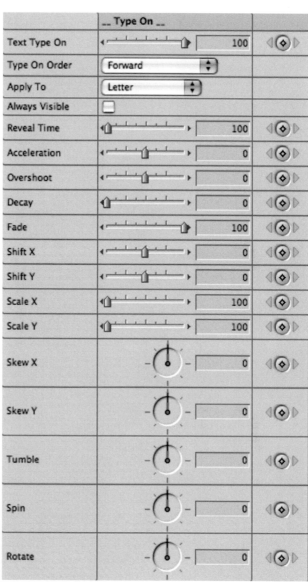

Geometry				
Position X/Y	⊕	360 ,	240	◁◉▷
Distance			0	◁◉▷
Lock To Scale X	☑	Ins/Del Keyframe		
Scale X			100	◁◉▷
Scale Y			100	◁◉▷

FIGURE 12.15
Keyframing Distance, Scale X, and Scale Y.

Animating Title 3D

Let's make a simple motion animation:

1. In the Controls tab of the Viewer, type *300* and press **Return** to move the playhead to the 3-second mark in the title.
2. Click on the diamond keyframe buttons for Distance, Scale X, and Scale Y, as in Figure 12.15.
3. Type +1, and press the **Return** key to go forward by one second.
4. Set the Scale X value to 270 and the Distance value to −16.
5. Render out the animation so you can play through it.

The title is static at the beginning of the scene and then zooms up and flies past the camera. The finished sequence is in the Browser and is called *Fly Through*.

Type On

Type On allows you to create a typed-on effect with Title 3D's full text controls, making FCP's Typewriter obsolete. The Type On controls are at the bottom of the Title 3D controls tab. Figure 12.16 shows you the amazing amount of text control you have for your animations. To type text on the screen, first you need to animate the **Text Type On** value.

1. To start, open the sequence in the Browser called *Type On*. It contains a piece of prepared text made in Title 3D.
2. Put the playhead at the beginning of the sequence (**Home**), and double-click on the text in the sequence to open it into the Viewer.

Type On		
Text Type On	100	◁◉▷
Type On Order	Forward	
Apply To	Letter	
Always Visible	☐	
Reveal Time	100	◁◉▷
Acceleration	0	◁◉▷
Overshoot	0	◁◉▷
Decay	0	◁◉▷
Fade	100	◁◉▷
Shift X	0	◁◉▷
Shift Y	0	◁◉▷
Scale X	100	◁◉▷
Scale Y	100	◁◉▷
Skew X	0	◁◉▷
Skew Y	0	◁◉▷
Tumble	0	◁◉▷
Spin	0	◁◉▷
Rotate	0	◁◉▷

FIGURE 12.16
Type On controls.

207

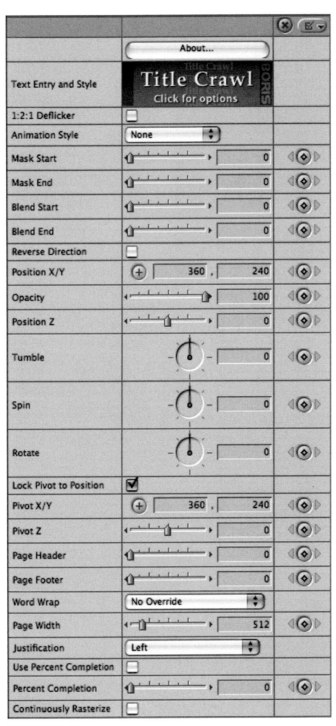

	About...	
Text Entry and Style	Title Crawl	
1:2:1 Deflicker	☐	
Animation Style	None	
Mask Start	0	
Mask End	0	
Blend Start	0	
Blend End	0	
Reverse Direction	☐	
Position X/Y	360 , 240	
Opacity	100	
Position Z	0	
Tumble	0	
Spin	0	
Rotate	0	
Lock Pivot to Position	☑	
Pivot X/Y	360 , 240	
Pivot Z	0	
Page Header	0	
Page Footer	0	
Word Wrap	No Override	
Page Width	512	
Justification	Left	
Use Percent Completion	☐	
Percent Completion	0	
Continuously Rasterize	☐	

FIGURE 12.17
Title Crawl controls.

208

3. Go to the Controls tab, and scroll down to the Type On area of the text.
4. The first value, Text Type On, is the one we'll animate. With the playhead at the beginning of the clip, click on the little diamond button, turning it green.
5. Drag the Text Type On slider all the way down to zero, or dial 0 into the value box. The text will disappear from the Canvas.
6. Go to the end of the clip. Using **Shift-O** right in the Controls window is the easiest way to do it.
7. Now drag the slider all the way up to 100, or type in the value.

You'll probably have to render this out. With the text clip selected, press **Command-R** to render it. Play it from the beginning, and you'll see your text type onto the screen. The rest of the controls in the section are for complex animation features for making the text bounce, curve, and scale.

TITLE CRAWL

Title Crawl is accessed from inside the Boris submenu of the **Generators** pop-up menu. It shares many of the same controls as Title 3D. The text window that's evoked when Title Crawl is called up functions identically in both Calligraphy title tools. The difference is seen in the Controls tab of the Viewer (see Figure 12.17). This has far fewer options: no Geometry, no Transformation. The Animation pop-up menu lets you set None (the default, and rather pointless), Roll (Scroll), and Crawl.

Mask Start, **Mask End**, **Blend Start**, and **Blend End** are interesting controls. These allow the scroll to fade in as it comes in off the bottom of the screen and fade out as it disappears off the top (see Figure 12.18). Mask Start and End control where on the screen the fades start and end. The Blend Start and End allow you to separately control the amount of fade at the top and the bottom of the screen.

FIGURE 12.18
Masking and Blending in scrolling title.

The **Reverse Direction** check box does just that: makes a roll reverse from the default bottom-to-top direction to top-to-bottom and reverses the direction of the standard right-to-left crawl to left-to-right.

To do a Crawl—a horizontal stream of text across the screen—first make sure **Word Wrap** is switched off in the second tab of the text window. The speed of the Roll or Crawl is determined by the amount of text in the text window and the duration of the text block in the Timeline: the longer the block, the slower the motion.

> **TIP**
> ***Interlace Flickering:*** If you're doing text animation on interlaced video, check the 1:2:1 Deflicker box to reduce interlace flickering.

You should be aware that although Title 3D is vector based, Title Crawl is not; it produces bit-mapped graphics.

Once you've made your Title Crawl, place it in the Timeline and try it out for speed. To test the speed without rendering the whole item, mark In and Out points in the Timeline, make sure nothing is selected in the Timeline, and press **Command-R** to render that section. Pick a piece in the middle of the title so you get a representative section. If it seems too fast, stretch out the title; if it's too slow, shorten it and test again.

NESTING

The power of FCE's titling tools is in their flexibility and the amount of control you have over your graphic elements. In the project Browser is a sequence called *Title and Background*, which consists of several FCE titling tools. The output appears in Figure 12.19, but if you open it in FCE, you'll see it in color. I'll show you how it was built up.

209

FIGURE 12.19
Title and Background.

If you open the sequence *Title and Background*, you'll see that it is made up of two layers. On V1 is a video clip twice, and on V2 is a text block called *Title Composite* and another called *Title Composite Japan*. These are nests. Nesting is an important concept to understand in FCE. Because you can have sequences within sequences in FCE, you can also group layers together into nests to form a sequence of their own. The Browser contains two sequences called *Title Composite* and *Title Composite Japan*. These elements appear on V2 in *Title and Background*. Let's build these nests together.

Text

1. Start by duplicating *Sequence 1* in the Browser. Select the sequence, and use **Edit>Duplicate (Option-D)**.
2. Rename the sequence *Title Composite 2* to distinguish it from the one that's already in the Browser.
3. Open *Title Composite 2* by double-clicking on it or by selecting it and pressing **Return**. Delete anything that may be in the sequence.
4. In the Viewer, from the Generator pop-up menu, select **Boris>Title 3D**.
5. Go to the Controls tab, and click on the **Title 3D** button to bring up the text window.
6. Go to the second tab in the Title 3D window, and change the pop-up menu to Wrapping.
7. Return to the first tab, and type in **KABUKI**.
8. You can use whatever text, color, or settings you want, but this is how I built the text:

Font	Arial
Style	Bold
Point Size	96
Color Fill	muted red: R 200, G 68, B 88
Edge Style	Plain, Inside, Black
Edge Width	3
Edge Softness	2
Drop Shadow	Default: Drop Shadow, Angle 45

Shadow Color	Green: R 20, G 96, B 19
Shadow Distance	6
Shadow Opacity	100
Shadow Softness	3

9. When you've finished making the text, click the **Apply** button.

10. Switch back to the Video tab in the Viewer, and edit the text onto V1 in the sequence.

Background

1. In the Timeline, move the playhead over the middle of the text block you just edited into the sequence.

2. From the Viewer, drag another copy to the Canvas Edit Overlay and drop it on Superimpose.

You now have two exact copies, one on top of the other. The top one will be our text, and the bottom one will be converted into the soft, white background layer.

3. Double-click on the Title 3D text block on V1 in the Timeline to bring it back into the Viewer.

4. Go to the Controls tab, and click on the Title 3D button to bring up the text window.

5. Select the text, go down to the Drop Shadow tab, and switch off the drop shadow.

6. Next go to the third tab, the color tab, and in the upper left corner, switch off **Fill On**.

7. Finally, go to the fourth tab, the edges tab, and set the edge as follows:

Edge Style	Plain, Center, White
Edge Width	Type in 80
Edge Opacity	80
Edge Softness	2.5

Why do I put the second edge on a separate layer? I do it for two reasons. It allows me to put the drop shadow on top of the soft background; otherwise, the drop shadow would be behind it and hardly visible. It also allows me to place elements between the text and the background. Your Canvas should now look something like Figure 12.20.

211

FIGURE 12.20
Text and background layer.

FIGURE 12.21
Add Tracks.

Color Mattes

1. Placing the cursor at the head of the V1 track, anywhere near the locks or auto select buttons, right-click, and from the shortcut menu, select **Add Track** (see Figure 12.21).
2. Do this three times so you have a total of three empty tracks between the two layers with the text blocks.
3. In the Viewer from the Generators button, select **Matte>Color**, as we did to make the color backing for the Page Peel transition in Lesson 8. Again, this will fill the screen with midtone gray.
4. Drag it to the Timeline, and place it on the empty V2 you created.
5. Double-click the Color Matte in the sequence to open it back into the Viewer.
6. Go to the Controls tab, and set the color to the same dark rose color as the KABUKI title. Use the color picker if the title is visible in the Canvas; it should be if the playhead is sitting over the clips.
7. After setting the color, go to the Motion tab and twirl open the Crop and Opacity controls (see Figure 12.22). I used these settings:

Top	62
Bottom	31
Opacity	75

FIGURE 12.22
Crop and Opacity settings in Motion tab.

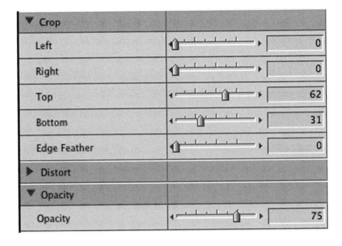

We'll look at the other controls in the Motion tab in detail in the next lesson.

8. Open another Color Matte, and place it on the track above the red bar you just created.
9. Make the color of this matte green as before (R 20, G 96, B 19). You can access the system color picker by clicking on the swatch and choosing the RGB sliders to set your color values.
10. In the Motion tab, set these Crop values:

Top	60
Bottom	38

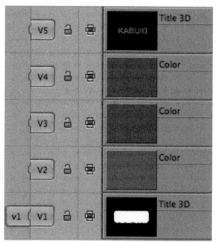

FIGURE 12.23
Timeline after Making Text and Matte Layers.

11. We have one more color matte to make. Generate the matte and bring it to the sequence below the uppermost Title 3D block.
12. Set the same green color and these Crop values:

Top	70
Bottom	32

213

Your sequence should have five layers in it (see Figure 12.23):

- Background blur made from the KABUKI Title 3D block on V1
- Three color mattes on the layers above
- At the top, the Title 3D block that holds the text KABUKI

Putting It All Together

1. Duplicate *Sequence 1* again.
2. Open the duplicate, and delete anything that may be in it.
3. Set V1 as the destination track in the patch panel, and deselect the patching so there are no audio tracks.
4. From the *Clips* bin, select the clip called *Kabuki3*. Use Overwrite in the Canvas, or drag it directly onto V1 of the empty sequence.
5. Move the playhead so it is over the clip on V1.
6. Drag *Title Composite 2* from the Browser to Superimpose in the Canvas to place it above the video clip.

Reusing the Title Block

Here's what else makes this beautiful: Suppose I've built this complex text block, and I want to change the actual text but nothing else.

1. Duplicate *Title Composite 2* in your Browser.
2. Change the name of the duplicate to *Title Composite Japan 2*, and open it by double-clicking on it.
3. Double-click on the top Title 3D block to open it into the Viewer, and in the text window, select the text and replace the word **KABUKI** with the word **JAPAN**.
4. Repeat for the Title 3D block on V1.

Nothing else changes, just the text block and the background layer. Easy, isn't it?

A nested sequence is like a clip in a sequence. If you want to apply an effect to a nest or reposition the block—lower in the frame, for instance—you can do this without adjusting each layer individually. We'll look at applying effects in a later lesson, as well as animating images about the screen.

STILL IMAGES

Often you must work with still images, photographs, or graphics generated in a graphics application such as Photoshop or Photoshop Elements. What you should first know about working in Photoshop is that you should use only the RGB color space—no CMYK, no grayscale, and no indexed color. They don't translate to video.

One problem with using Photoshop is the issue of square versus rectangular pixels when working with DV. Because Photoshop is a computer program, it works in square pixels primarily, but the DV format uses rectangular pixels— tall, narrow pixels that allow for greater horizontal resolution. This presents a minor problem in the earlier versions of Photoshop, but it has been corrected since the release of Photoshop CS, which allows you to preview images with rectangular pixels and has guides for both Title and Action Safe areas.

The important point is to understand how FCE handles still image files. It handles different types of images in different ways. Single-layer files are treated one way, and Photoshop files with multiple layers or transparency are treated another way. Single-layer files are treated as graphics files, and FCE understands that they come from a square-pixel world. Multilayer files are treated as sequences, and FCE would not presume to alter the dimensions of a sequence you created. It assumes that you did it correctly.

The recent versions of Photoshop and Photoshop Elements have presets for working in DV, NTSC and PAL, 4:3, as well as widescreen. These should be used whenever you're making a multilayer or transparent image for use with FCE. For HDV material, use either the HDV 1,440×1,080 Anamorphic preset if you're working in 1080i or the HDV 720 preset if you're working in 720p.

NOTE

Import Based on Setup: If you're creating your multilayer Photoshop file for DV, make sure you have DV as your setup before you import it. If you have HD or some other setting, FCE will use that to establish the correct frame and pixel aspect for the image. Similarly if you make an HD image in Photoshop, make sure you have the correct HD setting selected in your Easy Setup before you import the file into FCE.

You're not always making a graphic that needs to fit in the video format. Sometimes you're making a graphic that is much larger, one you want to move around or to make it seem as if you're panning across the image or zooming in or out of the image. To do this, you need to make the image much greater than your video format—perhaps 2,000 × 2,000 pixels or more.

If you are working with a Photoshop-layered image, you still should squeeze the image down to rectangular pixels before you bring it into FCE. Here's how you should make them:

1. Create your multilayer image or image with transparency, and before you save it, go to **Image>Image Size**.
2. Uncheck to switch off **Constrain Proportions**.
3. Switch the pixel value for the vertical height of the image to percentage, and then reduce the height of the image to 90 percent or, if you want to be precise about it, 89.886 percent.

You should only do this for Photoshop files that are multilayer or with transparency files that import as a sequence. This is not necessary for single-layer images without Photoshop transparency. FCE understands that these are square-pixel images brought into the video world and will handle them appropriately. If they are layered files with transparency, FCE treats these as separate sequences and does not adjust for square pixels.

FIGURE 12.24
Large image in the Canvas showing Scale in the Viewer.

When you import a graphic file into FCE and place it inside a sequence, FCE will scale the image to match the dimensions of the format you're working in. This is new in FCE4. Previously, graphics files would be scaled down to fit the screen, and images smaller than the screen would simply be placed in it. In the current version, images smaller than screen size also get scaled; they get expanded to fill the screen.

Take a look at the sequence called *HDV*. It contains a single graphics file. All HD is widescreen, whereas the still image is 4:3—thus the pillarboxing, the black bands on left and right.

1. Double-click on the image in the Timeline to open it into the Viewer.
2. Go to the Motion tab in the Viewer, and look at the Scale value. It's scaled up 227.37 percent. That's a great deal of scaling. The image will probably look quite soft and pixilated when seen on the screen.
3. To bring it back to normal size, set the Scale value back to 100. It's now much smaller than the size of the screen.

Different aspect ratio images will be treated in different ways. If the image is 400 pixels wide by 800 pixels tall, it's narrower, but taller, than a DV image. FCE will scale it to fit inside the window, as in Figure 12.24. Again, if you do want to use the image at its full size so you can move across it, you'll first have to return it to its normal size, as we just did.

Resolution

For people who come from a print background, an important point to note is that video doesn't have a changeable resolution. It's not like print where you can jam more and more pixels into an inch of space and make your print cleaner, clearer, and crisper. Pixels in video occupy a fixed space and have a fixed size, the equivalent of 72 dpi in the print world, which happens to be the Macintosh screen resolution. Dots per inch are a printing concern. Forget about resolution. Think in terms of size: The more pixels, the bigger the picture, just the way digital still cameras work. Don't think you can make an image 720×480 at a high resolution such as 300 dpi or 600 dpi and be able to scale it up and move it around in FCE. Certainly, you'll be able to scale it up, but it will look soft, and if you scale it far enough—to 300 percent, for instance—the image will start to show pixelization. FCE is good at hiding the defects by blurring and softening, but the results are not really as good as they should be. FCE is a video application and deals only with pixel numbers, not with dpi.

Scanners, on the other hand, are designed for the print world where dpi is an issue. Because scanners generate lots of pixels, this is very handy for the person working in video. This means that you can scan a four-inch by three-inch image at, say, 300 or 600 dpi, which is a quite small image, and your scanner will produce thousands of pixels, which will translate into video as a very large image. You now have an image that's much larger than your video format of 720×480 pixels.

If your scanner can generate an image that's 2,880 pixels across, it's making an image four times greater than your DV video frame. You can now move that very large image around on the screen and make it seem as if a camera is panning across the image. Or you can scale back the image, and it will look as if the camera is zooming back from a point in the image. Or reverse the process and make it look as if the camera is zooming into the image. We'll discuss these topics in more detail in Lesson 14.

Working with a single-layer file within FCE has one advantage: It's simpler! One of the issues that arises with Photoshop sequences in FCE is the problem of doing transitions between them. If you want to put together a group of still images with transitions between them, you can simplify the process in a couple of ways. When you import the files, make sure you leave enough room in your Still/Freeze Duration preference to accommodate the transitions. Sequentially number the stills you want to import, and place them in a separate folder on your hard drive. Next, import all your stills as a single folder, using **Import> Folder** so they come as a bin. Then drag the bin from the Browser straight to the Edit Overlay, and drop on Overwrite (or Insert) with Transition. All of the stills will miraculously dump out of the bin and appear in the Timeline with a cross-dissolve between them. The technique works beautifully with flattened PSD files or other image formats such as JPEGs.

Fading

Very often you'll want to fade in the graphic and fade it out again. Take another look at the sequence called *Title and Background*:

1. Click on the **Clip Overlay** button (**Option-W**), the button in the far lower left corner on the Timeline window.

The files now have lines in them near the top. This is the opacity value of the clips. With the lines all the way to the top, their values are 100 percent. You'll notice that the line ramps down at the beginning and end of each of the graphics clips in the lesson sequence. This will fade in and fade out the Opacity from 0 to 100 and back again. This works exactly like the control we used for audio levels.

2. Grab the level line, and pull it down to change the overall level.
3. Use the Pen tool (**P**) or the **Option** key as we did with audio to make opacity keyframes on the level line and to pull down the opacity as needed.

The global Levels tool, **Sequence**>**Levels** (**Command-Option-L**), also affects the opacity levels of multiple video or title clips. (We saw this feature in Lesson 10.) Unlike audio keyframes, you can also smooth the opacity keyframes to ease into the fade by right-clicking on the keyframe. In the sequence *Title and Background*, the first clip has had the fade smoothed, whereas the second has not.

Because FCE allows you to place sequences within sequences, such as these nested Photoshop or graphics sequences we've been working with here, it sometimes becomes necessary to create transitions between them. This presents some problems. FCE treats each sequence as a complete piece of media. So, as we've seen, if you have used the media to its limits, you can't create a transition.

Though each layer in a Photoshop sequence can be any length you want, when the sequence is laid into another sequence, the final sequence assumes that the limit of the media is the limit of the nested sequence. It will not go burrowing into the nest to extend the media for each layer to make room for the transition. So if you want to create a transition between sequences, you have to ripple the outgoing sequence and the incoming sequence to allow room for the transition.

SUMMARY

In this lesson we've gone through Boris Calligraphy's Title 3D and Title Crawl and looked at working with still images and Photoshop files. But that isn't all there is to titling. There's also LiveType, which is a truly powerful titling and animation tool. Take some time to try to learn it. We'll look at animation and creating moving images on the screen inside Final Cut Express in the next lesson.

LESSON 13

Animating Images

Final Cut Express has considerable capabilities for animating images. It allows you to enhance your productions and create exciting, interesting, and artistic scenes. In this lesson we concentrate on FCE's motion capabilities.

SETTING UP THE PROJECT

One more time, let's begin by opening up the lesson from your hard drive:

1. Open *Lesson 13*, and if necessary, go through the reconnect process.
2. Open *Sequence 1*, which is empty.
3. We're going to deal with only video tracks for much of this lesson, so the first step, as we did in the previous lesson, is to switch off the destination tracks for A1 and A2. In the patch panel, click on the a1/a2 buttons at the head of each track.
4. Next drag a clip—let's say *Archers 1*—from the *Clips* bin and drop it onto Overwrite or Insert in the Edit Overlay.

Because the audio tracks were untargeted, only the video portion of the clip will appear in the Timeline.

5. Use the **View** pop-up menu at the top of the Canvas to select **Image+Wireframe** (see Figure 13.1). Or use the keyboard shortcut **W** to toggle it on and off.

Select the clip in the Timeline, and the image in the Canvas will appear with a wireframe indicator. The large X through it defines the corners and boundaries (see Figure 13.2).

FIGURE 13.1
Canvas View pop-up menu.

FIGURE 13.2
Image + Wireframe clip
in the Canvas.

FIGURE 13.3
Compositing window arrangement.

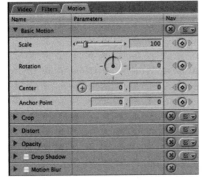

FIGURE 13.4
Motion tab.

220

Let's also set the window arrangement for compositing:

6. Go to the Window and choose **Arrange>Compositing**.

Your window layout should now look something like Figure 13.3.

7. Double-click on the clip in the Timeline to open it in the Viewer, and then click on the Motion tab at the top to open it.

The **Motion** tab (see Figure 13.4), which we've seen briefly before, holds all of the motion parameters that can be animated in FCE. Most of them, with the exception of Opacity, Drop Shadow, and Motion Blur, can be keyframed in the Canvas. Motion Blur cannot be keyframed at all. We saw one way to keyframe Opacity at the end of the last lesson.

Once you start twirling open the little triangles, which the FCE manual calls *disclosure triangles*, you might need to stretch down the window. Notice that each of the sections—Basic Motion, Crop, Distort, Opacity, Drop Shadow, and Motion Blur—has a button with a red X on it. This allows you to reset the values for that parameter.

KEYFRAMING

The basic concept of keyframing is that you mark the properties for a clip at a particular frame. You do this by setting a *keyframe*. If you go further forward or backward in time by moving the playhead and changing the parameter values for the clip, another keyframe will automatically be set. The application calculates how fast it must change the values to go from one state to the other. If the keyframes are far apart in time, the change will be gradual. If the keyframes are closer together, then the change will be more rapid.

It's easy to set a keyframe in FCE. With the clip selected in the Timeline, click the **Keyframe** button (the little diamond at the bottom right of the Canvas), or press the keyboard shortcut **Control-K** (see Figure 13.5).

This sets an initial keyframe for those properties in the Motion tab that are keyframeable. It will not set keyframes for Opacity or Drop Shadow. When a keyframe is set, the wireframe for the clip turns green in the Canvas. The wireframe will also display a number that indicates the track number of the track where the clip is. To delete a keyframe that you've set, go to the keyframe and right-click on the image in the Canvas and select Delete point from the shortcut menu (see Figure 13.6). You can also add keyframes in the Motion tab of the Viewer, so let's look at the parameters in the Motion tab that can be keyframed and what you can do with them.

FIGURE 13.5
Keyframe button.

FIGURE 13.6
Keyframe shortcut menu.

Scale

The first keyframeable property in the Motion window is **Scale**; a simple slider and value box let you set a size. Because FCE deals exclusively in bitmapped images once they're set in the Timeline, stills, video, and text files made up of pixels, it's generally not a good idea to scale upward, not much above 110 to 120 percent.

> **TIP**
> **Finding Keyframes:**
> With snapping turned on and the clip selected in the Timeline, if you drag the Timeline playhead, it will snap to keyframe points on the clip. Also with the clip selected in the Timeline, Shift-K will take you to the next keyframe on the clip, and Option-K will take you to the previous keyframe.

Although the sliders and value boxes in the Motion tab give you precise control, the easiest way to scale or control the other motion parameters is in the Canvas. With the Canvas set to Image+ Wireframe, grab one of the corners and drag. The image will, by default, scale proportionately. If you want the image to be distorted, hold down the Shift key while you drag (see Figure 13.7).

If you hold down the Command key while you drag an image's corner to scale it, you add the Rotation tool so you can scale and rotate at the same time.

FIGURE 13.7
Image scaling distorted.

TIP

Controlling Sliders: Because there is so little travel in the Scale slider's useful range, I use it while holding down the Command key, which gives smaller increments of movement. The Command key works like this in many drag movements in FCE, such as dragging clips to lengthen and shorten them in the Timeline. If you hold down the Shift key, you'll get increments up to two decimal places. Also try using your scroll wheel to move the sliders.

Rotation

Rotation is controlled with the clock dial or with values. There is a limit to how far you can take rotation; no more than 24 rotations are possible. To get there, you can either (1) keep dialing in more turns of the screw or (2) type in a value. Each notch of the "hour" hand is one revolution. It would be nice if separate value boxes for revolutions and degrees had been included, but at the moment, you must either (1) twist the dial around lots of times or (2) calculate, such as 22 revolutions times 360 degrees equals 7,920 degrees.

FIGURE 13.8
Rotation tool.

As with Scale, Rotation can be created in the Canvas. As you move the cursor near one of the edges of the image, it changes into a rotation tool (see Figure 13.8). You can grab the image and swing it around the anchor point, which we'll see in a minute. For the moment, rotation is happening around the middle of the image. It's a little easier to rotate the image if you grab nearer to the corner, but don't get too close or the cursor will change to the Scale point.

Center

Center is the position of the clip, where the image is on the screen. FCE counts the default center position, 0, 0, as the center of the screen and counts outward from there, minus x to the left, plus x to the right, minus y upward, plus y downward. The crosshairs allow you to position an image with a click in the Canvas, just as we did with text.

STRAIGHT MOTION

Let's set up a simple motion for a clip. You should have the clip *Archers 1* at the beginning of an empty sequence and have it loaded in the Viewer open to the Motion tab.

1. If you have done any movement to the clip, reset the parameters by clicking on the red X buttons in the Motion tab.

2. Make sure that the Canvas is in Image+ Wireframe and that the playhead is back at the start of the sequence.

We're now going to move the clip off the screen.

If you need to position an image outside of the Canvas, first reduce the size of the display in the Canvas.

3. Go to the **Zoom** pop-up menu (see Figure 13.9). The easiest way to do this is to set the pop-up menu to **Fit All**, which should reduce the size of the image, revealing some of the grayboard around it. You might want to stretch out the Canvas area a little to give you even more room or reduce it further, maybe down to 25 percent, to see lots of the outside area.

4. Grab the image and move it off the screen (see Figure 13.10). Or click on the Center crosshairs in the Motion tab and then mouse down out in the grayboard and drag to reposition.

5. Make sure the playhead is at the beginning of the Timeline. Press the **Home** key if it isn't.

6. Once the clip is positioned off the screen, use **Control-K** to set a keyframe, or click the **Keyframe** button in the bottom right of the Canvas.

> **TIP**
> **Rotation Tip:** Holding down the Shift key will constrain the dial to 45-degree increments, and holding down the Command key will give you a little finer control over the movement of the dial.

FIGURE 13.9
Zoom pop-up menu.

Notice in the Motion tab that all of the motion properties have keyframes that have become green, and if you look closely in the area to the left of the motion properties called the *keyframe graph*, you can see a keyframe has been added to the graph (see Figure 13.11).

7. To make our animation, go forward five seconds in time. To do this, make sure the clip in the Timeline is deselected (**Command-Shift-A**),

FIGURE 13.10
Moving an image off the screen.

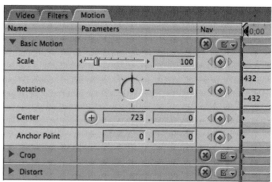

FIGURE 13.11
Keyframes in the Motion tab.

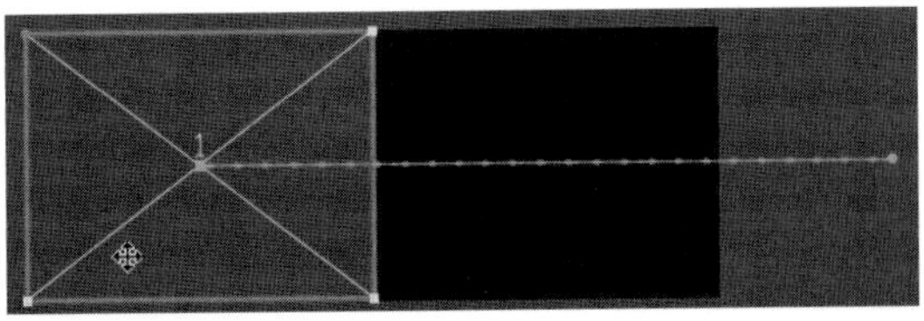

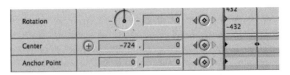

FIGURE 13.12
Linear motion path.

FIGURE 13.13
Center keyframes and keyframe graph.

type 5., and press **Return**. You'll see both playheads in the keyframe graph and in the Timeline move. You can also hold down the **Shift** key and tap on the **Right** arrow key five times to move forward five seconds.

8. Drag the clip across the screen to the other side, creating a line with a string of dots on it.

You have created a straight linear motion of the image across the screen (see Figure 13.12). Notice that while at the first keyframe, the wireframe was green, and at the second keyframe, only the dot in the center of the wireframe is green because only the Center position value has changed. Also notice in the keyframe graph and the Center parameter that a new keyframe has been added (see Figure 13.13) but only for that parameter because the Center position parameter is the only one that has changed. In the Canvas, the center point turns green when the playhead is on the keyframe. It's visible only when the clip is selected. When the clip isn't selected, there is no indicator.

> **TIP**
> **Straight Lines:** If you hold down the Shift key while you drag the image, its movement will be constrained to right angles, either straight horizontally or straight vertically, depending on which direction you drag the clip.

CURVED MOTION

You can create a curved path in two ways: (1) pull out the path from the linear motion, or (2) create a curved path by using Bezier handles. In the first method, when you place the cursor on the line, it changes from the regular Selection tool into the Pen tool. You can drag out the line so that it's a curve (see Figure 13.14). This creates a new keyframe. Notice also the two bars sticking out from the dot on the curve. The bars have two handles each, represented by little dots, one slightly darker than the other. These bars are called Bezier handles. The second method doesn't create an intermediate keyframe. There are normally no handles to adjust the arc on either the start point or the end point of the motion, but you can quickly add these by right-clicking on the point and selecting Linear from the shortcut menu (see Figure 13.15).

FIGURE 13.14
Curved motion path.

FIGURE 13.15
Linear menu.

TIP

Speed of Motion: The spacing of the little dots along the motion path indicates the speed of the motion. If the dots are close together, the motion is slow, whereas if they're more separated from each other, the motion is fast. The dots don't actually represent frames of video. Think of it rather as a graphical representation of a motion vector.

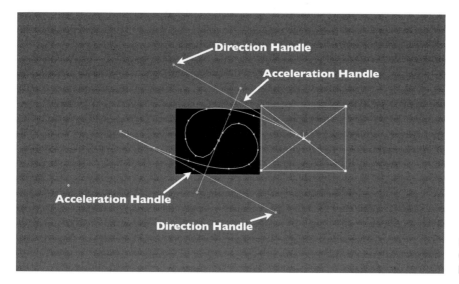

225

FIGURE 13.16
Curved motion with Bezier handles.

When you select either Linear or Ease In/Ease Out, the Bezier handles will appear. These can be used to pull the line into an arc (see Figure 13.16). Pulling the knob on the end of the handle allows you to adjust the arc of the curve. Each side of the arc—at the start, end, and any intermediate points—can be adjusted separately to make complex movements.

Changing Speed

In the real world, objects don't arrive at speed instantly, nor do they stop instantly; they accelerate and decelerate. So if your image is starting or stopping on screen, you probably want it to accelerate or decelerate rather than jerking into motion. In graphics animation this is called *easing*: You ease into a motion, and you ease out of a motion. This easing is controlled by the darker set of points halfway along the Bezier handles (see Figure 13.16). These handles allow you to adjust the acceleration and deceleration of the motion. They control the speed at which the image moves through the keyframe, the rate of deceleration as it approaches the keyframe, and the acceleration as it leaves the keyframe. If you pull the handles apart, the motion will be faster. If you push the handles inward toward the keyframe point, the acceleration will be more gradual. The image will decelerate as it comes to the keyframe and then accelerate away.

If you want the motion to smoothly pass through the point without changing speed, make sure those handles are not moved, or right-click on the keyframe and choose Linear. In the sequence in your Browser called *Curved Motion Path*, I have created a simple motion path that shows this feature. On a slower computer you might have to render this out, depending on your RT settings.

You'll clearly see the deceleration and acceleration as the image passes through the intermediate keyframe. Notice that the image moves much quicker in the first part of the movement and slower in the second portion. This happens because the first portion of the movement is shorter both in time and distance.

TIP
Starting Off-Screen: If your animation starts off the screen, generally you use the Linear selection to create the Bezier handle. This adds the handle but no easing. The assumption is that the object arriving from off-screen is already in motion at full speed and does not accelerate as it enters the frame.

One handy feature of FCE is the ability to move the entire motion path you've created. You can move the whole path as a single entity to whatever position on the screen you want. This can be very useful if you've made a horizontal movement— say, left to right across the screen—that slides a clip through the upper portion of the screen. If later you decide it would be better for it to slide across the lower portion of the screen, rather than resetting

TIP
Adjusting Bezier Handles: If you want to make the curves or the motion even more complex, you can adjust each end of the Bezier handles independently. If you hold down the Command key and grab a handle, it will move separately from the other handle (see Figure 13.17).

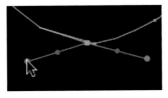

FIGURE 13.17
Separate Bezier control handles.

all the motion path keyframes, simply move the entire path. To do this, make sure the Canvas is in Image+Wireframe mode. Hold down **Command-Shift**, and when the cursor is over the clip, it will change to the Hand tool (see Figure 13.18). Grab the clip and move it. The whole motion path will move as a single group.

FIGURE 13.18
Using the Hand tool to move a motion path.

OTHER MOTION CONTROLS

Anchor Point

The **Anchor Point** is the pivot point around which the image swings. It's also the point around which scaling takes place. For reasons that escape me, Anchor Point, unlike Center, does not have crosshairs for positioning it, but, fortunately, there is a way to move it in the Canvas (see Figure 13.19).

1. Select the Distort tool (keyboard **D** for distort), and grab the center point of the clip. Drag it to where you want to position the anchor point. The point you're moving with this tool is actually the anchor point.

We'll look at the Distort tool soon.

2. Apply a rotation to the image.

FIGURE 13.19
Anchor Point moved with the Distort tool.

Notice that it doesn't swing around the center of the image but rather around this new point. If you pull it out to the upper right corner, that's where the image will pivot. Take a look at *Anchor Point Sequence*. Two images swing through the frame with opposing anchor points.

Notice also that on the second clip, I have animated the center as well as repositioned the anchor point. It moves slightly differently, more tumbling than simply rotating. Be careful with animating multiple parameters; once the anchor point has been moved, it can lead to unexpected results.

TIP
Anchor Point Keyframe:
If the clip is deselected, the anchor point keyframe is not indicated in the Canvas. If the clip is selected, however, the track number will turn green to show that the playhead is over an anchor point keyframe.

Crop

Crop allows you to cut the image from the sides. In addition to the Canvas, this can be done in the Motion tab with the Crop controls hidden under the

227

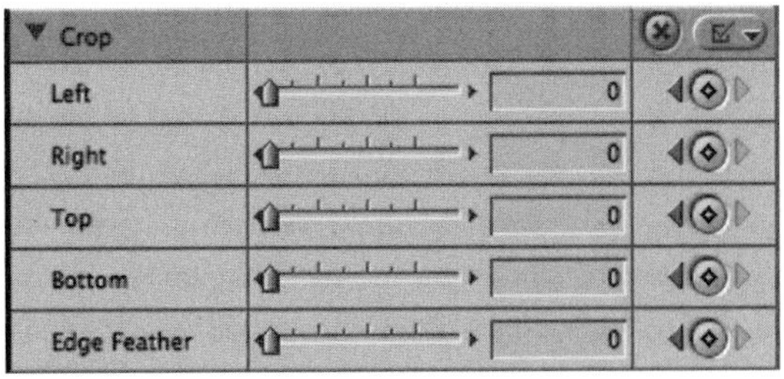

FIGURE 13.20
Crop controls.

FIGURE 13.21
Crop tool.

228

twirly disclosure triangle (see Figure 13.20). Notice that each of the sides in the Crop function can be keyframed separately.

If you have specific values, or if you want to reduce the image by precise amounts, then this is the place to do it. To crop in the Canvas, you'll need to use the Crop tool. The Crop tool is in the tools and can be called up with the letter **C**, just as in Photoshop (see Figure 13.21), and uses the same icon. As with the other motion controls in the Canvas, it will work only while you're in Image+Wireframe.

The Crop tool in FCE doesn't work very much like Photoshop's. You can't simply drag a marquee across the image to define the section you want to keep.

1. Select the image, and with the Crop tool, grab one edge of the image. As the cursor gets near the edge, it changes into the Crop icon, indicating that the cursor is acting in Crop mode.
2. Grab the edge and pull in the image to crop (see Figure 13.22). Or you can grab the corner and crop adjacent sides at the same time.

Notice at the bottom of the Crop control panel in the Motion tab the slider for Edge Feather. This softens the edges of the image and can be very attractive, particularly when there are multiple images on the screen (see Figure 13.23).

FIGURE 13.22
Cropping the image in the Canvas.

FIGURE 13.23
Two clips in the Canvas cropped and feathered.

Distort

The **Distort** tool allows you to squeeze or expand the image, either maintaining its shape or pulling it apart. Be careful, though. Remember that these are pixels you're dealing with, and making pixels bigger can make them blocky and ugly. What's remarkable is how much you can distort the image and still get away with it. As with other tools, there are two or more places to do everything. We already saw one way to distort the image by grabbing a corner with the Selection tool and dragging the image around while holding down the **Shift** key. This distortion alters the aspect ratio of the image but maintains its rectangular shape. This can also be done with the slider at the bottom of the Distort control panel (see Figure 13.24).

Moving the **Aspect Ratio** slider to the left, into negative numbers, will squeeze the image vertically so it mashes down into a narrow slit. Pulling the slider to the right into large positive numbers will squeeze it horizontally so it's a tall, thin image. The slider ranges from −1,000 to 1,000. The image can't be squeezed until it's gone, but it does come close.

TIP
Crop Line: If the clip is selected in the timeline, when the playhead reaches a Crop keyframe, the crop line shows as mauve. If the clip is not selected, no indicator appears in the Canvas.

TIP
Double Crop: If you hold down the Command key while you drag one edge of the image with the Crop tool, the opposite side will be cropped equally. And if you use the Command and Shift key and drag from one of the corners, you can crop all four sides proportionately and simultaneously.

229

You could dial in values into the corner-point boxes, which will move the corner points to any position you want, but the easiest way to use Distort is with the Distort tool, which is underneath Crop in the tools. Select it with the **D** key. The Distort tool lets you grab a corner in the Canvas and pull it around and really mess up the image, if that's what you want (see Figure 13.25).

Distort			
Upper Left	−360	−240	◀◈▷
Upper Right	360	−240	◀◈▷
Lower Right	360	240	◀◈▷
Lower Left	−360	240	◀◈▷
Aspect Ratio		0	◀◈▷

FIGURE 13.24
Distort control panel.

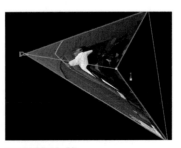

FIGURE 13.25
Distorted image in the Canvas.

TIP

Proportional Distortion: If you use the Distort tool and grab one corner while holding down the Shift key, you will distort the image proportionately. Dragging the upper left corner in, for instance, will make the upper right corner move inward the same amount. It's an easy way to create perspective. It's also an easy way to bend the image inside out so half of it is flipped over on itself.

Anything becomes possible with these kinds of tools. Now that images are digital, they can be twisted and distorted, shaped and sized, and blended any way you can imagine. I hope you see the potential for creating almost any possible transition. I've made a simple one using Distort, Scale, and Center animation. Look at *Transition Sequence*. A few pulls on Distort tool, a little scaling, and the image shoots off. If you apply motion or any other effects to a clip, the whole clip must be rendered out, even if all of the values remain at default for the greater part of its duration. The simplest way to get around this problem is to cut the clip—**Control V** or **Blade**—and separate the normal section from the twisted section. You can see what I did in *Transition Sequence*. Just be careful you don't move elements around so the two parts get detached from each other. Let's look at a few more elements in the Motion panel.

Opacity

The uses for **Opacity** are pretty obvious. The transparency of the image can be decreased from 100 percent opaque to zero opacity. It's a useful way to do simple fades, as we saw in the Timeline with titles in the previous lesson. Whatever is adjusted in the Timeline with the Pen tool will also appear reproduced in the keyframe graph in the Motion tab, or you can keyframe and control the Opacity in the Motion tab.

Drop Shadow

Drop Shadow gives a multilayered image a three-dimensional appearance, and it gives titles and moving images some depth and separation (see Figure 13.26). FCE's Drop Shadow is pretty basic, but it works fine. The control panel has all of the expected features of Offset, Angle of offset, shadow Color, Softness, and Opacity (see Figure 13.27). Note that Drop Shadow must be activated with the little check box in the upper left corner of the control panel.

FIGURE 13.26
Drop Shadows against white matte.

▼ ☑ Drop Shadow		⊗ ☑▾
Offset	2	◁◉▷
Angle	135	◁◉▷
Color		◁◉▷
Softness	10	◁◉▷
Opacity	50	◁◉▷

FIGURE 13.27
Drop Shadow controls.

What might seem puzzling about the **Offset** slider is that it goes into negative numbers. Angle would seem to do the same thing as Offset, but when you animate them, they behave differently. Open *Shadow Sequence* from the Browser and play through the first two shots. In the first shot, Offset is animated, and the shadow slides underneath the image. In the second shot, Angle is animated, and the shadow circles the image.

The **Angle** control lets you change the direction in which the shadow drops onto the underlying layers. **Softness** lets you control the amount of blurring on the edges of the shadow. Though the slider goes up to 100, I'm quite disappointed in how little effect it has. Shadow softness in FCE reaches no more than about 10 percent into the shadow area, so you're forced to rely on Opacity to soften the shadow area, which is not the same look. It lacks the subtlety of other compositing applications.

Look at the third clip in the *Shadow Sequence*. It uses the shadow to help create the illusion of three-dimensionality in two-dimensional space. By hardening the shadow and reducing the offset, while increasing the opacity of shadow as the clip becomes smaller, you can create the impression that the clip is getting closer to the gray background.

The default drop shadow value has changed in this version of FCE and now works well with text. For stills and other large images, you'll probably want to increase the values to around 10 or so. If you're making text with drop shadows, you should probably use the drop shadow functions in Title 3D. They're in real-time, whereas drop shadow in the Motion will most likely have to render for viewing unless you're in Unlimited RT. If you are using this drop shadow with the basic Text tool, you should bring down the Offset value and push up the Opacity value. For thin objects such as text, the first is too high and the second too low.

231

Motion Blur

Motion Blur is also activated with a check box in the upper left of its control panel. This is not a keyframeable property. Figure 13.28 shows FCE's Motion

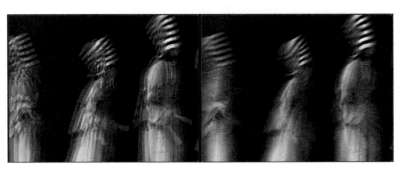

FIGURE 13.28
Motion Blur set to 1,000.

Blur at a setting of 1,000 with 4 samples and with 32 samples. This was created by applying Motion Blur to a panning shot. It gives the clip the appearance of great speed because of the added blur. Sampling goes down to 1, which produces no Motion Blur at all. The stepping that occurs in the lower sampling rates is ugly and best avoided. The low sample settings can be used, though, to produce interesting effects in images that contain fast-moving objects. You will see a ghosting effect as the object moves through the screen.

Use Motion Blur if you're trying to make it look as though your animations are moving very quickly, but be warned that Motion Blur adds considerable time to all renders. It's a very long and slow calculation for each frame. If you are going to apply it, always add it last, just before you're finally going to render out your sequence.

SUMMARY

This lesson gives you an overview of the motion parameters in FCE:

- Scale
- Rotation
- Center
- Anchor Point
- Crop
- Distort
- Opacity
- Drop Shadow
- Motion Blur

In the next lesson, we'll look at some ways to use these animation parameters to create motion effects.

LESSON 14

Animation Effects

Now that you know how FCE's motion parameters work, let's see what you can do with them. We'll go through several exercises to learn different techniques, beginning with motion control, easing and pan and scan issues, creating split screens, picture in picture, and making the motion graphics open for a classic TV show.

233

SETTING UP THE PROJECT

For this lesson we'll use the Lesson 14 project, launch the project, and reconnect the media if necessary. The project contains several sequences, including *Sequence 1*, which is empty and should be open. The Browser also has two master clips, *Archers* and *BB.mov*, as well as two bins, *Clips* and *Graphics*.

Because we're going to be working in the Viewer a good deal, let's change our window arrangement. Use **Windows>Arrange>Compositing**, and adjust the windows to suit yourself and your monitor.

MOTION CONTROL

One question that new users often ask is how to recreate what's called in iMovie "the Ken Burns effect." This name was coined by Apple to describe a technique that antedates Ken Burns's outstanding work by many decades. The technique used by the documentary filmmaker is called motion control and is traditionally done using cameras mounted vertically to shoot down on images as the cameras move across them. These days, motion control is done on special rostrum cameras that are computer controlled and can be programmed to make very complex motions with great precision. Some of this can now be simulated in inexpensive desktop software. Though not as simple as in iMovie, it's relatively easy to do in Final Cut Express. We'll do a slow push into two still images. Let's begin by bringing the two files into the Timeline:

1. Start by dragging *LongShot.jpg* into *Sequence 1* onto V2.
2. Next, Overwrite *Leaves.jpg* from the *Clips* bin into the Timeline after the first still.

The images are both 1,500 × 1,125 pixels in size, much larger than the size of the regular NTSC DV frame, which is 720×480 pixels. Whenever you bring a still image into an FCE sequence, the application will always try to fit the image to the sequence size as best it can. If the image is tall and narrow—a vertical shot—the application will scale it so it fits vertically in the frame. In this case, the images are scaled down to 48 percent to fit into the Canvas.

3. We'll work on *LongShot.jpg* first, so double-click on the image in the Timeline to open it into the Viewer, and look at the Scale value in the Motion tab.

To create the motion control effect, we're going to want to animate this Scale value.

234

4. To do this, make sure the playhead is at the beginning of the clip. Press the **Home** key.
5. Click on the keyframe button in the Motion tab that's opposite the Scale value.

Because I know I'm going to add a Cross Dissolve to this, I don't want the animation to stop at the end of the shot. The end of the shot will be the middle of the transition. The handles to create the overlap will be added to the shot to make the transition, and I want the motion to continue through to the end of overlap needed for the transition. A one-second transition will add 15 frames onto the still image. The still image is five seconds long, so I want to put my end keyframe at 5:15.

6. To go to the end point where we want the animation to end, type **515** and press **Return**, and the playhead in the keyframe graph (and the Timeline) will move to that point, 15 frames past the end of the still (see Figure 14.1).

We now want to change the Scale value of that first shot to do a slow zoom-in. Over the five-second duration of this shot, plus the transition, we'll scale the image by 20 percent.

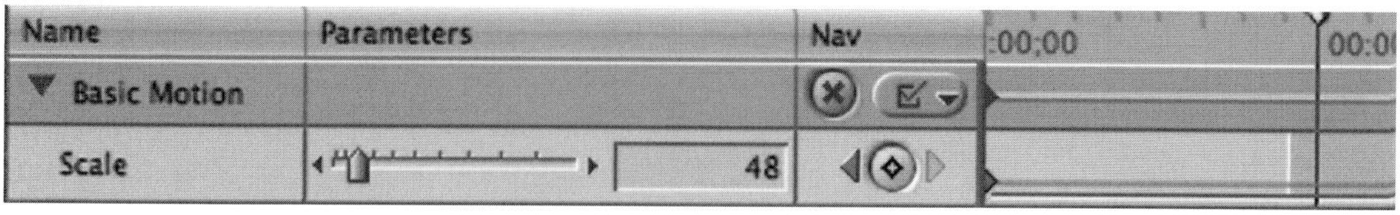

FIGURE 14.1
Playhead in the
keyframe graph.

7. Set the Scale value up to 75 percent.

You don't need to set another keyframe because the value has changed, so FCE will automatically add the keyframe when you change the value. If you play the Timeline, you'll see the slow push-in, which does not end at the end of the shot.

Let's work on the *Leaves.jpg* shot next. We want the motion to begin before the beginning of the clip so when the transition creates the handles it needs, the animation will have already begun.

8. Double-click on *Leaves.jpg* in the Timeline to bring it into the Viewer.

9. The shot begins at 5:00 in the Timeline, and we want the motion to start half a second earlier, so type **415** and, press **Return** to move the play-head before the start of the clip.

10. Click the **Scale** keyframe button to add a Scale keyframe.

11. Go to the end of the clip, using **Shift-O**.

12. Set the Scale value to 75.

13. Play through the Timeline.

To complete the animation, we just need to add the Cross-Dissolve between the two shots.

14. Select the edit point in the Timeline, and press **Command-T** to add the default transition.

That's it! If you step through the transition, you'll see that the animation is continuous, which would not happen if you put the keyframes right at the end of the first shot and the beginning of the second. The motion would stop for one shot in the middle of the transition and start for the other. In the *Motion Control* sequence I've laid out the animation both ways, with these step-by-steps first and then without the motion overlap—a subtle difference but quite noticeable to the viewer.

> **TIP**
> **Transition Glitch:** If you're working in real time, you will probably notice a little glitch in the transition's start and end. This is FCE's Dynamic RT changing resolution on-the-fly to keep real-time playback. To see it play smoothly, render it out using Sequence>Render Only>Preview.

Pan and Scan

Pan and scan is another slang term for motion control on large-size still images. It does raise some issues working in Final Cut, both Express and Pro. I have set up a sequence that illustrates some of the problems. If you open *Pan Sequence*, you'll see that it contains four copies of a still image. It's a PICT file called *Pict*, but it could just as easily be a Photoshop file, PNG, or TIFF.

In Lesson 12, I said you should forget about image resolution as far as video is concerned and think only in numbers of pixels. In the print world for which scanners are designed, resolution is critically important. If you're scanning images such as this one to use in FCE, you can scan it at a high resolution, like 300 or 600 dpi. Ideally, you'd want to calculate the area you're going to zoom into based on an image that's a multiple of 720 pixels across at 72 dpi. Often it's simpler just to scan more than you need and adjust it in Photoshop or even leave it to Final Cut. By scanning at high resolutions, the scanner will generate lots of pixels. FCE will translate this into a very large image, not a small image at high resolution as a print system would do.

In the *Pan Sequence*, I've done motion control on *Pict* four times. Look at them one at a time. On real-time systems, these movements will not need rendering to play back on the computer screen.

In the first image, the image starts out centered in the screen and zooms into a point in the upper right corner of the image. A couple of problems are apparent:

- The image jerks into motion; acceleration is not smooth.
- The zoom-in seems to get slower and slower as it progresses.

The latter one is a difficult problem and pretty much impossible to deal with when using the motion controls in Final Cut. It is totally unnatural and the bane of trying to create motion that looks like a camera moving over an image and zooming as it goes. First, however, let me show you how to add easing:

1. Copy the first *Pict* image inside the *Pan Sequence*. Select it and press **Command-C**.
2. Switch to *Sequence 1* and clear any content in the sequence by deleting it.
3. Paste the image into the empty sequence with *Command-V*.
4. Select the image, and in the Canvas **View** pop-up menu, switch on **Image+Wireframe**.

If you're partway through the motion, you'll see a trail of dots as well as the wireframe indicating the motion path of the center animation. If you set the Canvas in the **Zoom** pop-up to **Fit All**, you'll also see both green start and end center keyframes at the beginning and end of the motion path (see Figure 14.2).

> **5.** To add easing to the movement, right-click on each of the green dots on the ends of the motion path, and from the shortcut menu, choose **Ease In/Ease Out** (see Figure 14.3).

FIGURE 14.2
Image with motion path.

This will add the easing as well as the Bezier handles we saw in the last les-son, which allows us to bend the motion path. If you play this back, you'll immediately see a problem: The image overshoots the motion and then comes back into the screen.

To alleviate this, we'll add easing to the Scale value as well:

FIGURE 14.3
Easing center point.

> **6.** Double-click the *Pict* image in the sequence, and go to the Motion tab in the Viewer.
>
> **7.** To give you more room to work with, pull down the separator bar between the Scale and Rotation value controls, as shown in Figure 14.4. You can do this for any of these areas, but it's most useful for Scale.
>
> **8.** Next, right-click on each of the Scale keyframes, and from the shortcut menu, select Smooth (see Figure 14.5). This is equivalent in the Motion tab of easing for Center animation and will give you a curved value ramp that indicates the acceleration and deceleration of the scaling.

237

This is better, but it's still not right. The animation doesn't shoot as far off the screen, but it still swings off a little. This is because the smoothing rate of Scale and the Ease In/Ease Out rate of center-point animation are different, so the image still shoots off the Canvas and slowly comes back into frame. You can see this in the second animation in the *Pan Sequence*.

The third version of *Pict* in the *Pan Sequence* compromises by limiting how far into the corner the keyframes allow the motion to go. By leaving room

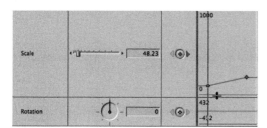

FIGURE 14.4
Separating Scale and Rotation values.

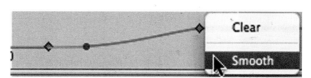

FIGURE 14.5
Smoothing Scale keyframes.

for easing to overrun and swing back, the move is more acceptable. At least it doesn't shoot off the Canvas. Scaling takes place around the anchor point, so if you scale to zoom and pan off to one corner at the same time, the image is moving farther and farther away from the point on which the scale is changing.

In the fourth animation, to correct this issue and the problem of the mis-matched animations, another animation is added—the anchor point—which is not normally animated. Using the Distort tool, I dragged out the anchor point so instead of moving farther and farther off the screen as the image moved, it remained centered in the screen. This produces a different result—not great but acceptable, and still subject to overshoot, especially on very large images.

The bottom line is you have three basic choices:

- Live with the jerky motion and lack of acceleration and deceleration.
- Apply easing to the center keyframes, and leave room for the overshoot on the zoom-in.
- Animate the anchor point as well to try and compensate for the overshoot.

Which option you use probably depends on the situation. Sometimes one might work better than another.

SPLIT SCREEN

A split screen is desirable for many reasons: for showing parallel action, such as two sides of a phone conversation, or showing a wide shot and a close-up in the same screen. It's easy to do if the video was specifically shot for a split screen. For a phone conversation, for instance, it should be shot so one person in the phone conversation is on the left side of the screen and the other person is on the right side.

FIGURE 14.6
Split screen with bar

Look at the *Split Screen Sequence* in your Browser. Don't bother rendering it out; they're just still frames. In the first clip, Rich was shot on the left of the screen and Anita on the right. I had to crop the picture of Anita from one side, and because neither image left enough space for the other person, I had to move Rich farther to the left and Anita farther to the right.

Some people like to add a bar that separates the two images, as in Figure 14.6. That's easy to do. Use the

Generators to create a color matte and place it on the top track, as in *Split Screen Sequence*. Crop the matte left and right so only a narrow stripe is visible over the join of the two frames.

Picture in Picture

By now you've probably figured out how to make a Picture in Picture (PIP). You just scale down the image to the desired size and position it wherever you want on the screen. One note of caution about PIPs: Many video formats, such as material converted from analog media, leave a few lines of black on the edges of the frame, as we saw when doing transitions. These are normally hidden in the overscan area of your television set and are never seen. However, as soon as you start scaling down images and moving them about the screen, the black line becomes apparent. The easiest solution is to take the Crop tool and slightly crop the image before you do your PIP so you don't get the black lines, which give the video an amateur look. You might also want to add a border to the PIP to set it off, but that's for Lesson 15 when we look at beveling borders.

A nice touch to add to PIPs is a drop shadow from the Motion tab. This will help separate it from the underlying image and give the screen a sense of three dimensionality.

BRADY BUNCH OPEN

This is one of the classic show opens on American television. It's relatively easy to reproduce in FCE using the techniques we've learned here. In the Browser is a clip called *BB.mov*. Play through it. This is the sequence we're going to build, which is based on the timing of the original show's open. (If you know the *Brady Bunch* song, feel free to sing along.) In building this sequence, we'll use still images rather than movie clips to conserve storage space.

1. Open the *Brady Bunch Sequence*.
2. You might have to render it out to play it at real speed, but it shouldn't take very long. Or use **Option-P** to play through the sequence as quickly as your computer can.
3. We're going to replicate this sequence. Look through it closely to get an idea of where we're going.
4. Make a copy of the *Brady Bunch Sequence* and open it. This sequence has markers set in where events will occur.
5. Use **Command-A** to select everything in the sequence, and delete it.
6. To begin, you might want to lay *BB.mov* on V1 in your Timeline and lock the track. That way, it can act as a guide.

Sliding White Bar

The first step is to create the white bar that slides across the screen. That's easy enough.

1. From the Generators, make a color matte. In Controls, change the color from the default gray to full white.

2. This bar moves across the screen very quickly, so set the duration to about two seconds. You'll need even less than that, but if you make it too short, it may be difficult to work with in the Timeline.

3. Crop the top and bottom with the Crop tool in the Canvas. In the Crop controls, the Top value is 48.75 and the Bottom value is 47.92, creating a narrow bar. You could bring it into the Timeline first and then bring it back to the Viewer to crop it, but we know we're going to create a thin white line, so we may as well do it before loading it into your work sequence.

4. Drag the bar onto V3 at the head of the Timeline, leaving a video track free below it.

I'm assuming that you've placed *BB.mov* on V1 as a guide and have locked that track.

5. Slide the bar off the screen to the left so you start in black. Open the white bar from the Timeline into the Viewer so you can set its Center coordinates to $x -720$, y 0.

6. Make sure the playhead is at the beginning of the clip, and set a Center point keyframe. This is the value we'll animate to make the motion.

7. Move the playhead to about 22 frames into the sequence.

8. With the Canvas in Image+Wireframe mode, using *BB.mov* as a guide, slide the bar across the screen to its end position, which is when about half the bar is off the screen on the right side. Hold down the **Shift** key as you slide it to constrain the movement to horizontal. Its Center coordinates should now be x 360, y 0.

9. In the Motion tab, add an Opacity keyframe. We are going to do a quick fade-out, so move three or four frames forward in time, and then drag the Opacity slider down or type in a value of 0.

The keyframes you're adding are visible in FCE's keyframe graph.

10. Move the playhead back to where the bar begins to fade out before you bring in the first image.

Fixing the Headshot

1. Open the bin in your Browser called *Graphics*.

It's probably best to leave it open. In the *Graphics* bin are the head-shots of this sequence and the image for the pan and scan sequence we dealt with earlier. These are mostly PICT files and a few titles made with Title 3D. We'll get to those later.

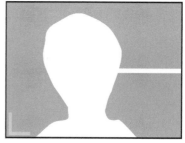

FIGURE 14.7
Headshot and white bar.

2. Drag *HeadshotPink.pct* to V2 to the point where the bar begins fading out (see Figure 14.7).

At this point, the headshot will fill the frame with the white bar over it. We have to scale down and reposition the headshot.

3. Open *HeadshotPink.pct* into the Viewer from the Timeline and pull down the Scale value. I scaled it down to 52.3.

4. In the Canvas, slide the image to the right. For precision, set the Motion tab values to *x* 166, *y* 0.

Next we have to crop the image.

5. Select the Crop tool from the tools (keyboard shortcut **C** for crop). With the Crop tool, pull in the left and right edges a little bit. Crop the top and bottom until the headshot is a narrow slit hidden underneath the bar. Or hold down the **Command** key as you drag with the Crop tool to proportionately crop the image from both top and bottom. The settings used in the sequence are as follows:

Left	6.38	Right	11.28
Top	50	**Bottom**	50

6. In the Viewer, set keyframes for the Top and Bottom Crop values.

7. Go forward about 14 frames into the clip. Type +14 and press the **Return** key.

Be careful you don't do this in the Timeline, because if you don't drop any selected clips, you'll move the clip 14 frames in the Timeline rather than moving the playhead 14 frames.

8. Open up the image by changing the Top and Bottom Crop values back to 0.

FIGURE 14.8
Scaled and positioned headshot.

You've made the first part of the animation: The bar slides across the screen, stops, and fades out, and the headshot wipes open to reveal the picture as in Figure 14.8. Don't worry about the lengths of the clips yet. We'll fix that later.

241

Middle Headshots

Now we're ready to bring in the next set of headshots.

1. Go down to *Marker 1* in the timeline by using **Shift-Down Arrow** to take you to the next marker; **Shift-Up Arrow** takes you to the previous marker.

This is the point where the three headshots of the girls appear on the left.

2. From the *Graphics* bin, drag in the image *HeadshotGreen.pct* and place it on V3, the track above the pink headshot.

3. Again, first we have to scale and position it so that it's in the lower left corner of the screen. The settings I used are as follows:

Scale	29.59
Center	x −231, y 147
Crop Right	3.85

Next we need to fade in the image by ramping up the opacity. This again is a fairly quick fade-in, about 14 frames.

4. Set an Opacity keyframe at the beginning of the clip, and pull the value down to 0.

5. Move forward 14 frames, and bring the Opacity slider back up to 100.

We need two more copies of this image to make up the three headshots on the left of the screen. We'll do this by duplicating the one in the Timeline.

6. Hold down **Option-Shift** and drag *HeadshotGreen.pct* in the Timeline from V3 onto V4 to duplicate it.

7. Repeat the **Option-Shift**-drag from V4 to make another copy on V5.

At this stage, all three copies of *HeadshotGreen.pct* are on top of each other.

8. Select the clip on V4, and in the Canvas drag it upward, holding down the Shift key to constrain direction, and position the image about the center line of the screen.

9. Repeat for the clip on V5, dragging it up vertically to the top third of the screen. I used these Center position settings for the three layers:

V5	x–231, y–148
V4	x–231, y–1
V3	x–231, y 147

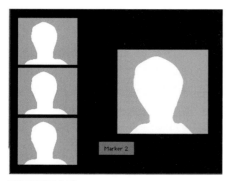

FIGURE 14.9
Four headshots on-screen at *Marker 2.*

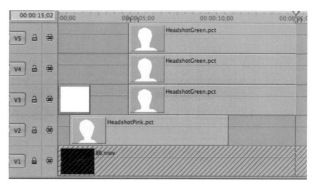

FIGURE 14.10
Timeline at *Marker 3.*

At *Marker 2*, where the fade-ups on the green headshots end, the screen should look like Figure 14.9.

Extending

So far, so good. Next you should extend the image files in the Timeline all the way down to *Marker 3*. You could drag them out to *Marker 3* with the Selector tool (A), or you could do an Extend edit.

1. Position the playhead at *Marker 3*.
2. **Command**-click on the edit points at the end of each clip in the Timeline, the green headshots as well as the pink headshot.
3. Press E to do an Extend edit.

Voila! All of the clips will be extended to *Marker 3*, as shown in Figure 14.10.

At *Marker 3*, all four shots end, and we cut to black—but not for long. Next we have to bring in a new white bar from the right side.

4. Copy the white line from the beginning, and paste it at the next marker on V3.

The line will appear with all of its motion and opacity just like the first time you made it. The only problem is that it's moving in the wrong direction.

You can simply copy and paste a clip on one track to another position on the same track. If you need to copy a clip from one track to another, you have to use the Auto Select buttons. To do this, select the clip you want and copy it. Then switch off all the Auto Select buttons except for the track you want to paste to. The easiest way to do this is to Option-click on the Auto Select button on the track you want to paste to. This switches off Auto Select for all the tracks except the track you Option-clicked on.

The patch panel has several distinct functions. One of them, Destination Track selection, controls how material gets placed into your sequence. Auto Select is similar; it controls how edits—such as an Add edit—are executed, which items are copied, and even where items are pasted. If you copy a clip from the Browser and paste it into a sequence, this is controlled by the Destination Track selection. However, if you copy a clip from inside a sequence, either the one you're working in or another one, and paste the clip or clips into the Timeline, the Destination Tracks do not determine where the pasted material goes. That is set by the Auto Select function.

5. Open the copied clip at *Marker 4* into the Viewer.
6. Holding down the **Shift** key, slide the clip in the Canvas, which should still be in Image+Wireframe mode, across the screen and off the right side. This is the bar's new start position, which should be at x 720, y 0.
7. Go to the point where the fade-out begins, which should be at 16:00.
8. Slide the bar to the left to its end position, mirrored from the first time you did it. The Center position should be x −360, y 0.
9. From the *Graphics* bin, drag *HeadshotBlue.pct* onto V2 in the Timeline, placing it at the point where the bar begins its fade-out.
10. Select the clip *HeadshotPink.pct* that's on V2 and copy it.
11. With *HeadshotBlue.pct* selected in the Timeline, go to the **Edit** menu and choose **Paste Attributes (Option-V)**. This brings up the dialog box in Figure 14.11.
12. Select **Basic Motion** and **Crop** from the dialog box. Because we've lengthened *HeadshotPink.pct*, make sure the check box at the top of the window for **Scale Attribute Times** is deselected. The default is for the box to be checked.

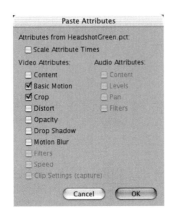

FIGURE 14.11
Paste attributes.

This duplicates the position and animation of the earlier shot. This ability to copy the attributes of a clip and paste these attributes to one or more clips—pasting the copied clip's motion, filter, and audio settings—is a very powerful tool in Final Cut Express.

Now we have to reposition the blue headshot clip to the left side of the screen.

13. Holding down the **Shift** key, slide the image in the Canvas to the left so it's underneath the white bar with a Center value of x −174, y 0.

Adding More Headshots

1. Right-click in the Timeline Ruler, and from the shortcut menu, select *Marker 6* to jump down to that point.

2. Bring in the clip *HeadshotRed.pct* from the *Graphics* bin and place it on V3.

3. Copy the green headshot that's earlier on V3.

4. Select the new red headshot, and again use **Paste Attributes (Option-V)**. Apply **Basic Motion, Crop,** and **Opacity** with **Scale Attribute Times** deselected, as previously.

5. Now reposition its center so it's on the opposite side of the screen with a Center value of *x* 232, *y* 147.

6. Again, Option-Shift-drag the copies of the clip from V3 to V4 and V5.

7. Holding down the **Shift** key to constrain movement, reposition the clips so they appear one above the other on the right side of the screen. The Center values I used for these three shots are as follows:

V5	x 232, y −148
V4	x 232, y −1
V3	x 232, y 147

8. Again, extend the green headshots and the blue headshot all the way down to *Marker 7*.

The screen cuts to black as before.

245

New Headshots

1. Go down to *Marker 8*, and bring in the clip called *Head Pink Small.pct* and place it on V2.

Though the image is the right size for the start of this section, the application will want to scale it for some reason. It's also in the wrong place.

2. First, open the clip into the Viewer and reset the Scale value to 100.

3. In the Canvas, drag it straight up to the top of the frame so the top edge of the image is at the top edge of the screen. My setting for the Center was *y* −129.

4. Go to *Marker 9*, and in the Viewer set a keyframe for the Crop Bottom value.

It's often easier to work backward in animation: to start with the end position on the screen and then animate the wipe on.

5. Now go back to *Marker 8*, and push the Crop Bottom value up to 100.

That's your start keyframe position to give you a quick wipe-on of the picture.

Marker 10 is where the next image comes in.

6. At *Marker 10*, place *Head Blue Small.pct* on V3.

7. Reset the Scale value for the new clip back to 100, and reposition to the bottom center of the screen. My Center value was *y* 125.

8. Go to *Marker 11* to set a Crop Top keyframe.

9. Go back to *Marker 10*, and again push the crop value up to 100.

At *Marker 11*, both pictures should now be on the screen as shown in Figure 14.12. We're ready now to bring in the rest of the headshots.

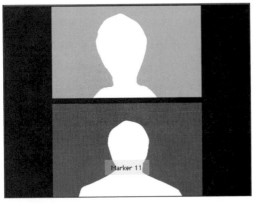

Final Headshots

At *Marker 12*, we'll first have to place keyframes on both the pink and blue headshots. Both images need to scale down slightly and have the left and right sides cropped so the images fit into their final position.

1. With the playhead at *Marker 12*, select both headshots and click on the **Keyframe** button in the Canvas to set a keyframe for the two headshots. This is the simplest way to add a bunch of global motion keyframes for clips.

FIGURE 14.12
Two headshots on-screen at *Marker 11*.

2. Change the scale of the Timeline window so you can see most of the Timeline. The simple way is to use **Shift-Z** for **Fit to Window**.

3. Position the playhead at *Marker 13* to place the next headshots. **Shift**-select the three green headshots from near the beginning of the sequence and copy them.

4. **Option**-click on the **Auto Select** button for V4 to make sure it is the only one selected.

5. Paste the clips into the Timeline. It doesn't matter if the other tracks aren't selected.

The clips will stack on top of each other based on the lowest autoselected track—V4 in this case. The three duplicate green headshots should be on V4, V5, and V6, leaving V2 and V3 for the pink and blue headshots. Next, do the same for the red headshots in the Timeline.

6. Select the red headshots and copy them.

7. Move the playhead back to *Marker 13*, and **Option**-click autoselect for V7.

8. Paste the clips into the Timeline.

Between *Marker 12* and *Marker 14*, where the green and red headshots reach full opacity, the pink and blue headshots scale, crop, and slightly reposition to their final locations.

9. For the pink headshot, set the following values at *Marker 14*:

Scale	58.08
Center	x 0, y−148
Crop Left	2.83
Crop Right	5.23

10. For the blue headshot, my values at *Marker 14* are as follows:

Scale	66.5
Center	x 0, y 139
Crop Left	8.23
Crop Right	11.16
Crop Top	11.22

247

When you've positioned the clips about the screen, you should end up with the Canvas that looks like Figure 14.13.

One more step still must be taken before we put in the titles: extend the headshots down to the end of the sequence.

11. Right-click, and using the shortcut menu, move the playhead all the way down to *Marker 24*.

12. Then **Command**-click on the edits at the ends of all the headshots: pink, blue, the three greens, and the three reds.

13. Now do an Extend edit to stretch them out to the playhead.

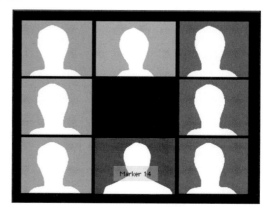

FIGURE 14.13
Eight headshots on-screen at *Marker 14*.

Titles

We're finished with almost all of the headshots. Next we have to get the titles on the screen. I've prebuilt them for you using Title 3D. They are made with the Marker Felt font, which is the closest in the current Apple font collection to the original title style.

1. Lay the first title, *Main Title* in the *Graphics* bin, at *Marker 15* on track V10.

You'll see that it's at its full size and the right duration for the open, but we'll do a small scaling animation.

2. Go to *Marker 16*, open the title from the Timeline, and in the Motion tab set a Scale keyframe. This will be the end point of the main title animation.
3. Go back to *Marker 15*, and set the **Scale** value down to 47.83.
4. Go down to *Marker 17*, and with the **Blade** tool (**B**), cut the title and throw away the rest of it.

At *Marker 18*, the next title, *Starring Title*, appears.

5. Drop *Starring Title* onto the same track as the main title.
6. Cut this title off at *Marker 19*.
7. At *Marker 20*, bring in *Mom Title*. Because it overlaps with the final head-shot we're going to bring in, it must be placed on a higher track, V11.
8. At *Marker 21*, set an Opacity keyframe on *Mom Title*.
9. At the frame before *Marker 22*, set the Opacity down to zero. This will fade it out quickly.
10. Cut *Mom Title* with the Blade tool at *Marker 22*.

Final Polishing

We're in the home stretch now; just a few more steps! At *Marker 21*, while *Mom Title* is fading out, one more headshot is fading in.

1. At *Marker 21*, drag one more copy of the green headshot onto **V10** underneath *Mom Title*.
2. The final green headshot must be positioned, scaled, and cropped left, top, and bottom to fit the center square in the screen. I used the following values:

Scale	33
Center	x −5, y 0
Crop Left	1.6
Crop Top	5.12
Crop Bottom	6.11

3. Set an Opacity keyframe for the green headshot at *Marker 21*, and set the value to 0.

4. Ramp up the Opacity to 100 at *Marker 22*.

5. At *Marker 22*, the last title, *Alice Title*, just cuts in. Place it on V11.

6. Cut off both *Alice Title* and the center headshot at *Marker 24*.

Fade to Black

The last step we want to do is to fade to black. We could keyframe and ramp down the opacity on each of ten layers now on the screen, but there's an easier way:

1. Make a short slug—three seconds will do—and place it on the topmost video track at *Marker 23*.

2. Set its Opacity down to zero, and add a keyframe to the slug in the Motion tab.

3. At *Marker 24*, set the slug's Opacity up to 100 percent so black fills the screen.

Congratulations! You've made the Brady Bunch open.

SUMMARY

In this lesson we looked at Final Cut's animation capabilities. You can use these tools to composite images one on top of another, using FCE's multilayer capabilities. We'll look at more compositing techniques in a later lesson, but first let's see how to use Final Cut's filters.

LESSON 15
Adding Special Effects Filters

In this lesson we look at and work with Final Cut's filters to create some special effects. FCE offers a great variety of excellent effects, including many new ones using Apple's FxPlug architecture. You should be aware that these new filters rely on the graphics card for processing. What this means is that on slower computers, you won't get very good performance with them and that on some marginal computers, they won't work at all.

Unlike transitions that go between clips, filters are applied to single clips or parts of clips. In addition to the filters included with the application, other programmers are creating effects using Final Cut's scripting software, both the original FXScript and the new FxPlug.

In the *Extras* folder of the DVD is a folder with demo versions of the filters from Klaus Eiperle's *CGM DVE Complete* package. Check out the HTML files and the demo movies that explain them. To add new filters to FCE, place them in the *Plugins* folder while the application is closed. Drag the plug-ins into *Library/ Application Support/Final Cut Express Support/Plugins*.

SETTING UP THE PROJECT

As before, begin by loading the material you need onto your media drive and reconnect the media if necessary. For this lesson we'll use the materials in the *Lesson 15* project. Inside your project, you'll find in the Browser the *Clips* bin, a *Video Filters* bin, a master clip called *Dance.mov*, and other sequences. One of the sequences is called *Effects Builder*, which demonstrates some of the filters

251

we'll see in this lesson. As we go through the lesson, I'll show you how the effects in this sequence were made.

The *Video Filters* bin contains 16 sequences, one for each category of filter in FCE. In each sequence is a two-second portion of *Dance1*, with each of its filters applied with its default settings. Two filters are not included—the two Color Smoothing filters—which we'll see in the next lesson. These have no adjustable controls anyway. For quite a few filters, such as the color correction filters, the default settings do nothing, but having them laid out like this lets you easily look at any filter and twiddle its knobs to see what it does.

You probably thought there were an awful lot of transitions. Well, there are even more filters—160 of them, in fact—almost twice as many as in the previous versions of FCE. Some of the filters aren't very useful, and there is quite a bit of redundancy, but a lot of them let you do some pretty amazing things with video. Because of this redundancy in the filters—different filters that do basically the same things—I'll only go through some of the important ones. In this lesson we'll look at some of the useful FCE filters, but in the next lesson, we'll examine some of the most important ones: Color Correction, Key, and Matte filters.

EFFECT AVAILABILITY

If you're observant, you may have noticed that I said there are 160 filters, but by default only 138 of them are visible. That's because you can view your filters three separate ways, which can be selected from the bottom of the **Effects** menu (see Figure 15.1) or by right-clicking in the Effects window of the Browser and selecting what filters to display. You can choose **Only Recommended Filters**, which is the default and displays 138 effects; **Only My Preferred Effects**, which displays only selected items; and **All Effects**. I suggest that you spend a little time and look through the filters, not only the recommended filters. This selection removes some of the filters that are duplicated between the FXScript filters and the FxPlug filters. Even if they have the same names, the filters often are not the same. For instance, if you select **All Filters**, you'll see in the Blur section two **Gaussian**

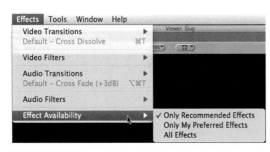

FIGURE 15.1
Effects>Effect
availability.

Blur filters. If you select **Only Recommended Filters**, you'll only get the FXScript filter. The two filters have different features, and you may want to have both available. This is where **Preferred Filters** comes in.

If you set your filters to **All Filters** and go to the Effects window of the Browser and double-click on the two Gaussian Blurs in turn, you'll see the differences.

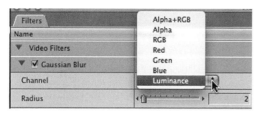

FIGURE 15.2
FXScript Gaussian Blur.

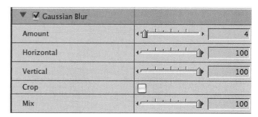

FIGURE 15.3
FxPlug Gaussian Blur.

The FXScript Gaussian Blur (see Figure 15.2) lets you blur individual Red, Green, and Blue channels, or the Luminance value as well as the whole image. The FxPlug Gaussian Blur (see Figure 15.3), on the other hand, lets you blur the whole image or blur it horizontally or vertically. Notice the Mix slider in the FxPlug filter, which is a feature of every FxPlug filter. It allows you to mix the original clip in with the filtered effect. For some filters it's pretty useless, but for others it's a great little feature that can enhance your work.

So how do you tell which is an FXScript filter and which is an FxPlug filter? It's very simple. In the Effects window there is a Browser column that displays in list view which ones are FxPlug filters (see Figure 15.4). If the filter has no name in the Effect Class column, it's an FXScript filter.

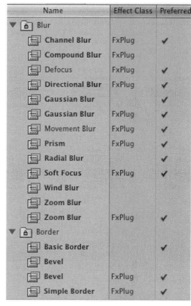

FIGURE 15.4
Effect Class and Preferred columns.

In Figure 15.4 you can also see the Preferred column, which lets you check which filters you want to display. This lets you go through he filters and select what appears both here in the Effects window and in the Effects menu. When you switch to Preferred filters, you will see only the checked items. I have only checked items in the Blur and Border sections, so when I switch to Preferred filters, that's all that will appear in the menus, as shown in Figure 15.5. Be warned that the Preferred selection applies to ALL effects—that's all the transitions and filters for both video and audio and all the Generators. So make sure you check those on as well. The filters aren't lost, of course, and any applied filters still work and can be controlled even when the filters are hidden.

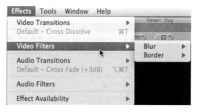

FIGURE 15.5
Preferred effects.

Selecting Preferred is a good way to hide a lot of extraneous material, such as many of the QuickTime filters or many transitions that you don't want. Also, it's a way to switch off third-party filters when you don't need them and want to keep them hidden so your Effects menu doesn't run off the bottom of your computer screen. Many third-party effects are available, and some people have a lot of them.

APPLYING A FILTER

Applying an effect in Final Cut Express is very easy:

1. Select the clip in the Timeline or in the Browser, and from the menu bar select **Effects>Video Filters**.
2. Pick a submenu and pick an effect.

If they're applied in the Browser, then every time that clip is used, the filter will go with it. If the effect is applied in the Timeline, it's applied only to that one copy of the clip. It is immediately applied with its default settings to the clip. If you prefer, you can drag the effect from the *Video Filters* bin inside the Effects panel of the Browser.

It's just as easy to remove an effect. Open the clip into the Viewer, go to the Filters tab, select the effect by clicking on its name, and press the **Delete** key. You can also select a clip(s) in the Timeline, and from the **Edit** menu choose **Remove Attributes** (keyboard shortcut: **Command-Option-V**). Make sure the Filters box is checked in the Remove Attributes dialog box (see Figure 15.6), and the filter or multiple filters will all be removed. Notice that other clip attributes can also be removed or reset with this function.

FIGURE 15.6
Remove Attributes.

Any number of filters can be added to a clip. The order in which the filters are applied can be important. The filter order can be changed by dragging the filters up and down to new positions in the order. Filters can also be turned on and off with a little check box. This allows you to leave a filter in place while you toggle its effect on and off to see what it's doing to the picture.

Filters can also be copied and pasted. If you select a clip that has a filter applied, you can copy the clip and use Paste Attributes (**Option-V**) to paste that filter or filters and their settings to any number of other clips simultaneously.

Filter values can be animated just like motion parameters by adding keyframes so they can be altered over time. Look at the clip at *Marker 1* in the sequence *Effects Builder*. The middle portion of the clip, *Dance 2*, has the effect applied to it, so the whole clip does not need to be rendered (see the *Selective Filtering* tip). Partway through the clip, the Gaussian Blur filter comes in and ramps up from 0 to 30, holds, and then ramps back down to 0.

Let's begin looking at the filters by opening the empty *Sequence 1* and dragging one of the clips from the *Clips* bin into it. We'll start with *Dance 1*. We'll apply some filters to this clip to see how they work.

NOTE

Favorites are a great way to save effects because you can both save them as their default settings and as an effects pack—several effects that work together to produce a result. It's simple to do. Apply the effects and adjust them as you want them, and then with the Filters tab of the Viewer open, drag them to the Favorites bin, where you can rename them (see Figure 15.7). Notice that I created a bin within the Favorites bin, in which I put the filters, and that the stack order in which the filters were created is maintained in the bin by numbering them.

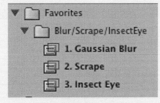

FIGURE 15.7
Filter pack in Favorites bin.

The Favorites bin sounds great, but it has one serious downside, which is that Favorites are part of the application's preferences. So if you have to trash your prefs file, your favorites are going to go with it. See "Saving Favorites" in Lesson 8 for one good solution to this problem.

SOME USEFUL FILTERS

Blur

Who knew there were so many ways to blur an image? There are 13 of them, and most of them are FxPlug filters. The most commonly used is the **Gaussian** (pronounced *gousian*) **blur**, named after the nineteenth-century German mathematician Karl Friedrich Gauss, which in its default settings produces a smooth blurring of the image. As we already saw, it also allows you to blur channels separately through a pop-up menu. Selecting different channels can produce some interesting and unusual effects. Try applying the filter. With the clip in the Timeline selected, choose **Gaussian Blur** from the **Effects>Video Filters> Blur** menu. If you want to blur a couple of channels, apply the effect twice.

Some of the other Blur filters, like **Channel Blur**, are also very useful. This filter lets you blur specific RGB channels and also lets you blur them or the image vertically and/or horizontally or a mix of the two (see Figure 15.8). **Compound**

▼ ✓ Channel Blur	
Amount	4
Blur Red	✓
Blur Green	✓
Blur Blue	✓
Blur Alpha	✓
Horizontal	100
Vertical	100
Crop	☐
Mix	100

FIGURE 15.8
Channel Blur controls.

Blur lets you blur with an image-specific area of the image, using a well like the Page Peel transition. **Movement Blur** gives you an excellent motion blur for your clips. It's especially useful for slow-motion clips to smooth out the motion. It's better than the internal Motion Blur setting in the Motion tab of the Viewer. **Prism** provides an interesting effect with color edges to the content of your clip. It's more a special effect than a practical filter. **Soft Focus** will give you a softening of the image blended with the sharp image for an interesting effect. **Wind Blur** shouldn't be used at all; use the direction controls of the FxPlug blurs instead. If you use the excellent FxPlug **Zoom Blur**, make sure you activate the Crop function if you turn up the Amount.

TIP

Selective Filtering: You can add a filter to only a section of the length of a clip, which can be useful if you want to ramp up an effect while most of the length of the shot remains unchanged. To avoid having to render out the entire shot, you can apply the filter by selecting a section of the clip you want to effect with the Range Selection tool (GGG). To make the selection, stroke along the clip, the group of clips, or the sections of the Timeline where you want to apply the filter. Choose the filter from the Effects menu, and you'll immediately see that only that portion of the Timeline picked with Range Selection will change the render color. You can also do this by marking In and Out points in the Timeline.

FIGURE 15.9
Bevel Border with a width of 15.

Border

Bevel Border is a nice touch to Picture-in-Picture effects (PIPs) and can be used to mask those nasty black edges we talked about in the previous lesson. Bevel creates a nice edge for scaled images (see Figure 15.9).

In the filter controls, the color picker is called Light Color, like the color of the gel a lighting director might put over a light that's falling across the beveled edges. You can also set the angle from which the light is falling.

At *Marker 2* in the *Effects Builder* sequence, I have a short animation in which one image sucks back into a PIP, and as it does so, the Bevel Border appears around it. The image then pulls out to fill the screen again, and the border closes down.

Channel

The Channel filters allow you an amazing degree of control over color and compositing. We'll look more closely at compositing in Lesson 17, but here the channel effects allow you to combine clips and apply color effects to them combined with compositing modes.

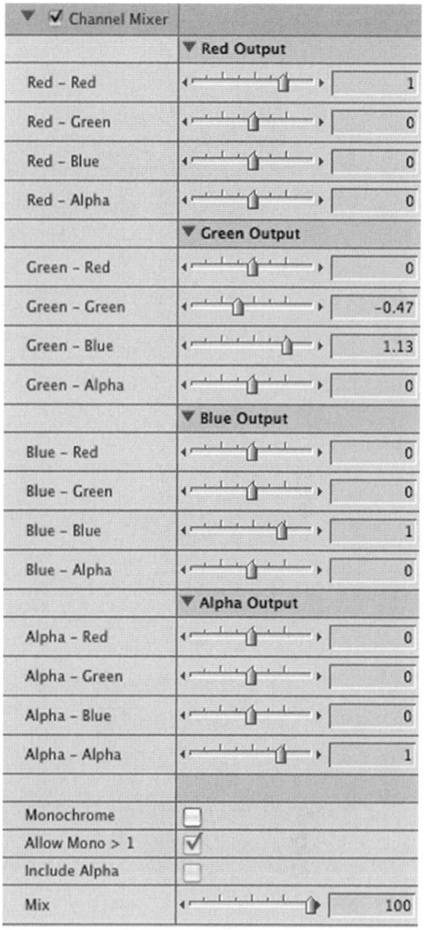

Channel Mixer gives you a huge amount of controls (see Figure 15.10) to blend the separate RGB channels and swap them around. It's really great for making monochrome images. Note the check box in the controls. Usually one channel will produce the best-looking black-and-white image. When Monochrome is checked, only the Red channel controls are active, and only one channel be controlled: red, green, or blue; the other channels will respond to it. **Channel Swap** lets you replace different channels with other channels or with the inverse of the channels. **Channel Offset** is a cool filter, although you can easily take it to great extremes where strange effects will happen, especially if you use the **Repeat Edges** pop-up menu. The clip at *Marker 3* in the *Effects Builder* sequence shows you Channel Offset as applied in Figure 15.11. **Compound Arithmetic**, like Compound Blur, is based on an image placed in the Well. The **Operator** pop-up menu produces little effect. It does not change by compositing with the layer below, only with itself. If an image is in the Well, the operator will apply to the image. Try it with text such as that on the clip at *Marker 4* in the *Effects Builder* sequence.

▼ ✓ Channel Mixer	
▼ **Red Output**	
Red – Red	1
Red – Green	0
Red – Blue	0
Red – Alpha	0
▼ **Green Output**	
Green – Red	0
Green – Green	-0.47
Green – Blue	1.13
Green – Alpha	0
▼ **Blue Output**	
Blue – Red	0
Blue – Green	0
Blue – Blue	1
Blue – Alpha	0
▼ **Alpha Output**	
Alpha – Red	0
Alpha – Green	0
Alpha – Blue	0
Alpha – Alpha	1
Monochrome	☐
Allow Mono > 1	✓
Include Alpha	☐
Mix	100

FIGURE 15.10
Channel Mixer controls.

257

Distort

We'll skip the Color Correction, Keying, and Matte filter groups for the moment and devote the next lesson to them in detail. The **Distort** group has some interesting new FxPlug filters like **Earthquake**, which I've put in the *Effects Builder* sequence at *Marker 5*. You really have to see it in motion to understand what it's doing. **Insect Eye** is another cool filter with nice controls. It refracts the image with a crystalline overlay (see Figure 15.12). The others are fun and can be used for strange effects to make the image ripple and wave and bulge with a fisheye, and, remember, they can all be animated.

FIGURE 15.11
Channel Offset three
times with large offset
and repeat 8.

FIGURE 15.12
Insect Eye.

FIGURE 15.13
Dazzle.

Glow

The entire group of **Glow** filters are new FCE4. They produce some excellent effects that can add pizzazz to a program, especially filters like **Dazzle** (see Figure 15.13) and **Overdrive**, though you might have to tone down some of the default values if the image is bright. **Light Rays** is an exciting addition to the collection. Let's build a little Light Rays animation.

1. Begin by opening *Dance1* from the *Clips* bin and making its duration five seconds.
2. Switch off the audio by decoupling A1 and A2, and Overwrite the clip into *Sequence 1*.
3. Next, use the basic Text tool to make the word JAPAN in big, bold letters. I used Gill Sans set to Bold and a point size of 148. Leave the other settings.
4. Make sure the playhead is over the video in the Timeline, and use the Superimpose function to edit the text on top of it.
5. Use the Superimpose edit again to put a second copy of the text into the Timeline above the video.
6. Open the text on V3, and change the color to something nice, perhaps a bright red that matches the red on the dancers' hats.
7. To the text on V2, apply the Light Rays filter. Open the Filter tab controls in the Viewer, and go to the beginning of the clip.
8. Set keyframes with the diamond keyframe button for both **Amount** and **Center**.
9. Click on the Center crosshair button, and then click in the Canvas on the far right of the frame so the light rays are all shooting off to the left.
10. Set the Amount value down to zero.
11. Go forward to the 1:00 second mark, and set the Amount value up to 200.

12. Next, go to the 4:00 second mark, and add another Amount keyframe. This will hold the light rays value to 200 between 1:00 and 4:00.

13. Use **Shift-O** to go to the last frame of the clip, and set the Amount value back to zero.

14. Finally, click on the Center crosshairs button, and in the Canvas click on the far left of the screen so the light rays are pointing off toward the right side of the screen.

Watch the light rays sweeping across the screen behind the text. I've built the effect for you in the *Effects Builder* sequence at *Marker 6*.

Perspective

This group includes the **Basic 3D** filter, and basic it is. However, it does the job and can be used effectively for making customized effects such as bow ties and for animating effects. The controls for the *x, y, z* axes are self-explanatory (see Figure 15.14). Notice the Center and Scale controls. Set these functions here and not in the Motion window. If you scale or reposition in Motion, the 3D will be cut off by the bounding box, as in Figure 15.15.

A *bow tie* is a broadcasting term for two images on the screen at the same time, often tilted toward each other to create the illusion of perspective (see Figure 15.16). Take a look at the stack at *Marker 7* in *Effects Builder*. That's a bow tie, most commonly used in two ways (interviews from a remote site).

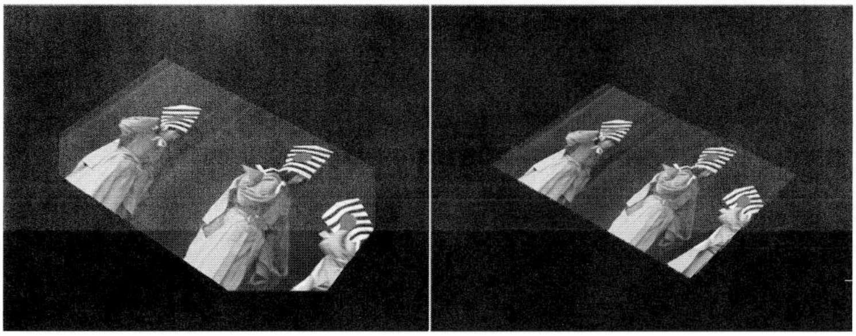

FIGURE 15.14
3D controls.

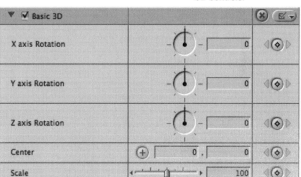

FIGURE 15.15
3D Scaled in Motion tab and scaled in 3D controls.

FIGURE 15.16
Bow tie.

Both clips are tilted backward on the *y* axis, one by 45 degrees and the other by −45 degrees. The center points are shifted to move the images left and right, and both are scaled down to 60 to fit the screen. You can add all sorts of graphical embellishments such as borders, bars, and logos across the bottom and top.

The **Flop** filter can be a real lifesaver. If you have ever shot something in which someone is looking right to left when they should be looking left to right, Flop can fix that. It reverses the direction of the image. Just be careful and watch out for words that might appear backward, or hair parting that swings from side to side, and similar telltales that would give you away. The only control is a single pop-up menu, which lets you flop the default Horizontal and also allows you to reverse the image vertically or both horizontally and vertically at the same time.

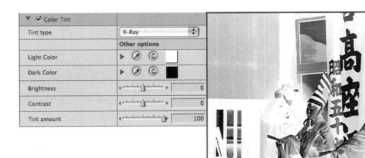

FIGURE 15.17
Color Tint controls with x-ray image.

The new **Curl** filter is also very neat. It acts like a page peel, but it lets you hold the curl, so it can start, hold for a while, and then go back or continue. I've used it in the past for chapter headings as at *Marker 8* in the *Effects Builder* sequence.

QuickTime

Most of the QuickTime filters don't have much value or are redundant in FCE. But one useful filter is **Color Tint**, which has a feature that is difficult to duplicate with any other tools. It allows you to create an x-ray negative effect (see Figure 15.17). One downside of the QuickTime filters is that when you're using the Safe RT setting, none of the filters give you real-time playback and always have to be rendered. Or you can switch to Unlimited RT.

Stylize

The **Stylize** section has a whole slew of interesting new FxPlug filters, including **Add Noise** and **Bad TV**. The first lets you add an overlay of noise or grain to the image, which can help to give it a film look. This used to be a complicated procedure with composite modes, but it is much easier with this filter. The **Circles** or **Crystallize** filters can be used for a mosaic effect to disguise someone's face. **Diffuse** can also be used for this, but it adds a lot of pixelization to the image and may be hard to compress.

Extrude allows you to create a three-dimensional look to images, like text, that have transparency. The extrusion makes the text look like a block of letters (see Figure 15.18) and can make the text stand out. It has a lot of controls for tweaking the look, but be careful with animating the Distance value because it can make the text appear to wobble a bit.

FIGURE 15.18
Extrude with controls.

Find Edges (Figure 15.19) and **Line Art** (Figure 15.20) are neat filters that give you a nice, stylized look. Try Find Edges with the Invert check box turned on, which puts a hard, black outline on the edges. Both have their uses and can work well. They can be used to create interesting effects, especially when composited over other images or blended with themselves.

The new FxPlug **Posterize** is easier to use and works better than the original. Remember that smaller levels of posterization have more effect, and increasing the value reduces the effect. The original Posterize filter does let you Posterize different RGB color channels separately.

Replicate is a cool filter. The default output produces only four images on the screen, but if you push the sliders, you can get 16 horizontal and 16 vertical.

FIGURE 15.19
Find Edges.

FIGURE 15.20
Line Art.

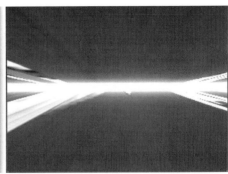

262

FIGURE 15.21
Slit Scan and controls.

That's 256 very small images on the screen. It's a nice effect when it steps back 2, 4, 8, and 16. You can easily create an interesting transition by animating the replicate values. Look at the two clips in *Effects Builder* at *Marker 9*.

Try **Slit Scan** to create that *2001: A Space Odyssey* look of rushing through time and space (see Figure 15.21). It has some really nice controls that can be animated to enhance the effect. **Slit Tunnel** is similar, except it's a circular, spinning vortex, a bit like the *Dr. Who* time-travel effect.

The new **Vignette** filter can be very useful. Using vignetting to emphasize the center of the screen or to frame the scene has become very popular, and you can see subtle uses of it in many shots. This filter gives you nice control over the edges of the image, allowing you to blur and darken the edges of the frame to suit your taste and the material.

Tiling

Tiling is a whole new category of four filters and includes **Kaleidoscope** and **Kaleidotile**, which can be animated to produce kaleidoscopic effects. They work especially well on images with motion in them as they rely on movement in the frame to create movement in the effect. With a still image, the kaleido effect will simply be stuck on the image unless you animate the properties.

Time

Time is also a new category with five filters that affect the playback of frames in a clip. Echo duplicates and delays frames to create ghosting. **Scrub** lets you move back and forth in time but you have to animate the Frame offset value so it can be difficult to use. The **Strobe** effect gives you the look of dropped frames, as if the video is skipping in playback. **Trails** and **Wide Time** are subtler forms of the Echo filter; the first emphasizes edges in the image, while the second repeats the edges but blurs them for a softer look. They're similar but produce slightly different results for different looks. I've laid the three of them, Echo, Trails, and Wide time, out back-to-back at *Marker 10* in the *Effects Builder* sequence. You should render them out first to see the proper time-displacement effect.

FIGURE 15.22
De-interlaced still frame.

Video

This last group of filters has nothing new in it, but **De-interlace** and **Flicker** are two of the most frequently used filters in FCE, if for no other reason than to remove video interlacing when making freeze frames. If you place a freeze frame of a clip with a lot of motion in it, the freeze will twitch horribly as the interlacing switches between the lines. The way around this problem is to apply the De-interlace filter to the freeze frame. The de-interlaced freeze frame will play back smoothly when edited into video. The filter has only a single control: a pop-up menu that lets you select a field. Choose whichever looks better. You can also use the Flicker filter to do this, which gives you three separate settings, letting you choose how much flicker removal to apply if there is only a minimal amount of jittering in the freeze frame. Flicker is also used to overcome that horrible shimmering effect you get when thin, horizontal lines are on the screen, such as serif fonts, thin lines of newsprint on the screen, stripes in a shirt, Venetian blinds in the distance, and so on. De-interlace or Flicker should also be used before you export a still frame with motion. In that case, the frame will look like Figure 15.22. If you don't remove the interlacing on an image with movement, you get a still that looks like Figure 15.23.

FIGURE 15.23
Interlaced still frame.

263

The other use for the De-interlace filter is to help make video look more like film. Removing interlacing is the first step toward trying to recreate that ever-popular film look. The best way to create a film-look effect, though, is to use the G Film Effects filters from Graeme Nattress.

SUMMARY

This is just the tip of the iceberg of some of the filters in FCE. I urge you to look through them and use the sequence in the *Video Filters* bin to explore their capabilities. By now you should have a fairly good idea of what you can do with this application and should be well on your way to creating exciting, interesting, and original video productions. We still have to look at an important group of filters for Color Correction, Keying, and Mattes, which we'll do next.

LESSON 16

Color Correction, Keys, and Mattes

We skipped over some groups of filters: **Color Correction**, **Image Control**, **Key**, and **Matte**. We'll look at them now, but first we need to load up the project. One more time, begin by loading the material you need onto your media drive, and reconnect the media if necessary. For this lesson, we'll use the materials in the *Lesson 16* project. Inside your project, you'll find in the Browser the *Clips* bin, a master clip called *Dance.mov*, and other sequences, *Keying* and *Color*, that we'll look at here.

COLOR CORRECTION

Good exposure and color begins in the shooting. It's always easier and better if you do it correctly from the beginning rather than trying to fix it in postproduction. That means lighting the scene well, exposing it correctly, setting your white balance correctly, and not leaving the camera's auto exposure and white balance to do the guessing.

If you're producing work for output on a television set, it is essential that you view your color correction work on a properly set-up production monitor, not the computer monitor. The color and luminance values on television sets are very different from computer monitors. Do not trust the computer screen to display the colors and luminance values the way they will appear on TV. Watch your video monitor while you work, or at least a TV set. Don't try to rely on your computer monitor.

The color correction tools are professional-strength tools, so use them carefully. All of the color-correction tools should be real-time capable, which can really speed up your workflow.

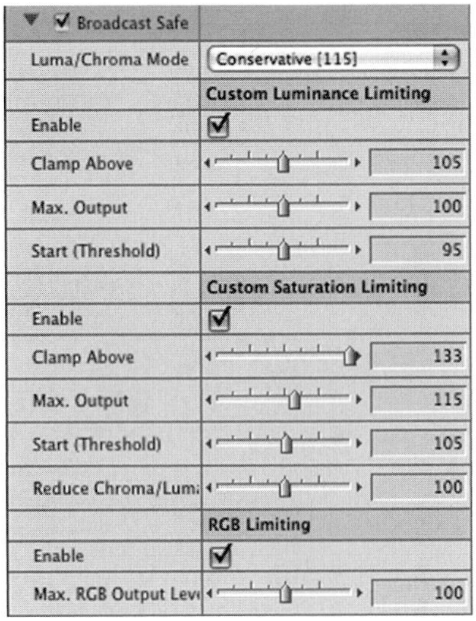

FIGURE 16.1
Broadcast Safe controls.

Broadcast Safe

Broadcast Safe is the perfect tool to use if you suspect your video is too bright for television. Just drop it on a clip, and you'll immediately see if it reduces the video level. It will have no effect if the image does not need correction. Although Broadcast Safe can be used as a magic bullet, you do have quite a bit of control on the filter to set it to whatever parameters you want (see Figure 16.1). The default is **Conservative**. The values controlled by the sliders are based on luminance value standards from 0 to 100. A value of 100 is considered peak white, and 0 is pure black. In practice, most cameras, especially consumer camcorders and prosumer equipment, shoot at levels much higher than 100, up to 109 and beyond, what's called superwhite. Televisions are designed to accept a video signal with peak white at 100, although they too have a good deal of tolerance, and most newer TV sets can readily accept values around 110 and 120.

Notice that as the default, you limit both the luminance values and the chrominance values. If you want to keep the luminance in an acceptable range but do something outrageous with the color, you have to make sure **Custom-Use Controls Below** is selected from the pop-up menu. Then uncheck the Saturation Limiting check box, and go to town!

Color Corrector

Unlike most filters, both Color Corrector and the Chroma Keyer in the Key sub-menu have two panels in the Viewer (see Figure 16.2). One, marked Filter, has sliders and numerical controls to adjust the values, and a useful button at the top lets you switch to the **Visual** display. The second panel with the name of the filter has the visual interface that you are most likely to use (see Figure 16.3).

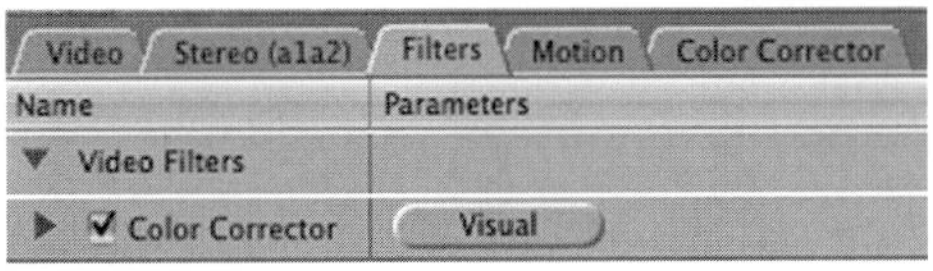

FIGURE 16.2
Top of the Viewer window with Color Corrector tab.

Let's look at the visual controls for Color Corrector. At the top is a grouping of useful buttons. The **Numeric** button takes you to the Filter panel. There is also the little check box that allows you to toggle the filter on and off. The eye icon tells you that you're in the Visual panel, in case you didn't already know that. A small timeline contains the basic timeline controls and timecode reference.

A grab handle that lets you pull the effect onto a clip, similar to the grab handle in the Audio panel, is available. On either side of the grab handle are some very useful buttons. The first to the right, with the number **1** on it, allows you

266

to copy your Color Corrector settings to the next clip in the Timeline. The second button to the right, marked with the number 2, can be even more useful. This copies the settings not to the next clip in the Timeline but to the second clip down the Timeline. For instance, if you have a two-camera setup for a wedding or a theatrical performance that basically switches back and forth between the two cameras, and you want to color-balance one camera to the other, you need to color-correct every other shot in the Timeline. Clicking the 2 button will copy the settings to the next shot for that camera. You can quickly copy the settings to every other shot in the Timeline.

The two buttons marked with a 1 and 2 to the left of the grab handle act similarly. They let you copy the Color Corrector settings to the clip you're working on either from the shot before, the 1 button, or from the shot before last in the Timeline, the 2 button.

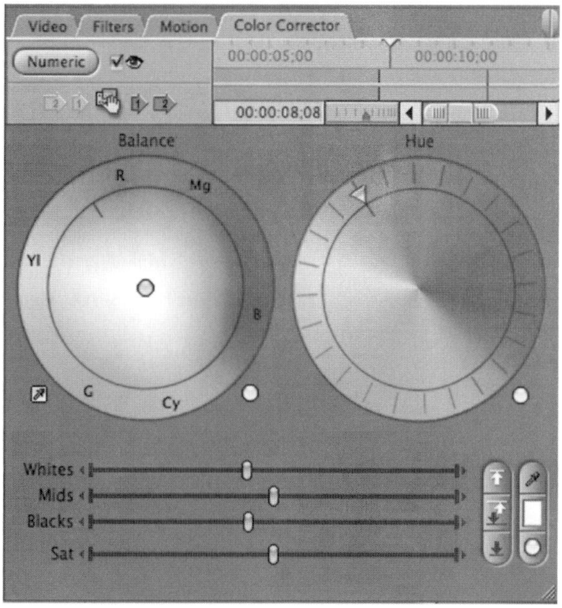

FIGURE 16.3
Color Corrector Visual display.

Let's look at the central control panel in Color Corrector, which has two color wheels, four sliders, and a few buttons. The left wheel controls the color balance of the image, and the right changes the hue, just like the hue control on older television sets. Below are four self-explanatory sliders. The first controls the white levels; the second, the midtones; and the third, the black level. The fourth slider adjusts the Saturation, or amount of color in the image. The three buttons stacked together on the right are auto setting buttons. From the top, the buttons are Auto White, Auto Contrast, and Auto Black. To the right of that is the Match Hue function with an eyedropper, a color swatch, and a white **Reset** button. The Match Hue function doesn't really work correctly in FCE. It would work if there were color selectors for blacks, mids, and whites, but with only a single white balance selector it usually doesn't work effectively.

> **TIP**
> **Before and After:** With the visual display active in the Viewer, you can quickly toggle the filter on and off to switch between before and after views with the keyboard shortcut Control-1.

In the *Color* sequence, look at the pair of images at *Marker 1*. The first is probably a bit darker than it should be. The image right after it has the Color Corrector filter applied. To use the filter, you should begin by clicking the **Auto Contrast** button, the middle of the three-button stack. Do not click on it repeatedly. You'll just keep shifting the contrast. Just click once. Next, set the **Auto Black** and then the **Auto White**. (Again, just one click for each button.) Always adjust the luminance values before you start adjusting the colors. A little adjustment there will spread the contrast levels nicely and brighten the image without increasing the overall level. Remember, as with almost all FCE sliders, if you hold down the **Command** key, you'll "gear down" the drag, giving you finer control.

The image at *Marker 2* in *Color* has been overexposed. With it is an attempt at fixing the problem. As you can see, you'll usually get a better result trying to fix an image that's been underexposed than one that's overexposed and washed out.

TIP

Reset: To reset the filter in the Color Corrector visual display, hold down the Shift key and click on either of the white buttons to the lower right of the color hubs.

Color Corrector obviously is for color as well as luminance and contrast. At *Marker 3* in Color is another still image. Something's certainly gone wrong here. It looks like the white balance hasn't been set correctly. Color Corrector is the easiest tool to use to fix this problem. To correct it, start with the **Auto Contrast** button, and set your luminance levels to what looks correct to you. It's not going to take much work. The exposure is correct; just the color is wrong.

What we're going to do is pick white in the picture and use that to set the correct color balance. There are a couple of tricks to this.

1. Take the Saturation slider and crank it way to the right, terribly oversaturating the image.

This emphasizes any color cast in the image, making it easier to pick out what's wrong. The second trick is to find the right bit of white. The temptation is to use something that's very bright, but the problem is that what's very bright often is quite washed out and has almost no color information in it. Look for something that's white but not at full luminance or something that's neutral gray. Here's how you do it with Color Corrector.

2. Just to the bottom left of the **Balance** wheel is a tiny eyedropper. (This is not the eyedropper next to the **Auto Contrast** button.) Use this to pick something in the scene that should be white or gray. In this image nothing is very oversaturated, so I'd pick something off the white roof of the van.

This will immediately pull the color back toward a truer representation of the image. You'll also notice that the button in the center of the Balance wheel has shifted toward the yellow-red direction. When I pulled the white, it gave the image a slightly more magenta tinge than I would have liked. Again, this was apparent because the Saturation was turned up. You'll want to fine-tune the color more toward the yellow-red direction of the Balance wheel.

3. Before you do that, slide the Saturation slider back down to normal, and you'll see that the image is close to looking correct.

4. Push the button in the center of the Balance wheel a little further to yellow-red.

There's a little gotcha here. All of the color wheels are geared down by default. So you have to move the button a lot to get any effect. In the color wheels, as with Balance, you use the **Command** key to gear up. This is the only place in FCE that this occurs.

TIP

Applying Filter to Multiple Clips: If you have a Color Corrector setting that you want to apply to a number of clips in the Timeline, set the filter for the first clip, and then copy it. In the Timeline, use Command-F to search for all the clips with the same name. Type in the name of the clip in the dialog box (see Figure 16.4), and click Find All. This will select all the clips in the Timeline with the same name. Hold the Command key, and click on the first clip that has already been color corrected to deselect it. With the remaining clips selected, use Paste Attributes (Option-V) to paste the filter settings to all the other clips with the same name.

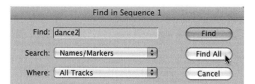

FIGURE 16.4
Sequence Find dialog.

269

Limiting Color Effects

Some important functions are on the Filter panel only. These are the whole group of controls for Limit Effect Controls, Edge Control, and Mask Control. Without having the visual interface for the Limit Effect Controls and the other functions, they are quite tricky to use, although with some care you can effectively

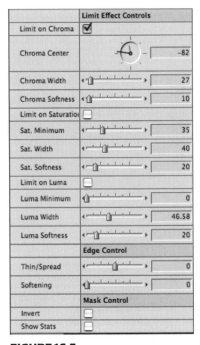

Limit Effect Controls		
Limit on Chroma	☑	
Chroma Center		-82
Chroma Width		27
Chroma Softness		10
Limit on Saturation	☐	
Sat. Minimum		35
Sat. Width		40
Sat. Softness		20
Limit on Luma	☐	
Luma Minimum		0
Luma Width		46.58
Luma Softness		20
Edge Control		
Thin/Spread		0
Softening		0
Mask Control		
Invert	☐	
Show Stats	☐	

FIGURE 16.5
Limit Effects Controls.

270

limit color control to only particular portions of the image. Look at the two images at *Marker 4* in *Color*. The color effect is changing the color of the woman's jacket. I did this by turning on the Limit Effect Controls and isolating the color of the jacket. The settings I used are in Figure 16.5.

1. To begin to isolate the color of the jacket, turn down the color saturation to zero.
2. Turn the Chroma Center dial until you find the color that's being desaturated.
3. Then by increasing the chroma width, isolate just that area of color.
4. Once the jacket color is isolated, turn the saturation back on.
5. Then use Phase Shift in the upper portion of the controls to change the jacket color from its original lime green to a more conservative tan. You could also do this with the Hue hub in the visual panel.

Notice that two clips are stacked in the *Color* sequence. That's because I used another filter—the Four-Point Garbage Matte—to limit the area that I had to color select.

IMAGE CONTROL

The **Desaturate** filter is the quickest, easiest way to remove color. FCE4 has two of them with different capabilities. The original FXScript filter sets the default Amount of 100, which is a fully desaturated image, pure black and white. I find this makes a somewhat flat-looking black and white. This Desaturate filter not only *de*saturates, but it will *over*saturate. Desaturate can go into negative values, which can add chroma to the image. It won't take much of a push into the negative numbers to get excessively colorful, especially if the scene already has a lot of color, particularly reds. The FxPlug filter, on the other hand, lets you

FIGURE 16.6
FxPlug Desaturate controls.

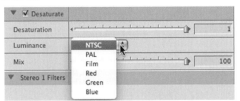

select which channel to use for black and white (see Figure 16.6). Generally the green channel will work best, but it depends on the image, and you should try the other channels. You can also select monochrome balances that are more suitable for NTSC, PAL or even for film.

Gradient Colorize

Gradient Colorize is brand new to FCE and is a great tool for creating wonderful duotone looks. The controls are different from the FXScript controls. Figure 16.7 shows the gradient colors that you can adjust. Right-click on the end stop for each end to call up an interactive HUD (Heads Up Display) that lets you select the color you want. These controls allow you to pick the white and

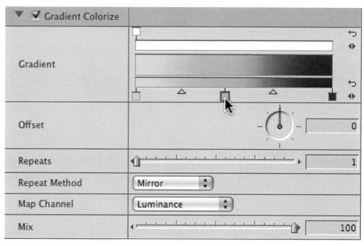

FIGURE 16.7
Gradient Colorize controls.

the black colors separately. The great thing about the HUD is that it changes the color in the Canvas while you scrub through it. You can also add multiple stops to the gradient, as in the Title 3D gradient tool. At the first marker in the *Effects Builder* sequence is a Color Gradient effect applied to a clip. Open the controls to see what you can do with this filter.

Sepia

FCE4 has two **Sepia** filters, but the original FXScript filter is probably the better of the two. One nice feature of this filter is that if you want a monotone effect, as opposed to the complexity of Gradient Colorize, you can set Sepia to whatever midtone color you want. It doesn't have to be sepia toned. The filter also allows you to blend in the underlying color, which makes an interesting look. Sepia also has a Highlight slider, which increases the brightness in the highlight areas, punching them through the tint color. Pulling the Highlight slider into negative numbers will deepen the shadow areas.

271

FIGURE 16.8
Threshold.

Threshold

Threshold is new to FCE4. This filter lets you create a high-contrast black-and-white image (see Figure 16.8). The default is to make the image very high contrast, but by pushing up the Smoothness value, the contrast will reduce. It should be used only for special, high-contrast effects. For monochrome effects, the FxPlug Desaturate gives better results.

KEYING

Keying is used to selectively cut out areas of the image. The most efficient way to do this is chromakeying, the technique of removing one specific color from an image. (You see this when meteorologists stand in front of weather maps.) The two most commonly used colors are blue and green. Because of the way the DV format works, it's easier to chromakey green than blue. On the other hand, if your subject has to wear green for St. Patrick's Day, you'll have to use blue.

The key to keying is to shoot it well. Poorly shot material just will not key properly. For chromakeying, the background blue or green screen must be evenly lit and correctly exposed so that the color is as pure as possible. Video, and DV especially, has many limitations of color depth and saturation that make good keying difficult.

FCE has tools to do keying, the best of which (in my opinion) is the Chroma Keyer. In your Browser is a bin called *Keying*, which holds the elements we'll work with in this part of the lesson. Open the *Keying* sequence, which has a couple of still images to work with. On V1 in the sequence is a still of the Stanford University's Hoover Tower called *Background.pct*, and on V2 is the image to chromakey called *Blue.pct*. We're going to work with a quite difficult blue-screen image.

Color Smoothing—4:1:1

Color Smoothing—4:1:1 and Color Smoothing—4:2:2 are used to smooth color compression artifacts in heavily compressed material like DV. These filters are designed to reduce the effects of pixelization in digital video. When working in FCE with DV-resolution, you should use the 4:1:1 filter, which is the color space used by DV. You should apply the filter first to any clip that you want to key. The filter has no controls. You just drop it on the clip first and apply the Chroma Keyer filter to remove the green or blue that you want to key out of the image.

HDV and DV PAL material, however, use a different color space—4:2:0—for which no suitable color smoothing filter is available in FCE. If you need to key HDV or DV PAL material, I would suggest you look in Graeme Nattress's Film Effects filter, whose G Chroma Sharpen will do smoothing for 4:2:0 material.

Chroma Keyer

If the material is properly shot and lit, there is no special trick to chromakeying in FCE, just a lot of shifting of sliders. I would ignore the Blue and Green Screen and Color Key filters and just work with the **Chroma Keyer**. Let's start by examining some of the controls in this perhaps daunting-looking filter.

1. Begin by applying Color Smoothing −4:2:2 to *Blue.pct* on V2. This may be the only instance in which you'll use this filter because FCE does not normally work with full-color space video.
2. Apply Chroma Keyer to the same clip.
3. Open the clip into the Viewer, and go to the Chroma Keyer tab (see Figure 16.9).

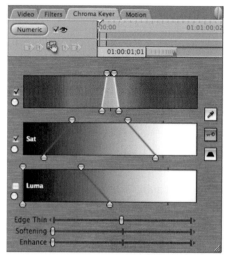

FIGURE 16.9
Chroma Keyer controls.

The controls show a Color Range slider at the top: the rainbow-colored bar. Below that is the Sat (saturation) control and Luma (luminance) control. Each has a round radio button that allows you to reset the parameter and a square check box that lets you toggle the parameter on and off. Each of the controls has handles that can be adjusted. Pulling the buttons on the top of the sliders will increase or decrease the range of the effect, and pulling on the buttons at the bottom of the slider will control the tolerance—how widely the parameter will be applied to adjacent colors or saturation or luminance values.

On the right are three important buttons (see Figure 16.10). At the top is the critical eyedropper. Below that, in the middle, is a three-way toggle switch with a key icon. Its default position is colored gray, which shows the final output of the image. Click it, and it will change to white, which will show you a black-and-white representation of what you're keying. Click it again, and the button turns blue, which shows you the original source material. The bottom button with the keystone icon will invert the key, which can be useful in some instances.

FIGURE 16.10
Chroma Keyer buttons.

4. Click on the eyedropper, click in the blue screen behind the flowers in the Canvas, and you're practically done. Almost instantly the bulk of the blue will disappear.
5. Check the matte by clicking on the **Matte/Key** button.

You'll see most of the background has been keyed out, as in Figure 16.11. This is a grayscale representation of transparency. What is white is opaque in the *Blue.pct* clip, and what is black is transparent. You'll see the black if you switch off the visibility for the background layer on V1.

6. Widen the Color Range slightly with the button pulls at the top, and broaden the Luma controls a bit; you'll have a pretty good key.
7. Push up the Edge Thin control a bit.

273

TIP
Color Selection: If you hold down the Shift key, you can
click on multiple points, and the Chroma Keyer controls will extend the
range of values, color, saturation, or luminance as needed. Also, if you hold down
the Shift key and drag a line through the area you want to sample, the tool will use
the range of values along the line to set up the controls.

FIGURE 16.11
Matte display.

If you look closely at your key in FCE, you'll probably see a rather unnatural color fringe around the edges of the flower. This can be a little tricky to eliminate.

8. At the very end of the Softening control is a tiny little triangle. Give it a few clicks. This will move Softening incrementally.
9. Try adding a little Enhance, but not too much, or the edges will start to turn yellow.

Spill Suppressors

There are now three **Spill Suppressors**. The FxPlug filter will work for either blue or green, while there are separate FXScript filters for blue and green. They are pretty much interchangeable and are used if there is a blue or green cast on the edges of the image. This often happens when you get reflected light from the blue screen wall falling on the edges of a curved object, like a person's shoulders. The Spill Suppressor replaces the blue in the image with black, like a shadow area. This is fine on the object you want to leave, but if the background color has not been keyed out sufficiently, it can leave a dark edging on the screen. You might have to pull down the Amount slider substantially, although usually only a small amount will be sufficient to do the work.

Matte Choker

Adding another tool in the mix here may be helpful. The **Matte Choker** is useful, but it isn't in the Key package. It's in the Matte package, which we'll see in a moment. There are two Matte Chokers, which are very similar and are most commonly used as a keying tool. Adding one of the filters to the key can improve the image.

The controls are basically the same as the Edge Thin and Softening controls in the Chroma Keyer, but now you are adding a second line of choking to the key's edges after the Spill Suppressor has done its work. If you find that your keying is cutting into the image too much, you can also use the Matte Choker to bring back some of the cutoff image by pushing the slider down into negative numbers. You can also try the new **Matte Magic** filter, which is a type of choker with feathering. It gives you subtle control and can be more useful than the two Matte Chokers on some images.

MATTE

Eight-Point Garbage Matte

A Garbage Matte allows you to roughly cut out a section of the image by selected points on the screen that define corners of the picture. In addition to the **Eight-Point Garbage Matte,** there is a Four-Point Garbage Matte as well, the only difference being the number of points available (see Figure 16.12). Notice that all of the points and most of the other controls can be fully animated, so you can change the shape of the Garbage Matte over time.

The controls allow you to set eight points on the image, beginning with Point 1 in the upper left corner. The points go clockwise around the screen, starting with that corner (see Figure 16.13). It's best to try to keep the points in those relative positions. Because lines connect the points to each other, it's important to avoid having the

▼ ✔ Eight–Point Garbage Matte		⊗ ☑▾
View Mode	Preview ⬍	
	Corners	
Point 1	⊕ −360 , −240	◁◉▷
Point 2	⊕ 0 , −240	◁◉▷
Point 3	⊕ 360 , −240	◁◉▷
Point 4	⊕ 360 , 0	◁◉▷
Point 5	⊕ 360 , 240	◁◉▷
Point 6	⊕ 0 , 240	◁◉▷
Point 7	⊕ −360 , 240	◁◉▷
Point 8	⊕ −360 , 0	◁◉▷
	Edges	
Smooth	⬆————▸ 0	◁◉▷
Choke	◂——⬆——▸ 0	◁◉▷
Feather	⬆————▸ 0	◁◉▷
	Options	
Invert	☐	
Hide Labels	☐	

FIGURE 16.12
Eight-Point Garbage Matte controls.

FIGURE 16.13
Garbage Matte Canvas display.

lines cross each other. Bizarre shapes can be created with your image if the lines cross.

In the controls there are eight points that can be placed anywhere on the screen using the **Crosshairs** button. Click in the crosshairs for Point 1, and click in the Canvas. The point will be placed there. It's as simple, and as difficult, as that.

Three **View Modes** can be selected from the pop-up menu at the top of the controller:

1. **Final** is the output as seen on the screen along with the underlying layers but without any point markers.
2. **Preview** is the same as Final, only with the points indicated and with the point numbers. The number display can be toggled with the check box.
3. **Wireframe** shows you the matte outline, but only on the layer on which you're working, without cutting away the rest of the image to reveal any underlying layer.

Below the points are some important tools. The first is **Smooth**, which rounds out the corners in your matte. You can combine it with **Feather** to create soft-edged mattes with interesting organic shapes (see Figure 16.14). Without Smooth applied, **Choke** is a subtle adjustment of the matte shape. Moving Choke into negative numbers will slightly reduce the matte, and pushing the value up will increase the size of the matte.

FIGURE 16.14
Matte without Smooth and with Smooth and Feather at 20.

TIP

Setting the Point: The easiest way to apply the Garbage Matte point is to click one of the point's crosshairs in the Filter panel and then mouse down in the Canvas, which will update as soon as it can. If you hold the mouse down and drag the point around the screen, the image will be pulled around on the screen as quickly as your computer can manage it. The faster your computer, the sooner this will happen.

Finally, an important but often overlooked check box is **Invert**. This feature allows you to create a matte around an object that you want to remove and then, instead of keeping the area you defined, you can cut it out by checking the **Invert** box.

TIP

Do It First: It's a good idea to apply your Garbage Matte before you reposition or scale your image. The points are based on the image frame. So if you move the image before you apply the Garbage Matte, it's hard to pin down where the points should be because they're not referring to the new shape, position and scale of the image but to its original position in the frame. So apply your Garbage Matte, and make it the shape you want before you scale, center, or rotate the picture about the screen.

Extract

Extract is a neat little filter. It's a bit unpredictable to work with, but with luck, it will create interesting combinations of matte shapes, especially when used with a Garbage Matte to define a core area. Extract gives you deceptively simple controls together with a three-up display in the Canvas, if needed (see Figure 16.15).

A pop-up menu lets you select if you want the extraction applied to RGB or to the alpha channel of the image. Applying it to RGB will make a high-contrast black-and-white image. By adjusting **Threshold, Tolerance**, and **Softness**, you can vary the image substantially. It gets really interesting when you apply it to the alpha channel instead of the RGB value. Then you cut through to an underlying layer with a great amount of control. It's useful for pulling an alpha channel from an image that doesn't have one.

FIGURE 16.15
Extract controls.

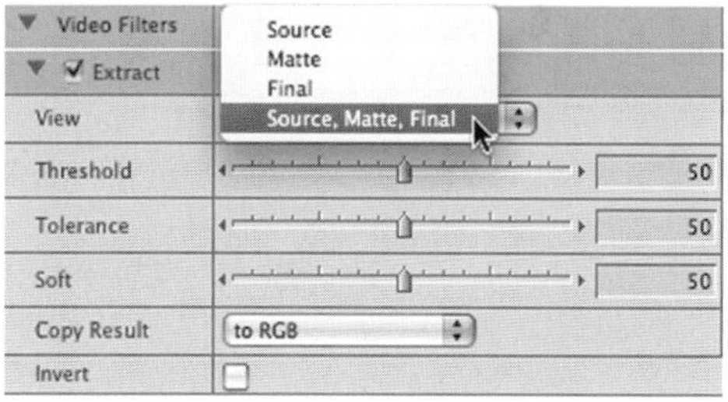

Look at the file in the Browser called *TIFF.tif*. Apply the Extract filter to it with Copy Result to Alpha Channel, and you'll see that with hardly a tweak of the sliders, the white will disappear from around the word. It's set up at *Marker 2* in the *Effects Builder* sequence.

FIGURE 16.16
Mask Shape controls.

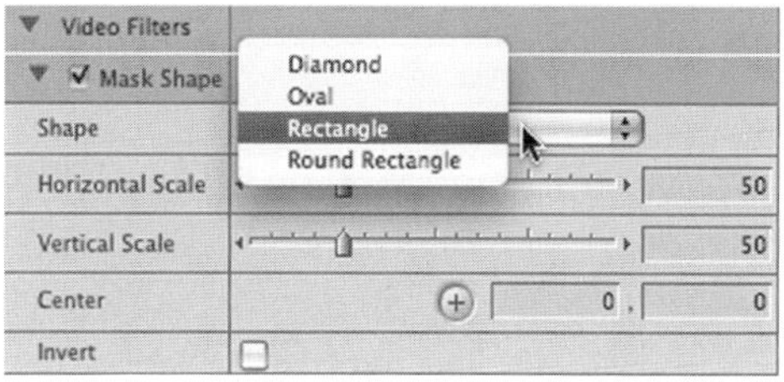

Mask Shape

Mask Shape is a useful filter that lets you easily control the shape of the image. The controls allow basic shapes (see Figure 16.16) and have Horizontal and Vertical sliders that let you adjust the default shapes. I'll show you a practical application.

TIP

NightScope: If you apply Color Corrector to a clip, taking down the black level a bit, and then use the Extract filter, followed by Color Corrector again with a green tint and the white level brought down considerably, as well as the mids choked down, you can create quite a credible Night-Scope look for your image. Look at the clip at *Marker 3* in Effects Builder. A touch of Gaussian Blur softens the hard-edged look of the Extraction. It needs a little fiddling, depending on the image, but it's fun, especially if you can add a little blurred glow to it with a composite mode, which we'll talk about in the next lesson.

An interesting use for Mask Shape is to create borders using color mattes. It's simple to do. Look at the clip stack at *Marker 4* in *Effects Builder*. On V1 is the *Dance2* clip with **Mask Shape>Round Rectangle** applied. On V2 is a color matte in pale yellow. The color also has Round Rectangle applied to it twice. The first time it's applied inverted, which leaves the matte with the picture showing through and fills the rest of the screen with the color. Applying the shape again, only slightly larger and not inverted, will cut the color outside in the Round Rectangle. I also used **Anti-alias** to soften the stair-stepping around the mask.

Mask Shape also allows you to create an animated highlight area. At *Marker 5* in *Effects Builder*, I have created an effect with a highlight area that follows an individual in a group as the camera pans over them.

1. To do this, first place two copies of the clip one on top of the other.
2. To the top layer, apply the Mask Shape filter. Nothing will appear to happen because the two images are identical.
3. To the bottom layer, apply the **Color Corrector** or **Brightness and Contrast** filter from the **Image Control** submenu. Now you can see the area being masked off on the top layer.
4. Next, move to the middle of the clip where it's easiest to see the layer you have to affect. In the Filters tab for the image on the top layer, use pop-up and the Horizontal Scale and Vertical Scale sliders to set the shape you want, as well as the Center point to position it roughly.
5. To animate the shape, start by setting the Canvas to **Fit All** in the Zoom pop-up or by setting a value that lets you see the grayboard around the Canvas.
6. Go to the point on the screen just before the subject starts appearing as the camera pans, and using the **Crosshairs** button, set a Center value that's off the screen.

TIP
Matte Boundaries: Although you can extend the points out into the grayboard, the matte doesn't extend out there. If only it would! The matte is still bound by the edges of the frame. So if you are hoping that extending the points out from the screen will prevent Feather from affecting one edge of the image, give up. Feather will unfortunately occur around the frame edges.

7. In this case we only need to animate the Center value, so set a keyframe there. If the image changed shape or size, you could animate the horizontal and vertical scales of the shape as well.
8. Because the pan is pretty constant, go to the point in the clip where the subject has exited the frame on the far side, and set a new Center value off the left edge of the screen.
9. Next, step through the clip and see how the animation flows, adjusting the position of the shape to match the movement of the subject and the camera.
10. I also added a **Mask Feather** filter from the **Matte** submenu to soften the edges of the shape.
11. Finally, I animated the Brightness and Contrast filter to ramp down and back up the value of the Brightness to darken the image as the shape moves onto the screen and bring it back to normal as the shape moves off.

Widescreen

This filter lets you take a standard 4:3 video and crop it to one of seven standard cinema shapes (see Figure 16.17) to create a letterbox effect. This is a crop, not an overlay, so the area outside the image is empty. If you want to place a color there, you should put a color matte underneath it, as I did in *Final Letterbox*.

The **Offset** slider allows you to move the image up and down without altering the position. Negative numbers drag the image downward, and positive numbers move the image upward, the opposite of the way the *y* axis functions in the Text tool.

FIGURE 16.17
Widescreen controls.

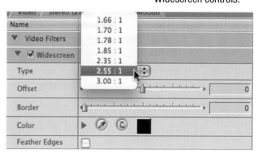

279

If you want to make a whole sequence widescreen—which is probably the point rather than applying it to individual clips—nest the whole sequence, and apply the filter to the nest.

1. Make a new sequence, naming it something useful, such as *Final Letterbox,* as I've done in the Browser for the *Lesson 16* project.

2. Drag your edited sequence into the new open Timeline window—in this case called *Edited Sequence* in your Browser. This is now a nested sequence, with the edited sequence nested inside the new sequence.

3. Select the nested sequence in the Timeline, and apply the Widescreen filter to it.

4. To access the settings for the filter, simply select the nest in the Timeline and press the **Return** key or with the **Option** key double-click to open it into the Viewer. You can now go to the Filters tab to change the settings.

If you need to use **Offset**, you may not want to do it here because it will offset all the clips in the nest. It would be better to open the nest, use the Motion tab of any shots you want to offset, and move them up or down in the frame as necessary.

You can create the widescreen effect in other ways, such as Four-Point Garbage Matte. Create the shape you want for the masked area, and use the **Invert** button. Or for a simple widescreen without the border, you could also use the Crop tool. Remember to drag with the **Command** key to get opposite sides to move equally. Or you could make a mask in Photoshop, a black area at the top and bottom with transparency in the middle. I like this way the best, particularly for projects such as commercials, because it lets me create interesting effects with the mask edges, such as graphic elements that overlap the widescreen line, different color masks, text, and logos.

280

TIP

Recursive: Nested sequences are recursive. That is, in any changes you make in the nested *Edited Sequence,* shortened or lengthened clips will also appear in the master sequence.

SUMMARY

In this lesson we looked at some of the most important filters in FCE: color correction, keying, and creating mattes for our clips. We need to explore one more aspect of FCE before we're ready to put our creations out on tape, the Web, or some other delivery format, and that is compositing, the topic of our next two lessons.

LESSON 17

Compositing

Compositing is the ability to combine multiple layers of video on a single screen and have them interact with one another. This capability adds great depth to FCE. Until now we have been looking primarily at horizontal editing. In compositing we're dealing more with vertical editing, building stacks of layers. Compositing allows you to create a montage of images and graphics that can explain some esoteric point or enhance a mundane portion of a production.

Good compositing work can raise the perceived quality of a production. Compositing is used for a great deal of video production work on television—commercials, of course—but also on news programs and for interstitials, the short videos that appear between sections of a program. Be warned, though, that compositing and graphics animation are not quick and easy to do. Most compositing is animated, and animation requires patience, skill, and hard work.

SETTING UP THE PROJECT

Begin by opening the *Lesson 17* project from your hard drive and going through the reconnect process. Inside your copy of the project *Lesson 17*, you'll find the *Clips* bin, two master clips (*Village* and *Ceremony*), and some sequences.

As in the previous lesson, a couple of sequences contain examples of effects used in the lesson. They're called *Composite Stacks, Composite Modes,* and *Renders & Shapes*. Before we get into compositing, we should take a quick look at the Generators because these provide us with some useful compositing tools, including some excellent new FxPlug generators with built-in transparency.

FIGURE 17.1
Generators pop-up.

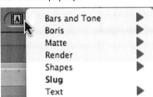

GENERATORS

We used the **Generator** pop-up menu to create text files as well as color mattes, but let's take a moment to look at what else is under that little A (see Figure 17.1). There are submenus for Bars and Tone for both HD; 1080 and 720; and DV, NTSC, and PAL. There are also submenus for Boris, Matte, Render, Shapes, and Text, as well as the Slug. We're going to look at a few of the Generators.

Render and Shape

Render and **Shape** are objects that allow you to create compositing tools that will alter the shapes and textures of video and graphics images. These generators are laid in the *Renders & Shapes* sequence. The default duration for these items is ten seconds, but I've put them in the sequence at five seconds in length, unless they have motion in them, in which case I've left them at the default ten seconds. Try out the different generators and especially explore their controls, which give them remarkable flexibility.

282

Transparency

Some, like **Caustics**, **Membrane**, and **Swirly**, have transparency, but most of them, like **Lens Flare** and **Two Color Ray**, and the four shapes, **Circle**, **Oval**, **Rectangle**, and **Square**, are against black. Be aware that the blackness you see in many Render items and in the Shapes is not the emptiness you normally see in the Viewer or Canvas around text or animated images. What you see in the gradients and shapes is actual opaque black without any transparency.

FIGURE 17.2
Gradient editor.

FIGURE 17.3
Opacity HUD.

Some Render items such as **Cellular** and **Clouds** are gradients that go from white to black but also have a FxPlug gradient editor that allows you to add transparency. The gradient editor has two portions: the color gradient area that goes from white to black and above it a white bar that controls transparency. If you double-click on the right end of the bar, you'll create a second stop or tag as in Figure 17.2. Next, right-click on the tag, and move the cursor over the grayscale HUD that appears (see Figure 17.3). Selecting black will make that tag area of the gradient transparent. What's bright or white in the image will be opaque, and what's black or dark will be transparent.

Grid has a slider that allows you to change the Background Opacity from fully opaque to fully transparent. Some such as Lens Flare require a composite mode, which we'll look at in a moment, to eliminate the background.

COMPOSITING MODES

One of the best ways to combine render elements with images is to use compositing modes. If you're familiar with Photoshop, you probably already know that a compositing mode is a way that the values of one image can be combined with the values of another image. Final Cut has 13 compositing modes, including two traveling mattes, which we'll look at in the next lesson. For the moment, we'll deal only with the first 11. These can be accessed from the **Modify>Composite Mode** menu. These are the composite modes:

- Normal, the way clips usually appear
- Add
- Subtract
- Difference
- Multiply
- Screen
- Overlay
- Hard Light
- Soft Light
- Darken
- Lighten
- Travel Matte-Alpha
- Travel Matte-Luma

Compositing Exercise

Let's begin by looking at the compositing modes available in FCE:

1. Open up the sequence *Composite Modes*.

This sequence contains 11 iterations of two clips, one on top of the other. Each clip on V2 is composited onto the clip on V1, using a different compositing mode. There's an extended marker on each clip that identifies the compositing mode applied to the clip stack. No two compositing modes are the same, although the differences are sometimes subtle. Some will make the output darker, and some will make it lighter, but all in a slightly different manner. It's a wonderful tool for controlling and combining images. The two last composite modes, Travel Matte-Alpha and Travel Matte-Luma, have special uses that we'll look at later.

2. To change the compositing mode of a clip, select the clip on V2, and from the **Modify** menu, choose **Composite Mode** and choose a type.

Screen

One of the most useful composite modes is **Screen**, which will remove black from an image. It screens out portions of the image based on luminance values. Pure black will be transparent, and pure white will be fully opaque. Any other shade will be partially transparent. This is great for creating semitransparent shapes that move around the screen and useful for making animated backgrounds. Many 3D and other animation elements are created against black backgrounds that can be screened out. Let's try the composite mode, and you'll see how it works, compositing the Lens Flare generator on top of another scene:

1. Open the empty *Sequence 1* if it isn't open already.
2. Again, we won't be working on the sound, so let's switch off A1/A2 in the patch panel.

3. Edit about six seconds of any of the *Village* shots into the Timeline. I used *Village1*.
4. With the playhead over the clip in the Timeline, from the Generators select **Render>Lens Flare**. Superimpose the generator so it's on top of the clip on track V2.
5. Select the Lens Flare on the upper track, and use **Modify>Composite Mode>Screen**.

Instantly, the black background will disappear, and the flare will appear over the village scene as in Figure 17.4. I used the Lens Flare controls to reposition the flare from the center of the screen. You'll find the effect laid out at the beginning of the *Composite Stacks* sequence.

FIGURE 17.4
Lens Flare over the village.

Animated Text Composite

One of the best uses of composite mode is with text, especially animated text that's moving on the screen. The composite mode will allow the text to interact with the layer underneath.

1. To start, edit five seconds of another clip into the Timeline on V1. I used *Village3*.
2. Next, using the basic Text tool, create a title with the word *Village*. Use a large, chunky font, and make it a bright color. I used Arial Black in 98 point in a fairly bright red.

3. Superimpose the text on top of the village shot.
4. Now we need to create the animation. Make sure you're at the beginning of the text block, and with the Canvas in Image+Wireframe mode, drag the text upward so it's off the top of the screen.
5. Add a keyframe to the text block, either with the global motion keyframe button in the Canvas or with the Center keyframe button in the Viewer.
6. Move the playhead to the end of the village shot, and drag the text block downward so it's off the bottom of the screen.

So far you just have a simple text animation that scrolls across the screen from top to bottom, but adding the composite mode changes everything. The text will change and be textured by the underlying image.

7. Select the text block in the Timeline, and use **Modify**>**Composite Mode** and pick one. I chose **Overlay**, but try some of the others and see what it does to the text as it moves across the screen.

The effect with the text animation is at *Marker 2* in the *Composite Stacks* sequence.

Instant Sex

Let's look at some more effects you can create with composite modes:

1. Let's open a clip from the *Clips* bin into the Viewer. We'll use *Ceremony2* because it has some nice highlight areas that will show off the effect.
2. Set the clip's duration down to five seconds, and edit it into your sequence.
3. In the Timeline, move the playhead back over the top of the clip that was just edited into the sequence.
4. Drag the same clip from the Viewer to Superimpose, making identical copies on V1 and V2.

You could also use **Option-Shift**-drag to copy the clip from V1 to the space above on V2.

5. To the top layer, apply a generous amount of Gaussian Blur, something like 30. The image looks very out of focus now.
6. Turn down the Opacity of the clip on V2 to something like 40 percent.
7. Go to **Composite Mode**, and change the clip on V2's setting to Add. I prefer **Add**, but try some of the others, such as Screen or Lighten.
8. Try adjusting the Blur amount and the Opacity levels to different settings.

This is a recipe for Instant Sex from the great After Effects artist Trish Meyer. Although it was created for After Effects, it adapts readily to Final Cut. The soft, blooming highlights make a wonderful, dreamy, romantic effect.

Noise Exercise

Now let's bring up the noise. We can use Noise to add a film-grain effect.

1. Go to the Generators pop-up, and from **Render** select the second **Noise** generator, which is the original FXScript generator.
2. Drag it onto V3, above the Instant Sex stack, or set V2 as the destination and use Superimpose to bring it into the Timeline.
3. Change the Noise layer's compositing mode to **Screen**.
4. Remember, the piece in the Timeline is a copy of the one you created in the Viewer, so double-click it to bring it back into the Viewer.
5. In the Controls tab, make sure the **Random** box is checked and the Color box unchecked.

In Color mode, Noise is too strong and generates too many sparkling bits to be useful for our purposes.

Toning It Down

286

At this stage the Canvas should look like a very snowy television screen (see Figure 17.5). Now we need to reduce the effect of the Noise.

1. In the Noise controls, set the **Alpha** level all the way to zero, and pull down the **Alpha Tolerance** to something around 10 or 20, depending on how much graininess you want to introduce.
2. Also try using the Soft Light composite mode, but with Noise's Alpha turned up to around 120.

FIGURE 17.5
Snowy Noise.

TIP
NTSC Warning: If you are going to output to NTSC analog to be seen on a television set, be careful in using compositing modes, particularly Add. It will brighten the image, often beyond the luminance and chrominance values allowable for broadcast transmission. If the image is too bright or oversaturated, especially in red, it may bloom objectionably and smear easily when analog copies are made, particularly VHS copies.

3. To see the effect the Noise layer is having, and toggle the track visibility on and off with the green button at the head of the track.

Text

Let's not stop there. On top of your video, which should still have strong, glowing highlight areas as well as a sprinkling of grain, let's add a text element.

1. For simplicity, use the standard Text tool to create the word *JAPAN* in any font you like in a fairly large size and a nice, bright color.

I used Optima, in bold and italicized, with a point size of 168 in a fairly bright red, R 200, G 18, B 18. Create whatever text block you like, using any available font.

2. Place your text block on V4. Use the Origin control to move it lower in the frame. I set the *y* value to 150.

3. **Option-Shift**-drag the *Text* clip to the space above to create a copy on V5.

Your stack should look like Figure 17.6.

4. Go to the controls for the text file on V5, and change the color to bright yellow, something like R 223, G 223, B 18.

5. Next, apply a Gaussian Blur filter to the top text layer, maybe something in the 30 range. This will make it quite wispy looking.

6. Change the composite mode for the text on V5 to **Add** so it combines with the layers beneath.

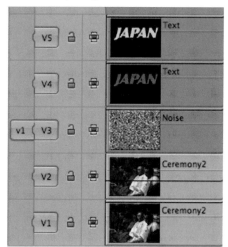

FIGURE 17.6
Two video layers, one noise layer, and two text layers.

Making the layer blurred and then compositing will make it look like a glow over the image (see Figure 17.7), but you may not want that top glow layer on the image all the time.

7. Ramp up the Opacity on the glow layer quickly over a few frames.

8. Hold the Opacity at full level for four or five frames.

9. Quickly ramp it down again. When you play it back, you should just get a quick flash of yellow glow.

Look at the sequence *Composite Stacks*. I've built the five-layer stack with the quick opacity animation at *Marker 3*.

FIGURE 17.7
Composited layers and effects.

287

FIGURE 17.8
Drop shadow glow layer
behind.

Drop Shadow Exercise

Another variation is to use a composite mode to create a different kind of drop shadow, using this type of glow layer technique, only behind the text rather than on top of it (see Figure 17.8). Rather than using yellow in the glow layer, we'll simply keep the same color as the text layer.

1. You should still have in your *Sequence 1* the five-layer stack we created. Let's start by deleting the top text layer that became our glow.
2. Once again, **Option-Shift**-drag the text on V4 onto the empty V5 to make two copies of the text stacked one on top of the other.

This time, rather than working with the upper text layer, let's work on the lower text layer.

3. Double-click the lower of the two text layers on V4 to open it into the Viewer. In the Motion tab, change the value Scale up to about 110 percent.
4. With the Viewer still in the active window, go to **Effects**>**Video Filters**> **Gaussian Blur**.
5. Set the blur value to something around 20.
6. At this point, the color will be too rich, so change the composite mode to **Overlay** or **Darken**. Try a few different ones to see what they look like.

The drop shadow glow layer stack is built in the *Composite Stacks* sequence at *Marker 4*. This is a different-looking shadow than you usually see. Instead of being directed to one side, it flares out from the text as though the light is coming from the front, projecting the text onto the background. These glow effects can also be created and animated using Title 3D's edges and drop shadow effects.

Bug

A bug is an insect, a mistake in software coding, and also that little icon usually in the lower right corner of your television that tells you what station you're watching. There are lots of different ways to make bugs, but I'll show you one using Photoshop and compositing modes. In your Browser in the *Graphics* bin is a Photoshop file called *Logo.psd*. Double-click it, and it will open as a sequence with two layers. The bottom layer has the bug already made up with the Photoshop effect. The top layer that is visible in the Canvas doesn't have the effect applied, and that's the one we're going to work on. If you want to just work with the bottom layer that's made up for you already, you can skip the first section of this tutorial.

PHOTOSHOP EFFECT

1. Make sure in your User Preferences that your External Editor for still images is set to Photoshop (or Photoshop Elements).
2. Right-click on the visible layer in the *Logo.psd* sequence, and from the shortcut menu choose **Open in Editor**.
3. Once Photoshop has launched, select *Layer 2*, and from the little F in the bottom left of the Layers palette, add a Layer Style, choosing **Drop Shadow** (see Figure 17.9).
4. Change the Drop Shadow Angle to 145 and the Distance to 15. Leave the other controls the same.
5. Check the Inner Shadow check box to add the shadow. Set the Distance to 5, and set the Choke and Size to 10.
6. Also add a Stroke. Set the Size to 6. I made the color blue (see Figure 17.10).
7. Click OK, and you've built the effect.

FIGURE 17.9
Add Layer Style>Drop Shadow.

There is one more step to take before going back to FCE. The effects have to be applied to the layer. The easiest way to do this is to add a layer underneath the effects layer.

289

8. Add a new layer to your Photoshop composition, and in the Layers palette, drag it below *Layer 2*, which holds the effects.

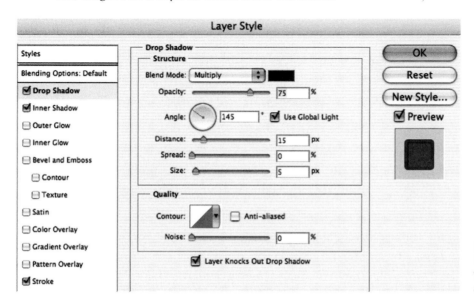

FIGURE 17.10
Drop Shadow panel with Inner Shadow and Stroke.

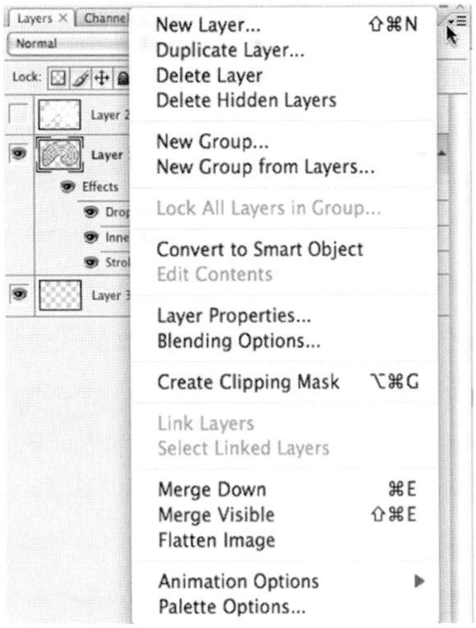

FIGURE 17.11
Merge Down.

9. Make sure *Layer 2* is selected. From the Wing menu, choose **Merge Down**, or use the keyboard shortcut **Command-E** (see Figure 17.11).

10. Save your file and go back to Final Cut Express.

COMPOSITING THE PHOTOSHOP FILE

Back in FCE *Layer 2* in the Photoshop sequence, *Logo.psd* will have been updated and will include your new effects.

1. Open a new duplicate *Sequence 1*, and drag some video into it. I used *Village2*.

Now normally you're going to want your bug to run the duration of your sequence, which might be an hour or more. Because you can't drag out still image layers to an unlimited duration once they're in a sequence, you need to set the duration of the bug while it's still in the Browser.

2. The simplest way to work with this is to first open the sequence *Logo.psd*. Now drag your newly minted effects *Layer 2* out into the Browser (or the original *Layer 1* if you prefer).

This will be a copy of the *Layer 2* in *Logo.psd*. With *Layer 2* as a single-layer image, before you place the bug into the final sequence, you can change its duration in the Browser. Here you can make the duration of the still image anything you want—or at least anything up to 12 hours, which is the duration limit of any FCE sequence.

3. Set the Duration for the bug logo to the duration of the sequence you want to cover. Now you can drag the layer into your final sequence.

FIGURE 17.12
Logo with Composite Mode>Multiply.

The next step is to change the logo's composite type. Several compositing modes will work for this, but I like to use **Composite Mode>Multiply** (see Figure 17.12). This will make the white of the logo almost transparent. For a slightly brighter look, try **Soft Light**, and for an even more transparent look, use Overlay.

At the current size, the logo is probably a bit intrusive. You might want to scale it down a bit and reposition it in the corner of your choice, bottom right being the traditional location on American television. It will now be your unobtrusive

290

> **TIP**
> ***Distinctive Logo:*** There are any number of different ways to give your logo a distinctive edge by using the power of layer styles. Rather than using the Inner Shadow and Stroke method, you could also use Bevel and Emboss. Change the Technique pop-up to Chisel Hard, and push the Size slider until the two sides of the bevel meet. This will give you maximum effect. Remember that the logo is going to be very reduced in size. Also, in the bottom part of the Bevel and Emboss panel, try different types of Glass Contour from the little arrow pop-up menu.

watermark on the screen. Some people also like to use effects such as displacements or bump maps, but for something this small, I don't really think it's necessary. The simple transparency effect of a composite mode is enough. The one I created is at *Marker 5* in *Composite Stacks*.

SUMMARY

This short lesson should give you a taste of and a little practice in using composite modes in Final Cut Express. They are a great way to blend images, text, and generators together into a single composition. But there's more: We still have to look at the two most important composite modes—the travel mattes—to which we'll devote the next lesson.

LESSON 18
Travel Mattes

Travel mattes, or traveling mattes, are a unique type of composite mode that uses the underlying layer in a composite stack to define an image's transparency. It allows the application to create a great many wonderful motion graphics animations. We'll look at a few that I hope will spur your imagination and get you started on creating interesting and exciting projects.

SETTING UP THE PROJECT

For this lesson you'll need to launch the *Lesson 18* project and go through the reconnect process, if necessary. Inside your copy of the project *Lesson 18*, you'll find the *Clips* bin, three master clips (*Village, Dance*, and *Ceremony*), and a number of sequences. As in the previous lesson, there is a *Composite Stacks* sequence.

TRAVEL MATTES

Technically these are compositing modes as well, although they function in a special way. The two travel mattes are **Luminance** and **Alpha**. In a travel matte, the layer to which it's applied will take its shape and transparency from either the Luminance value or the Alpha (the transparency) value of the layer directly beneath it. Because it tracks the layer, any animation or change in the layer below will be reflected in the tracking layer. This makes Travel Matte an extraordinarily powerful tool.

Soft-Edged Split Screen

Let's use a travel matte composite mode with a gradient to create a soft-edged split screen. Sometimes when doing a split-screen effect, you like to have a soft, blurred edge instead of the hard edge the Crop tool gives you, which we saw in Lesson 14. The Crop function does have an Edge Feather function; unfortunately, this feathers all of the edges, not just the edge that splits the two images. That's where gradients with composite modes come in. At *Marker 1* in *Composite Stacks*, I've created a soft-edged split screen. One clip is on V1, another on V3, and sandwiched in between is a custom gradient.

1. To build this effect, start out by laying the clips into the *Sequence 1* Timeline on V1 and V2. I used the still images *Rich.pct* and *Anita.pct* from the *Graphics* bin.
2. Offset each to left and right so the heads are separated enough to leave room for the soft-edged split. You'll have to toggle the Visibility of the top layer on and off as you make this adjustment.
3. From the Generators, select **Render>Custom Gradient**.
4. Make sure the playhead is over the two clips and V1 is set as the destination track. Use the Superimpose function to sandwich the custom gradient onto V2 between the still images.

5. To the clip on top, apply **Composite Mode>Travel Matte-Luma**. You will immediately see that much of the image has become transparent.

What immediately happens is that half of the top layer seems to disappear. The top layer's transparency is created by the composite mode that is looking at the layer directly beneath it to determine what should be transparent. Whatever is white in the layer below will be opaque in the top layer. Whatever is black will be transparent in the top layer. Different values of gray will create different levels of transparency.

In our exercise, what we need to control is the shape of the gradient, how quickly it falls off from white to black, and where that fall-off happens.

6. Double-click the Custom Gradient in the Timeline to open it into the Viewer, and go to the Controls tab.
7. To make things easier, grab the Video tab and pull it out of the Viewer, positioning it to the left. Now you can see the gradient on the left, its controls in the center, and the output of the effect on the Canvas to the right (see Figure 18.1).

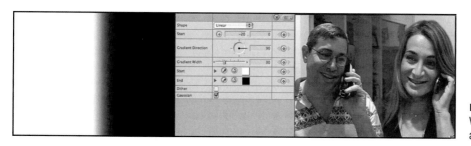

FIGURE 18.1
Viewer, controls,
and Canvas.

TIP

Clip Visibility: Rather than switching off the visibility for an entire track, which will lose your render files if you have any, simply switch off the visibility for a single clip. You can do this by using the Clip Enable function. In FCE4 you have to use a keyboard shortcut to do this; use Control-B. Another option is to Solo just the clip you want to see and switch off the visibility for other clips. You can do that from the Sequence menu or with the keyboard shortcut Control-S.

295

8. Begin by setting the Start *x, y* value to 0, 0, and pull down the Gradient Width to about 40.

That's about it; you just need to adjust the *x* value at it so the gradient doesn't bleed too much into the right image or maybe tighten the gradient a little more. Turning on the Gaussian check box will make it easier to get a tighter gradient fall-off from white on the left to black and transparency on the right.

Highlight Matte

Next we're going to create a **Highlight Matte**. This allows us to create a highlight area, like a shimmer that moves across an image or, as here, across a layer of text. Let's set up a simple animation:

1. Edit only the video of five seconds of one of the clips into the Timeline to use as a background layer. I used a section of *Ceremony 1*.
2. Next we'll add text on top of it. As in the previous lesson, for simplicity use the standard Text tool to create the word *JAPAN* in any font you like,

in a fairly large size, and in a nice, bright color. I again used Optima, bold and italicized, with a point size of 168 in a fairly bright red, R 200, G 18, B 18. Create whatever text block you like, using any available font.

3. Superimpose your text block on top of the video and use Image+Wireframe to move it higher in the frame.

4. Next, duplicate the text block and make a copy on the layer above, V3, by **Option-Shift** dragging it upward.

5. Open the top text layer, and make it a very pale version of the text color on V2. I made it a pale pink.

6. Set V2 as the destination track so you can superimpose between the two text layers.

7. Select **Highlight** from the **Render Generator** pop-up menu, and superimpose it onto V3 between the text layers.

Now let's work on the highlight:

FIGURE 18.2
Highlight under text.

8. Double-click the Highlight to bring it into the Viewer. Go to its Controls tab and move the Highlight Angle around to 35 degrees.

9. Set the Width and Softness to about 5 and 10, respectively, leaving off Dither and Gaussian (the latter only tightens the sharpness of the fall-off).

Your Canvas should look something like Figure 18.2.

Animating the Highlight

The next step will be to animate the Highlight. We'll do this in the generator's Controls tab.

1. Put the playhead at the start of the clip.

2. In the Controls tab of the Highlight, set the Center x axis to -600, which should take it off-screen left, at least away from the text file on V4.

3. Add a Center value keyframe in the Highlights Controls tab.

4. Move to the end of the clip (**Shift-O**). Now set the Center x point to 500.

Over the five seconds of the clip, the Highlight bar will sweep slowly across the screen. Of course, we still don't see the background layer.

5. Next, set the **Composite Mode** of the text file on V4 to **Travel Matte-Luma**.

If you're at the start or end of the clip, you'll see the red text layer on V2 as well as the background. As you scrub through the sequence, you'll see that the text highlight area will softly wipe onto the screen and then wipe off again as the Highlight layer slides underneath it. The pale text file's transparency is being directly controlled by the luminance value of the layer beneath it. The matte layer, the Highlight in this case, is invisible. The four layers are at *Marker 2* in *Composite Stacks*.

Glints

We've seen how we can put a highlight across an image. Next we're going to do something a little more complex—creating a traveling highlight—but one that goes only along the edges of a piece of text—a highlight that glints the edges.

1. We'll begin again with a base layer from one of the clips available in the Browser. I used the first five seconds of *Ceremony2* for this, editing onto V1.
2. Next we add the text to V2. Again, make it big, a fat font, such as Optima in bold, with a point size of about 180, right to the edges of the Safe Tide Area and beyond. Set it a little below center in the frame. For my font I used a *y* value of 70.

Next we'll create a moving highlight area:

3. Use FCE's Custom Gradient from the **Generators** pop-up menu, **Render>Custom Gradient**.
4. Superimpose the Custom Gradient on top of the text and background clip so it has the same five-second duration.
5. Open the Custom Gradient from the Timeline, and using the Control tab of the Viewer, change the Shape pop-up menu to Radial.

The Radial center is very large and on the left edge of the screen. We want the radial highlight to be much smaller and higher in the frame.

6. Set the Gradient Width to 35, and make sure both Dithering and Gaussian are not checked.
7. Change the gradient's Start coordinates to *x, y* of 0, −100, centering the radial in the screen as in Figure 18.3.

FIGURE 18.3
Radial gradient in the Viewer.

Animating the Radial

To animate the gradient, we want it to move from left to right across the screen and then back again, and remaining at its current height. At the start, you want the gradient off one side of the screen.

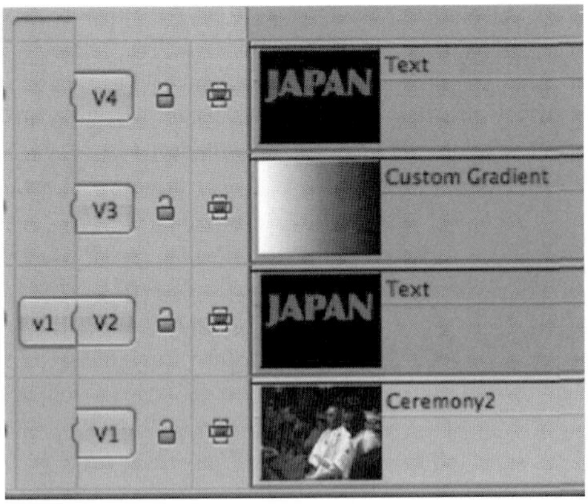

FIGURE 18.4
Four video layers in sequence.

FIGURE 18.5
Text with glow composite.

1. In the Custom Gradient's Controls tab, set the Start *x* point to −600, leaving *y* at −100.
2. Make sure you're at the beginning of the Timeline, and keyframe the Start value.
3. While in the Controls tab, type *215* to go forward to 2:15 (two and one-half seconds), about halfway through the clip.
4. Set the Start *x* value way over on the opposite side of the screen, about 600.
5. Go to the end of the five-second clip, and set the Start *x* value back to its start position of −600.

Over the five seconds of the clip, the radial gradient will sweep across the text and then back again. So far, so good. If you scrub the Timeline, or play through with **Option-P**, you should see the gradient swing from left to right and back again.

6. To make the glow appear only on the text, start by copying the text layer on V2 and placing the copy on V4, on top of the gradient. Do this with **Option-Shift**-drag. Your stack should look like Figure 18.4.
7. Open the top text layer into the Viewer, and use the controls to change its Color to white, pale yellow, or whatever glow color you want to use.

This layer will be the glow on top of the text; the radial gradient will be the matte it follows.

8. To the top text layer apply **Composite Mode>Travel Matte-Luma**.

Immediately, the gradient will disappear, and the glow will be composited on top of the bottom text layer. Figure 18.5 shows the text with the glow but with the underlying video switched off.

Polishing the Glow

That's a nice effect. You could be happy with it and stop there, with the glowing layer animated across the screen with the Custom Gradient layer. What we really want, though, is for the glow not to race across the whole text but to run just along the top edge of the text. It's not hard to do. We just need to add a few more layers.

1. **Option-Shift**-drag two more copies of the text layer on V2 up to the top of the stack onto V5 and V6.

These will completely hide the glow, so we want to create a mask that will hide most of the text except for the very edges.

2. Open up the Controls for the topmost layer, and set its Origin point slightly to one side, away from the side where the glow starts.
3. Also set it slightly lower on the screen if the glow is traveling above the text or slightly higher if the glow is traveling below the text.

I increased the values of both x and y by 6. This will make the text look slightly fatter than it is, so we want to make a matte that cuts off the bits of text that protrude beyond the correct shape of the text. That's what the layer beneath is for.

4. To the top layer apply **Composite Mode>Travel Matte-Alpha**.

The Travel Matte layer disappears, and you're left with just a glint that travels along the edges of the text (see Figure 18.6).

FIGURE 18.6
Glint on text.

299

> **NOTE**
> **Alpha Mattes and Luma Mattes:** An alpha matte uses the transparency of the layer below, like text layers, to create transparency in the layer to which the composite mode is applied. A luma matte uses the luminance values of the layer below for the composite mode. Generators, like render shapes, have no transparency, but they have luminance values. Whatever is white in the matte layer will be opaque in the layer above, and whatever is black will be transparent in the layer above. Shades of gray give different amounts of transparency.

One More Touch

At the moment, the glint brushes across the upper left edge of the letters as it moves back and forth across the screen. If you want to be really crafty and add a little something special, you can shift the glint side as it swings back and forth.

1. For the first pass of the Radial Gradient, leave the settings as they are.
2. When the glint reaches the far right side of the screen at 2:15, in the Controls tab of the text layer on V6, set a keyframe for the Origin point.
3. For the next frame, while the Radial Gradient is still off to the right, change that offset text layer's Center x value to -6, but leave the y value as it is.

Now when the glint passes back from right to left, it will be on the upper-right edge of the letters. The glint stack is at *Marker 3* in *Composite Stacks*.

Video in Text

I hope you're getting the hang of this by now and are beginning to understand the huge range of capabilities that these tools make possible. Next let's try an even more complex animation with traveling mattes, the ever-popular video-inside-text effect, the kind of technique that might look familiar from the opening of another old television program, *Dallas*.

To look at what we're going to do, open the *Composite Stacks* sequence and go to *Marker 4*. If you click on the clip on V2 called *HDV Sequence* and press **Command-R**, you will render out the section of sequence defined by the length of the clip. That's what we're going to build.

To make really enormous letters that fill right to the top and bottom edges of the screen and are wider than the screen, you could create this in Photoshop or Photoshop Elements. We can use Photoshop to create multilayer, oversized sequences that we can work with in FCE. If you're working in DV, you can also use FCE's HDV capabilities to generate an oversized sequence.

Making Text

We need to start with *really* big blocks of text.

1. Start by creating a new sequence and opening it.

I called the prebuilt one in your Browser *HDV Sequence*, so you should give yours a different name. Call it *Nest*, because that's what it's going to be: a nested sequence. It's probably in DV format, so we need to change it to HDV.

2. With the sequence open, go to **Sequence>Settings**, or use **Cmd-zero**.

3. In the lower left corner of the settings window, click on the **Load Sequence Preset** button, and from the pop-up choose **Apple Intermediate Codec 720p**. You could use 1080i as well, but 720p is a little closer to DV size.

4. From the **Generators**, go to **Boris>Title 3D**.

5. Go to the Controls tab, and click on the **Title 3D click for options button**.

6. In the text window, click on the **Reset Style** button to go back to the default white text, and then make your text.

> **TIP**
> *HDV Multilayer Sequence:* If you're working in HDV format, I've created an oversized Photoshop file with the text built into it that you can use in HDV. It's in the *Graphics* bin called *Stage1080.psd*. It's based on a 1080i format, but if you need it for 720p, simply scale it down to fit. There's a graphic called *Stage480.psd* that is suitable for use with DV material.

301

I created the text using the word *JAPAN*. Pick a chunky, broad font. Don't use a thin, wimpy, serif font. I used Arial Black, but you can use whatever you have at hand. Make the type size large, something like 96 point to start, but we'll make it even bigger. You will also need to open up the tracking a little or kern the letter pairs so the letters don't overlap vertically, particularly the P and the second A.

7. Click the **Apply** button in the text window, switch back to the video tab, and edit the text into the HDV sequence. It should be fairly large but still not fill the screen.

Nesting

We now have a large HDV-format sequence called *Nest*, as well as a standard-definition DV sequence called *Sequence 1*. We need to nest the large-format sequence inside the smaller-format sequence.

1. Begin by opening up *Sequence 1* from the Browser.

2. From the Generators button, select **Matte>Color**.

3. Make the Color five seconds long, and edit it into the sequence. This will be our background layer.

4. Open the Color from the Timeline, and in the Controls tab make it a nice bright color.

5. To add a little motion to the background, we'll add a render element: From the Generators go to **Render**>**Membrane**.

6. Make sure the playhead is over the Color in the Timeline, and drag your *Nest* sequence from the Browser to the Canvas in the Edit Overlay, and drop it on Superimpose. That will make the nested sequence five seconds long as well.

7. Double-click on the nested sequence inside *Sequence 1* so it opens into its own tab in the Timeline window.

8. Double-click on the text layer in the sequence to open it into the Viewer, and switch to the Controls tab.

9. Uncheck **Lock to Scale X**, which gives you separate vertical and horizontal scaling.

10. Push up the **Scale X** value as far as it will go, keeping the letters in the screen. Don't touch the *y* value for the moment.

11. Switch back to *Sequence 1* in the Timeline window.

The text should extend beyond the edges of the screen, which is fine. The Controls tab for the text should still be in the Viewer, and we'll use this to adjust the size of the text while watching the text in the Canvas for *Sequence 1*.

12. Now increase the **Scale Y** value until the text stretches up to the Safe Title Area guides in the Canvas.

We've now made the text for the sequence.

> **TIP**
>
> **RAM:** You will have difficulty doing this portion of the lesson if your system resources do not meet the minimum requirements to support HDV content. If that is the case, rather than creating an HDV sequence, use the *Stage480.psd* that's in your *Graphics* folder in the Browser.

Separating Letters

We're going to not only move images in the text but also going to move a different image in each letter of the text. We're going to do that inside the *Nest* sequence, adding images above each letter, which will all appear inside the nested sequence in *Sequence 1*. The text file will be the matte for the video that's on top of it. Because we want different video in each letter, we need to separate the word into its individual letters.

1. Inside your *Nest* sequence, **Option-Shift**-drag the text layer from V1 onto the layers above again and again, until you have a stack five text layers tall, or one for each letter.

After you've created the layer stack, then you need to crop each letter so that only it is visible.

FIGURE 18.7
Cropped text layer.

2. If the Canvas is not already in Image+Wireframe mode, switch to it now.

3. Select the text on V1, and use **Sequence>Solo Selected Item(s)** or **Control-S** to solo it so none of the other layers is visible.

4. Use the Crop tool to pull in the right side of the text layer that's in your sequence. Crop it between the J and the A until only the J is visible (see Figure 18.7).

5. Select the text layer on V2 and solo it with **Control-S** to make only that layer visible.

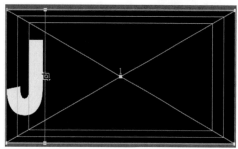

The number in the center of the Canvas will tell you which layer is selected.

6. With the Crop tool, move the right crop line from the right until you are between the A and the P, and then move the left crop line so that it's between the J and the A, isolating the second letter.

7. Select the text on V3 and repeat, moving the right crop line to the right until all of the P is visible, and move its left crop line so that it's between the second and third letters, A and P.

8. Repeat for the other two layers until each layer has one letter visible on it.

9. When you're done, be sure to switch off Soloing on the last layer with **Control-S** so that all of the letters are visible again.

303

Adding Video

We're now ready to put in some video. We'll work with only video here—no audio.

1. Decouple the audio patches, and set V1 as the destination track. Make sure the playhead is over the stack in your HDV sequence.

2. Find a clip in the Browser that you want to place above the text on V1. I used *Ceremony1*.

3. Drag the clip to the Canvas to Superimpose, slotting the clip into a new V2 between the J on V1 and the A now on V3.

4. Roughly position the clip in the Canvas so it's sitting on the left side of the frame over the letter J.

FIGURE 18.8
Distorted image
composited over text.

The next step will be to apply a Composite Mode.

5. With the clip on V2 selected, right-click on it in the Timeline to call up the shortcut menu, and choose **Composite Mode>Travel Matte-Alpha**.

The image doesn't have to be the whole size of the frame or positioned in the center of the frame. It can be placed anywhere at any size as long as it covers the letter.

6. Grab a corner of the image and resize it. Hold the **Shift** key and distort the image shape if you want (see Figure 18.8).

Next we need to add some more video to the other layers:

7. Set V3 as the destination track, and find a clip in the Browser to superimpose over it. I used *Village3* for this one.

8. Superimpose it onto V4, and change its **Composite Mode** to **Travel Matte-Alpha**.

9. Scale and distort the image in the Canvas, and position it so it covers the letter A.

The next clip will take its matte from the text now on V5 and fill the letter P. I used *Dance2*, beginning about three seconds into the shot.

10. Find the clip to use and Superimpose it above V5.

11. Set the **Composite Mode** to **Travel Matte-Alpha**.

12. Scale and position in the Canvas.

I used the beginning of *Ceremony2* to super above V7.

13. Repeat the process, which will create a new V8, above the second letter A.

I used *Dance1* for the next track.

14. Repeat the process to create a new V10 to be matted by the letter N on V9.

Your ten layers in the sequence should now be made up of five layers of text interspersed with five layers of video scaled and positioned to fit the text layer below it (see Figure 18.9).

FIGURE 18.9
Ten-layer stack.

Edging

One last thing we want to do in this sequence is add an edging that borders the letters and separates the text and the video from what will be the background layer.

1. Let's start by **Option-Shift**-dragging a copy of the text layer on V9 right up to the top of the stack to create a new text layer on V11.

2. Double-click the text layer on V11, and go to the Motion tab to reset the Crop values. Use the little red **X** button next to crop. This will cover all of the video with the letters.

3. Switch to the Controls tab in the Viewer, and click the **Title 3D click for options** button to bring up the Title 3D text window.

4. Stroke through the text to select, and then switch to the fourth tab in the text window, the Edges tab.

5. Activate one of the edges, and set an edge to taste. I used a plain edge, but I set the **Position** pop-up to **Outside** so it didn't cut into the video and used a rich blue.

6. Switch to the third tab on the left, the Color tab, and in the top left corner deactivate, uncheck, **Fill On**. This will leave the text fill open with only the edging around the letters.

Animating the Nest

Let's switch over to *Sequence 1*, which is 720×480, smaller than the nest inside it. We want to animate two elements: the nested sequence so it moves across the screen and the custom generator so the background has motion as well.

305

1. In the Canvas, make sure the View pop-up has Image+Wireframe turned on, and set the Zoom pop-up on the left to Fit All. Your Canvas should look like Figure 18.10.

2. Select your *Nest* sequence and press the **Return** key, which will open it into the Viewer. Double-clicking won't do it because that will just open the nested sequence in the Timeline window.

3. Go to the Motion tab, and with the playhead on the first frame of the sequence, set a Center point keyframe.

4. In the Canvas, holding down the **Shift** key to constrain the movement, drag the nested layer off the screen to the right. A Center value of 1,000 did this for me.

5. Use **Shift-O** to go to the last frame of the sequence, and holding the **Shift** key again, move the image over to the left side of the screen. I used a Center value of −1,000.

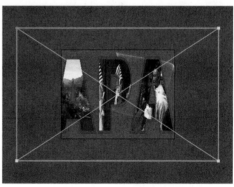

FIGURE 18.10
Nest sequence composited on background.

Over the course of the five seconds, the text will travel from right to left on top of your background. I have built the animation at *Marker 4* in *Composite Stacks*.

Day for Night

Color mattes don't have to be used only for backgrounds or graphical elements, as we saw in earlier lessons. They can also be used as a color filter. Day for Night is the now seldom-used technique of trying to shoot in daylight and make it look like a moonlit night. Old Westerns almost always used this technique. Basically, you stop down the camera and shoot through a blue or a graduated blue filter. Let's do something similar:

1. Start off by laying the clip you want to affect on V1 in a new sequence. I used *Village3* because it presents a typical daylight problem: the bright sky.
2. Darken the image, using a filter such as with Color Corrector.

FIGURE 18.11
Darkened image with a bright sky.

I pulled down all of the levels: Whites, Mids, Blacks, and even Saturation. Even with the levels pulled down quite far, the sky remains bright and pale (see Figure 18.11). Next we'll use the Color Matte to add the blue night filter.

3. Create a deep, dark blue color matte and Superimpose it onto V2.
4. Create a Custom Gradient, and with V1 set as the destination track, Superimpose it so it sandwiches itself onto V2 between the video and the color matte.
5. Set the **Composite Mode** on the color matte to **Travel Matte-Luma**.

All that's left to do is to set up the gradient.

6. Open the controls, leave the default at Linear gradient, and change the Direction to 180.

Next you need to use the crosshairs to place the start of the gradient. There is a start point but no end point for the gradient. If you start at the top of the Canvas, the blue will carry too far down into the image.

7. Zoom down the size of the Canvas to something like 25 percent.

8. Place the start point for the crosshairs out in the grayboard above the image.
9. Tighten the Gradient Width so it falls off more sharply.
10. Make the end color of the gradient somewhat less than pure black to give the lower part of the image a cold, blue cast.

The sky should be dark blue, but the center of the image should still show some light and color (see Figure 18.12). The stack is at *Marker 5* in *Composite Stacks*.

FIGURE 18.12
Day for night gradient filter.

SUMMARY

That brings us to the end of this packed lesson on compositing. We're almost ready to export our material from Final Cut Express out into the world, which is the subject of our final lesson.

LESSON 19

Outputting from Final Cut Express

Remember I said the hard, technical part of nonlinear editing was at the beginning, setting up and setting preferences, logging, and capturing; the fun part was the editing in the middle; and the easy part was the outputting at the end? Well, we're finally up to the easy part: the output. These are the two basic ways of outputting:

- Exporting, if you're going to another computer application or CD or DVD or Web delivery
- Going back to tape, if you're going to traditional tape delivery

Let's look at outputting to tape first. The two ways to get material from your computer to tape are record to tape and print to video.

RECORD TO TAPE

You can get your edited material back out to DV tape in several different ways. The simplest, and perhaps the most commonly used, way is to record to tape. This works only with DV material, not with HD material, but before you record to tape, you should always do the following:

1. Make sure everything that needs to be rendered in the sequence is rendered.
2. Make sure you are set to **FireWire** in the **View>Video Out** menu.
3. Make sure you mix down your audio. Go to **Sequence>Render Only> Mixdown (Command-Option-R)**.

Mix down the audio even if you have only a single stereo pair of audio. It's much easier for your computer and your drives to play back a mixdown file than it is to mix your audio on-the-fly. Also, the default audio quality play-back is set to Low. If you just record to tape without mixing down, you will get low-quality playback. However, whenever you mix down your audio, it's always done to high quality, and that's what you want when you record to tape.

To record to tape put the playhead at the beginning of the timeline, put your camcorder into VCR mode, switch on Record with its VCR controls, and press the spacebar. This is a fast, effective, and simple method. It's probably a good idea to have some black at the beginning and end of your sequence and have the playhead sitting on it at the beginning so when you begin recording, you're not recording a still image for a while. You should record at least ten seconds of black before pressing the spacebar to begin playing back your sequence.

There is one other trap in recording to tape, either manually or with Print to Video. If you have set your Render Controls in Sequence Settings down to low values to speed up rendering, that's the playback quality you'll get. You cannot now switch to high quality and automatically force a rerender. You have to switch to high quality and then reset each effect that was rendered at low resolution to force it to rerender at high quality. Or switch off the visibility for the base track and then switch it back on to force a complete rerender of your sequence. There is no other force rerender function—unfortunately. This is also true of exporting to tape and can also be an issue in Final Cut.

Using playback from the Timeline has some disadvantages. You don't get to put in things like bars, tone, neat countdowns, slates, black leaders, and trailers unless you physically add them to your sequence. If you want these features, you can use Print to Video.

PRINT TO VIDEO

Print to Video is under the **File** menu. This is the only way to go back to tape for HDV material. If you are working with original AVCHD material and have an HDV deck, you can output your program back to HDV tape even though it originated in AVCHD. Either way, DV or HDV, if you have a sequence selected in the Browser or an active Timeline, you can call up Print to Video from the **File** menu or use **Control-M**. This brings up the dialog box in Figure 19.1.

In this dialog you can set any number of options for program starts and ends. You can add bars and tone and set the tone level, depending on the system you're using. Several different digital audio standards are used, if you can call anything that has variables a standard. Different systems use -12, -14, -16, or $-20\,dB$ as digital audio standards. Analog uses a variety of other standards around $0\,dB$. If you are going to send your video to a duplication house, check with them before selecting a tone level.

The Slate pop-up lets you use (1) the clip name, (2) the text, which you can add in the text window, and (3) the file, which is any still image, video, or audio file. So if you want to record an audio slate, selecting the file and navigating to it with the little Load button will play the sound during recording. You can use FCE's built-in countdown, using a form of Motion Picture Academy leader. Or you can use a countdown of your own by selecting File in the Countdown pop-up menu.

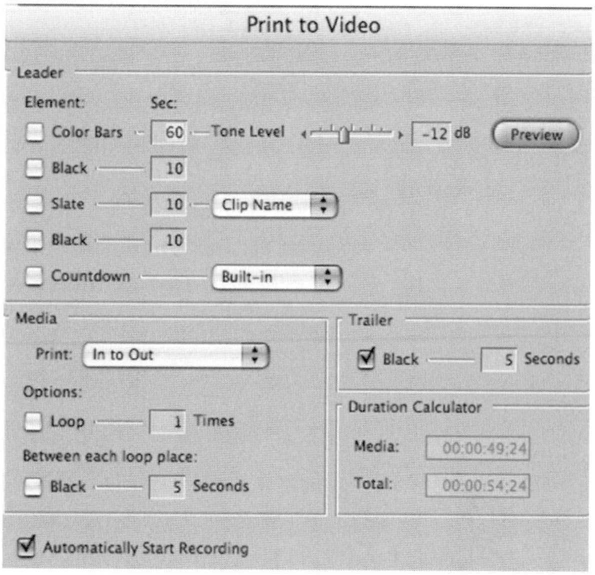

Notice the check box in the bottom left that provides the ability to automatically begin recording. This is essential for some cameras that do not have a manual record function.

FIGURE 19.1
Print to Video dialog box.

When you start Print to Video, FCE will write a video, and if necessary, it will write an audio file of any material that needs to be rendered. Every time you use Print to Video, it will have to do this, even if you've just used it. After it has finished writing the video and audio files, FCE will prompt you before it begins recording. Accept by clicking OK, and the computer will take control of the deck and send it into Record at whatever point it's parked on the tape.

You can use either Record to Tape or Print to Video to make a VHS recording. Connect your DV camcorder or deck to your computer, and connect its analog output to your VHS deck. It's probably a good idea to have the VHS deck in turn connected to a video monitor or TV so you can see what you're recording. Then set the VHS deck to Record, and use the DV device as a digital-to-analog converter to get your movie onto VHS.

TIP
In to Out: If you want to record only a portion of your sequence, select the portion you want to record by marking it with In and Out points in the Timeline. Then in the Print to Video settings window, select In to Out from the Print pop-up menu in the Media portion of window. When you press OK, playback will begin at the marked In point and run until it reaches the Out point.

EXPORT

You can access the different formats and ways of exporting from FCE from the File menu. From here you can export to **QuickTime Movie** or **Using QuickTime Conversion**.

QuickTime Movie

Let's start with QuickTime Movie, the first of the two Export options. When you export a QuickTime movie, Final Cut is listed as its creator type, so if you launch the resulting movie, it will launch FCE. Because Final Cut is a QuickTime-based application, the exported movie will also play using the QuickTime Player and will work in any other QuickTime-based application on the Mac, such as iMovie or iDVD.

You can export a sequence as a digital file in several ways:

- From the active Timeline window directly from the sequence you're working in
- From an active Viewer
- From the Browser by exporting a sequence or clip

Click on the item, and go to **Export>QuickTime Movie**. This brings up the dialog box in Figure 19.2. Here you can rename your sequence, and you can select whether you want to export **Audio and Video** or **Audio Only** or **Video Only** from the Include pop-up menu. Here you also have the option to export **Markers** through a pop-up menu (see Figure 19.3). To export chapter markers to iDVD, select **Chapter Markers** from the pop-up menu.

The check box at the bottom of the dialog box, **Make Movie Self-Contained**, is an important one. This check box defaults to being on, but if you uncheck it, FCE will generate a reference movie. This is a relatively small file that points back to the original media source files. It will play the contents of the sequence as you laid them out.

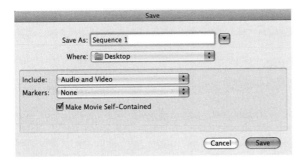

FIGURE 19.2
QuickTime Movie export dialog box.

FIGURE 19.3
Exporting Markers pop-up menu.

The reference movie will play back from the QT player, and it can also be imported into other applications such as iDVD or compression programs such as Episode. The reference movie is treated just like any other QT clip inside these other applications. FCE and the importing application do not need to be open at the same time for this to work.

The advantages of making reference movies are the speed in generating the file and the comparatively small file size. If anything in the FCE sequence needs to be rendered, it will still have to be rendered for the reference movie, and the audio files will also be duplicated as a mixdown of your tracks. You do need to have access to all of the source media included in the sequence because a reference movie only points to existing media source files on your hard drives. It's not a complete video clip in itself. Be warned: If you delete any of the media needed for the reference movie, it will not play. It will be a broken QuickTime file. If you send it to somebody on a CD, they won't be able to play it. It will play only on a machine that has access to the media.

Export to QuickTime Movie is an important tool because it is the only way to export a sequence from FCE without recompressing the video. All other exports, including Export Using QuickTime Conversion, will recompress the frames, producing some degradation of the video image, albeit very slight.

313

TIP
Anamorphic Material: iDVD still does not support the use of anamorphic material from DV, only native widescreen HDV. To get around this problem, you need to use software like Anamorphicizer or the excellent myDVDedit. You can also use the QuickTime Pro player or export to QuickTime Conversion and set the frame size to a 16:9 aspect like 854×480 for DV. With this last method you will not be able to export chapter markers however.

Making Chapter Markers

The last thing you should do to a project before exporting is set up chapter markers to use in iDVD. It could not be simpler to create them.

TIP
Export for Live Type: This function is the same as exporting to QuickTime Movie. The only difference is that exporting to LiveType defaults to make a reference movie. It is also preset to export all markers.

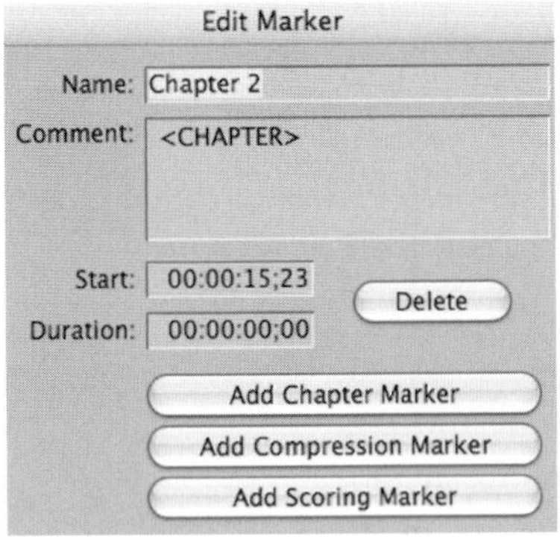

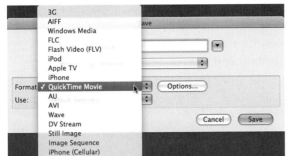

FIGURE 19.4
Edit Marker dialog box.

First, you need to ensure that the marker is in the correct location. It must be placed on the Timeline Ruler, not on a clip. To put a marker in the Timeline, make sure nothing is selected in the sequence. Use **Command-Shift-A** to **De-select All**.

Add the marker by pressing the **M** key. Press it again to call up the Edit Marker dialog box (see Figure 19.4). To create the chapter marker, click the **Add Chapter Marker** button. <CHAPTER> will appear in the Comment field. Do not alter this.

If you want to give the chapter a name that will carry over to iDVD, enter it in the Name field. That's it! Close the dialog box, and you're done.

You should bear in mind a few rules about chapter markers:

FIGURE 19.5
QuickTime Conversion
export.

- DVDs will accept no more than 99 chapter markers.
- Chapter markers cannot be closer than one second from each other.
- You can't have a chapter marker within one second of the start or end of the sequence.
- A chapter marker is automatically created for the beginning of the exported material.

It's probably a good idea not to put in chapter markers until after you have completely, positively, and finally finished editing your show. Otherwise, you may have to redo or at least reposition all your chapter markers to get them into the right place.

QuickTime Conversion

Export>Using QuickTime Conversion is the catch-all for every form of file conversion from FCE. I would have liked for Still Image export to be separate, but it's hidden in here as well (see Figure 19.5).

Video Export

Final Cut Express has several video export choices for QuickTime Conversion. The **Format** pop-up allows you to choose from a variety of formats, including the following:

- 3G, a format used by handheld devices such as cell phones
- FLC, an 8-bit format used for computer animations
- Apple TV, for sending to your Apple TV for television display

- iPhone and iPod, for podcasting size and format for display on those devices or on the Web
- QuickTime Movie
- AVI, a PC video format
- DV Stream, DV audio and video encoded into a single track for use with iMovie
- MPEG-4, a format designed primarily for cross-platform Web compression

These are the video formats. You will also have other formats such as Flash and Windows Media Video if you have third-party resources such as Flash encoder, Flip4Mac, or WMV installed on your system. Some of the available formats such as AVI and QuickTime allow you to use several different codecs. DV Stream is used by iMovie, not by FCE. Do not export to DV Stream if you're going to a video-editing application other than iMovie.

In QuickTime Conversion, the **User** pop-up is contextual—that is, what is offered here is determined by what's selected in the **Format** pop-up. If you select QuickTime in the Format pop-up menu, the **User** pop-up menu offers common Internet settings (see Figure 19.6) based on QuickTime using H.264 as the codec. This is a good place to start if you want to create a video to show on the Internet or put on your dotmac homepage.

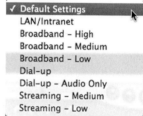

FIGURE 19.6
QuickTime Conversion User pop-up menu.

315

NOTE

Codec is a shorthand way of saying compression/decompression, defining the mathematical algorithm that's used to compress and play back your media. H.264 is a specific codec that became available in QuickTime 7. This is now the default compressor, and an outstanding codec, used by iPod video and one that will be used for high-definition DVD creation. It's highly scalable, while preserving image quality, and excellent for Web use in particular. It's not a production format and cannot be used in video-editing applications, but it's great for content delivery. The only problem is that it requires the user to have QuickTime 7 or later installed, which may limit its availability, particularly for PC users, who may not have the latest versions of QuickTime.

If you want more control, click on the **Options** button to bring up the Settings window (see Figure 19.7). The Video and Audio tabs give you full control over your media. It takes a great deal of practice and testing to become proficient at

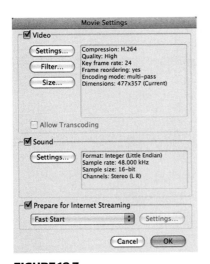

FIGURE 19.7
QuickTime Settings
window.

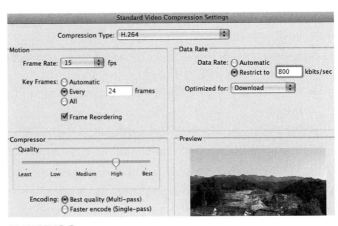

FIGURE 19.8
Standard Export settings.

compression for the Web. Try various data rates, frame sizes, and frame rates, and compare them to the default Web settings that come with selecting QuickTime in the **Format** pop-up menu.

Exporting with QuickTime Conversion allows you to use a variety of different codecs for compression in addition to H.264, including the following:

- Animation
- Cinepak
- DV-NTSC
- MPEG-4 Settings window
- Motion-JPEGA
- Photo-JPEG

To export to other QuickTime codecs, use the **Options** button and then click on **Settings** to select the correct video and audio settings (see Figure 19.8). Try various data rate settings: 800 kbps will give good results. Set the frame rate to 15 fps. Size should be set to 320×240.

You should also compress the audio. IMA 4:1 at 22,050 works well for most material. For music you might use a music compressor such as QDesign Music 2 and a sample rate of 44.1 K, the audio CD standard. These settings will produce a fairly large file, suitable for use on high-speed connections.

Photo-JPEG is an excellent codec used for file-size reduction. Another important codec is Animation, which has a high data rate. Animation is a lossless compression codec often used to transfer material between various applications. One advantage of the Animation codec is that it can carry alpha-channel information with the video. This allows you to create a sequence in one application and bring it into FCE without loss and with its transparency information. Or you could export an FCE sequence that has transparency and bring it into another application such as After Effects, keeping the transparency you created in FCE. When you export with the Animation codec with an alpha channel, make sure that for **Colors** you select **Millions+**. The plus is the alpha channel. Also make sure that your program that has transparency is *not* rendered, or the render file will get exported. If it's not rendered, the Animation codec will render the file with the transparency you want.

The Sound dialog box allows you to set an audio compression scheme as well as setting the sampling rate you want to use.

To create video CDs, you'll need an application such as Roxio's Toast that allows compression to the MPEG-1 codec. This is a heavily compressed codec but a remarkable one in that it can play back off the very low output of a CD and still produce a full-screen, full-motion image. To create a DVD, you need another application such as iDVD. When exporting to iDVD, you should use either a self-contained or a reference QuickTime Movie, and iDVD will do the compression to MPEG-2 for you.

To export to Flash, which is the most widely available video format on the Web, you'll either need to get the On2 Technologies export module, software like Episode that comes with it, or have Flash installed.

Exporting to QuickTime Conversion allows you to add filters to your clips or sequences. Most of the QuickTime filters are available directly within FCE, with one notable exception, **Film Noise**, which is under the **Special Effects** submenu (see Figure 19.9). This filter adds an old-time film look to your video, as if it were scratched and dirty. A small QT movie runs in the bottom left corner, showing how much schmutz you've added to the picture. Here you can set amounts of Hair that appear on your video, from very low to quite furry. Notice the buttons that allow you to Save and Load, letting you create favorite preferences for the filter that you can access again and again. In addition to Hair, the pop-up at the top

FIGURE 19.9
Film Noise Hairs panel.

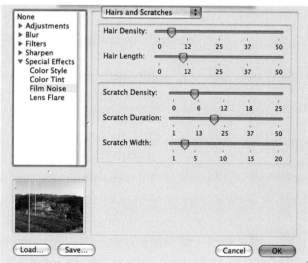

will take you to another panel to set Scratches, where you can set the amount of damage on your video, and another to set Dust and Film Fading, which allows you to tint the film. The sepia is quite subtle, and the 1930s' color film is suitably garish.

Still Image Export

Two other types of QuickTime Conversion export are often used: **Image Sequence** and **Still Image**. Image sequences are useful for rotoscoping, frame-by-frame painting on the video image, and other animation work, and they provide high-quality output without loss. You can set any frame rate, and exporting will create one picture for every frame you specify. Make sure you first create a folder in which to put your image sequence because this can easily generate a huge number of files.

Finally, QuickTime Conversion allows you to export still images. This is how you get frames of video out to your computer for Web or print use. Your stills will only be 72 dpi—probably not good enough for fine printing. Scaling up the image in Photoshop to achieve higher resolution will improve your print capability.

The **Options** button for Still Image export, which uses the same dialog box as Image Sequence, includes a Frame Rate box. Don't be confused; leave the Frame Rate blank if you want only one frame.

If you're going to export stills for Web or print work that come from video, especially video with a lot of motion in it, you'll probably want to deinterlace it. You can do this either in FCE or before you export the frame. As we saw in Lesson 15, you select **Video Filters**>**Video**>**Deinterlace** from the **Effects** menu. Or you can deinterlace in Photoshop as well. It's in the **Filters** menu under **Video**>**Deinterlace**. I normally do it in Photoshop because I think its Deinterlace feature works better than FCE's built-in one, which simply drops one of the fields. In the Photoshop Deinterlace filter, you have an interpolation option, which works very well.

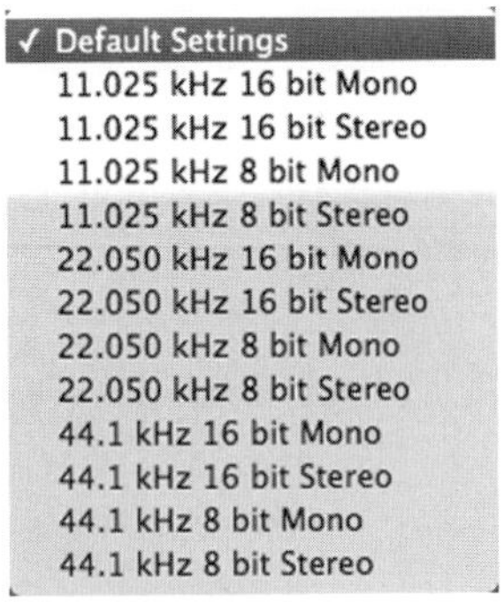

✓ Default Settings
11.025 kHz 16 bit Mono
11.025 kHz 16 bit Stereo
11.025 kHz 8 bit Mono
11.025 kHz 8 bit Stereo
22.050 kHz 16 bit Mono
22.050 kHz 16 bit Stereo
22.050 kHz 8 bit Mono
22.050 kHz 8 bit Stereo
44.1 kHz 16 bit Mono
44.1 kHz 16 bit Stereo
44.1 kHz 8 bit Mono
44.1 kHz 8 bit Stereo

FIGURE 19.10
AIFF Export Use
pop-up menu.

Audio Export

FCE can export to several different audio formats, including AIFF, AU, and Wave. It cannot export to MP3. If you select AIFF in the Use pop-up, you'll get common audio file settings (see Figure 19.10).

Notice that the selection does not include any of the DV sampling rates, although AIFF is the most commonly used format for audio files with

Final Cut. Instead of the Use pop-up, use the **Options** button, which is also context-sensitive and offers a wider range of options, including 32,000 and 48,000, the DV sampling rates. AIFF export options also offer a large number of compressors to reduce the file size of the audio. Generally, audio for video is not compressed, except for Web use or in DVD creation.

HD Export

So you've shot your movie on HDV or on AVCHD, and now you want to show it on an HD display. With HDV you can go back to tape and play your program back from tape, but with AVCHD, unless you also have an HDV device, you don't have that option. There are a few ways around this problem. One option, if you have it, is to export to Apple TV, which will create an HD format program that you can send to your Apple TV and put it on your HD screen. Another option is to burn your program onto a Blu-ray disc, but you must have a Blu-ray burner and Toast to do this. A third option, suggested by Dan Hawkins in the Apple FCE discussion forum, is to export an MPEG-4 file that is 1920×1080 with a high data rate like 18,000 Mbps and take that to a Sony PlayStation 3 for playback.

ARCHIVING

319

Now that you've finished your project, you should think about archiving your material. The original videotapes on which you shot the project should be your primary archive. Using the **Project** feature that we saw in the Capture window in Lesson 4, you can recapture all the video for your project.

You need to store the project file. This is most important because it allows you to recapture your material and rebuild your project. The best way to do this is to burn it onto a CD. You should also put on the CD whatever graphics files you created for the project. You should not do this with the FCE titles, which are retained in the project file, but with any Photoshop or other images you may have used. You should also save any music or separate sound you used in the project. And don't forget to save any Voice Over tracks you created. Everything other than the video clips that made up your movie should be burned onto your archive CD.

To restore the project, copy all the material back from the CD onto your computer. Open the project file, and reconnect the existing files. Next, run the capture process, clicking on Project in the Capture window to bring your video material onto the computer. The Capture window will prompt you for each tape it needs in turn. When all the material is back on your computer, your project will be restored and ready to be reedited.

Recapturing with Capture Project only works for DV material. If you're working in HDV material you will have to manually capture and reconnect your media. If you're working in AVCHD you can re-ingest your media from your archive DVD (see the Tip on page 72).

SUMMARY

We've now gone through the whole cycle of work in Final Cut Express Version 4, including setting up your computer, working with the interface, capturing your tape raw material, either analog or digital, editing, transitions, titling, special effects, and compositing. Now, finally, we have returned our finished project to tape or outputted it for everyone to see and enjoy. It's been a long road, but I hope you found it an exciting, interesting, and rewarding one. Good luck with all your future video projects and with your work in Final Cut Express!

Index

INDEX

INDEX

INDEX

The **CGM DVE Complete XXL** contains 186 filters, transitions, and generators for use in Final Cut Pro and Final Cut Express. In addition to the professional plug-ins, the package also includes a series of Final Cut workshops and 68 soft-wipe patterns.

All CGM transitions and filters are written in Final Cut's "native language" so they function seamlessly while fully supporting YUV rendering and multiprocessing in OSX. Additionally, they are designed to render at the subpixel level, which ensures smooth movement within the rendered clip.

Another advantage is that the 2D and 3D effects are "true" FCP transitions rather than After Effects filters (which may require cutting and pasting and often suffer from luminance shifts since they do not render in YUV space). All plugins support progressive video and the Intel Processor and RTExtreme HD architecture of FCP and FCE. Of course, rendering is optimized for maximum speed on all available Apple computers.

We can offer you four single volumes of plugins OR the complete package of all four volumes, the **CGM DVE Complete XXL.**

Available Packages (all prices in US Dollars):

– CGM DVE Complete XXL: $ 369.00
– CGM DVE Vol. 1: $ 99.00
– CGM DVE Vol. 2: $ 179.00
– CGM DVE Vol. 3: $ 179.00
– CGM DVE Vol. 4: $ 179.00

Online Store: http://www.cgm-online.com
We accept Mastercard, Visa, American Express, Diners Club and Paypal.